T0246201

HARD
TRUTHS

HARD TRUTHS

THINK AND LEAD ═══ LIKE A ═══ GREEN BERET

CONGRESSMAN
MIKE WALTZ,
U.S. ARMY SPECIAL FORCES (RET.)

ST. MARTIN'S PRESS
NEW YORK

First published in the United States by St. Martin's Press, an imprint of St. Martin's Publishing Group

www.stmartins.com

Designed by Omar Chapa

The Library of Congress Cataloging-in-Publication Data is available upon request.

ISBN 978-1-250-28618-5 (hardcover)
ISBN 978-1-250-28619-2 (ebook)

Our books may be purchased in bulk for promotional, educational, or business use. Please contact your local bookseller or the Macmillan Corporate and Premium Sales Department at 1-800-221-7945, extension 5442, or by email at MacmillanSpecialMarkets@macmillan.com.

First Edition: 2024

10 9 8 7 6 5

To my wife Julia, my partner and my hamsa, who encouraged me to capture my experiences in combat and in Congress for the next generation.

To Anderson and Armie, you inspire me to stay in the fight for the future of this great nation.

CONTENTS

INTRODUCTION

Hard Truths: Think and Lead Like a Green Beret reveals life lessons gained from thirty years of service leading Special Operations forces in combat, as an advisor in the White House, as an entrepreneur, and now as the first Green Beret to ever be elected to Congress.

Green Berets are unique in the world of Special Operations because they specialize in training indigenous peoples in guerilla warfare behind enemy lines. Alternatively, they also train and advise allied militaries in how to defeat insurgencies. In addition to possessing elite specialty combat skills, they are trained in multiple languages, local cultures, diplomacy, psychological warfare, and local politics. Often called *warrior diplomats*, they quietly operate in very small teams, in remote locales, with little support. In a single operation, Green Berets can find themselves gathering intelligence while also working with indigenous doctors to care for thousands of villagers and then using that intelligence to strike a key terrorist figure in the dark of night. They can build schools and clinics for tribes we seek to influence—and teach local militias how to destroy bridges ahead of an advancing enemy force. It takes a special mindset to influence warlords who could just as easily turn their guns on their American advisors if they thought it suited their interests.

I want to bring the reader the sights, sounds, intense emotions, immense complexities, and ways of thinking required to navigate centuries-old tribal feuds, interwoven with clever and evolving insurgencies. Those same skills are often necessary to navigate the stupefying bureaucracy also present in Washington, DC, and corporate America. I listen to an illiterate but wise tribal elder in the mountains of Afghanistan tell me how his secret weapon (educating his daughters) will ultimately defeat Islamic extremism—and then lead a town hall in north Florida where my constituents tell me about the problems with underresourced schools at home. I tell the horrifying story of the Taliban hanging a young boy in front of his family for refusing to fight alongside them, but also the triumph of swearing in an Afghan interpreter as a new U.S. citizen. I walk you, the reader, through my experiences in a deeply divided political system—and make the case for initiatives like returning America to national service. My own experience has taught me the value of young people serving a cause larger than themselves, alongside fellow Americans of all races, religions, and creeds.

Very few choose to endure the combined rigors of the Virginia Military Institute, Ranger School, survival training, and the Special Forces Qualification Course that together forge the mindset of the Green Beret. Yet the key attributes of a Green Beret, such as extreme determination, adaptability, and a commitment to bottom-up leadership, can apply to anyone's life, be it at school, at home, or at the office. An individual and a society that can handle hard truths, while thinking and leading like a Green Beret, cannot only master unconventional warfare but also business, politics, and life. As a nation, we can and must use the Green Beret principles of trust, resilience, restraint, and more to face our foes abroad—and overcome the internal strife that besets American society today.

I have spent much of this book bearing witness to the extraordinary heroism, decency, and character of the Green Berets I fought alongside from Africa to Afghanistan. I've tried to use the stories from training and combat to illustrate and explain some essential virtues—virtues that are in danger of being forgotten and abandoned—and how they apply to the tough political decisions I've had to make and to our broader national discourse. We face serious challenges today—and we will face others in the future. The key is for America to hear the hard truths it will need to hear in order to be prepared for both the anticipated and for the unexpected—and to be armed with the same philosophy that created the greatest fighting force on earth: the Green Berets. We must be vigilant. Perhaps that is the hardest, and most important, truth of all.

HARD
TRUTHS

1

THE MAKING OF A GREEN BERET

The guerilla chief stood over the captive, who lay bound and blindfolded on the ground.

The prisoner had once been a notorious commander in the government regime's secret police and had hunted down and brutally murdered countless guerillas, including this chief's own men. Now, he was defenseless—and by the looks of things, not long for this world. The chief spat at the man, then looked at me.

"This piece of filth raped our women, stole from my family, and tortured my people. Now, Captain, we will do the same to him. An eye for an eye."

My men and I had been marching for days, carrying one-hundred-pound rucksacks, to reach this remote corner of the earth. I was exhausted, and my mind was reeling. I knew I had to protest. "To execute this prisoner is a war crime, no matter how evil he is. My team cannot be a part of that. We cannot allow it," I said to the guerilla chief.

"Then walk away, Captain," replied the chief, stabbing his

finger toward the hills outside his camp. He was clearly irritated.

"We cannot allow it," I repeated. In the most compassionate voice I could muster, I added, "I understand your anger, sir."

"You understand nothing!" the chief exploded. "Don't lecture me, American! You would do the exact . . . same . . . thing if they killed your family!" He stepped forward, so close to my face that he was spitting on me. Out of the corner of my eye, I saw some of his men repositioning their hands toward their weapons. I sensed two of my men step out from behind me so they could have a clear shot if the situation continued to deteriorate.

This was a major test. The chief would not back down from the execution. He demanded my cooperation with it. Moreover, he let me know that the future of our relationship depended upon it. If I stood aside, I would make my team complicit in a war crime. If I continued to object, I would ruin the relationship with the chief and probably surrender precious American influence in an area where we needed it most. A tactical loss by me would lead to a strategic defeat for the United States in this part of the world.

One of the most consequential things a Green Beret does is make momentous moral calls, with strategic implications, in extreme circumstances. There is often no time for quiet reflection or to ask for guidance. I was hungry. I was tired. I had been on near-constant patrols. Now, I had to deal with an impossible situation. My mind raced. I asked the chief to speak privately, and thankfully, he agreed.

Man to man, I leaned in and said quietly, "He's worth more alive than dead. Think of the intelligence value this guy has. He is from the secret police. He knows how and where the government's security forces are operating."

The chief considered it silently, his gaze stony. Finally, he said, "Okay, Captain. Maybe you're right."

Inwardly, I exulted. The chief continued, "We will torture him for all he knows."

Exultation over. This was getting worse. I could no more allow this man to be tortured than I could allow him to be executed out of hand. That was also a war crime. Contrary to the imagination of many, we don't condone torture, even in dire circumstances. I had to think of something—and I had to think fast.

"The CIA," I blurted out, "has the best interrogators in the world!"

The chief furrowed his brow. Here I was grasping at finding a common interest. We both wanted intelligence from this prisoner. The CIA had a legendary and infamous status around the world. Our allies and foes believed the agency was full of James Bonds and Jason Bournes. Maybe I had an outside chance of playing on that.

"Can you get this man to the CIA?" the chief asked, interested but skeptical.

"Yes," I said.

"But how can the CIA do better than my men? We can cause him pain. He will talk," he said.

I had no choice but to lie. "The CIA has truth serum and methods that will make any man talk." I tried to imply that the methods might be too unpleasant to mention. "It is impossible to lie to them," I said, hopeful that Hollywood had penetrated even to this part of the world.

The chief considered the offer. The pause was painfully long. "Yes, that is a good idea." When your CIA is done with him, we will deal with him our way." He shook my hand and walked away. I breathed a sigh of relief. I had prevented an execution—and preserved the relationship. Mission accomplished—for now.

I looked past the chief. I saw the exercise evaluator leaning against a tree, spitting tobacco on the ground, listening intently. Standing beside him was an Army psychologist writing in his green waterproof notepad. I wasn't in Afghanistan or Chad or Colombia. I was in a remote corner of North Carolina, and this was the culmination of the Special Forces Qualification Course. Known as Robin Sage, it is the American military's premier unconventional-warfare exercise and is the final test for every aspiring class of Special Forces soldiers on their long march to earning the coveted Green Beret. Here, the mindset it takes to be successful in guerilla warfare gets baked in. In Robin Sage, we face extraordinary physical tests—and even more consequential moral and psychological ones.

In the exercise, aspiring Green Berets are formed into

twelve-man teams tasked with supporting a resistance movement in the fictional nation of Pineland. The exercise is one of the largest in the military, spanning twenty-five counties in North Carolina and three counties in South Carolina. Key role-players come from the local community—sheriffs, mayors, farmers, and hotel owners—who serve either as officials of the "oppressive" government or as informants and supporters of the "resistance." To add to the realism, the Army orders mechanics, supply sergeants, cooks, and clerks from various conventional units to serve as the fighters for our "guerilla" force. These soldiers are somewhat like what we face with our partner forces overseas: they have very basic weapons and tactical training, and most of them aren't thrilled about being tasked to run around the woods for weeks on end with prospective Green Beret candidates. Not surprisingly, our "guerilla forces" often have a poor attitude, are not exactly motivated, and certainly aren't keen to take instructions from us. By disposition, they are very close to what we often find out there in real-world missions.

The tribal leader who wanted to execute the prisoner was played by a "G Chief." G Chiefs are salty, retired Green Berets. With cunning and hard-won expertise, they play parts they know well and give us hell.

The characters they portray are very interested in the aid, counsel, and material support that only a team of Green Berets can provide. I will never forget my own experience working with my G Chief and his guerilla force during Robin Sage.

He seemed to take true joy in throwing me into all types of moral dilemmas that Green Berets typically confront in the gray areas of unconventional warfare. There is a misconception that special operations forces get to play by special rules. Green Berets and other operatives often grow their hair and beards long, which regular soldiers are not allowed to do.

Some assume that these allowances in clothing and grooming symbolize permission to also flout the laws of war that bind conventional forces. The truth is that Green Berets, SEALs, and Rangers have the same code of ethics as every other American soldier. There is no special unit that offers a pass to abandon morality. We do not win at any price. That's never been the American code. Even though the Green Beret must expect to be thrust into cultural and moral environments that are profoundly different from their own, they are never at liberty to ignore the ethics, morals, and laws that define what it means to be an American.

Now, I serve in Congress. I am no longer in the most inaccessible and dangerous corners of Africa, Afghanistan, or Pineland. I do not negotiate with tribal chiefs to stop them from putting prisoners to death. I walk the hallways of the Capitol rather than hike remote mountain trails. I carry briefing binders instead of a rucksack. Yet the lessons of the Q Course, and of the Green Beret career that followed, still guide my words and steps.

As a nation, we face hugely complex challenges at home and abroad. Our foreign enemies are real, and they are growing in their power. We underestimate them at our peril. At home, we are as divided as we have been at any time in living memory. There is mistrust, anger, and contempt. Too many Democrats and Republicans no longer know how to talk to one another. They don't seem very interested in finding out how to start the conversation, either. They trade cynical and bitter sound bites, lobbing barbs like grenades. They fight over the same patches of ground with no prospect that one side can achieve a final victory over the other. The fleeting thrill of a tactical victory—a witty line on a news network that leads to clicks online—replaces the hard but satisfying work of pursuing a successful strategy on behalf of the voters in the people's House. This ugly conflict seems to be everywhere, but it is nowhere more noticeable than Washington, DC.

I think often of that grizzled G Chief and the way he snarled at me and the moral dilemma he forced me to confront. The Robin Sage instructors wanted to see what we would do under stress. Would we adhere to our ethics? Would we stand by the rules of engagement, or would we let the pressure lead us to bend the rules? The greatest challenge of Robin Sage was to never let the strain become an excuse to forget who we were. The greatest challenge of DC is much the same.

A Green Beret is called upon to solve problems with strategic implications under extraordinary stress, and to do so without compromising their morals. The principles and practices of the Green Berets have something to teach us about how to solve our most urgent and intractable domestic conflicts. First, though, we need to understand what's at the core of what it means to be a Green Beret.

There's an urban legend in the special operations community. A new Secretary of Defense wanted to know the difference between the Green Berets, more formally known as the U.S. Army Special Forces, and the Army Rangers and Navy SEALs. The Secretary called a Green Beret general into his office and asked, "What makes you different from the other special operators?"

The Green Beret general replied, "Sir, Rangers and SEALs are some of the toughest, most elite infantry on the planet." He explained, "The Rangers operate under strict discipline in large, battalion-size units. They take on large-scale sensitive missions like seizing an enemy airfield or nuclear power plant." The general explained that SEALs operate in small units with a maritime focus—like clearing obstacles at night on an enemy-held beach, affixing mines to enemy ships, or swimming out of a submarine near the ocean floor.

"Mr. Secretary"—the general paused for effect—"the bottom line is that the Rangers and SEALs are fantastic at finding, fixing, and killing our enemies anywhere in the world. Green Berets are different. They like to find our friends and train them to kill our enemies for us."

The Secretary of Defense motioned for the general to continue.

The general gave a half smile. "Sir, let me demonstrate the

difference for you. I've brought a Ranger, a SEAL, and a Green Beret with me today."

The group stepped outside the Secretary's office to a construction site serving as part of a Pentagon renovation. The general pointed to a partially constructed wall and said, "Ranger, take down that wall." The young Ranger, over six feet tall and built like a linebacker, sized up the wall of drywall and studs, knelt in a three-point stance, and crashed through it. With his body covered in dust and blood trickling down his forehead, the Ranger nodded at the general and the man-size hole in the wall.

The general then pointed at the next partially built wall, looked over at the SEAL, and ordered, "Chief, take it down." The SEAL chief petty officer picked up a sledgehammer and, with a series of powerful, expert strokes, demolished the second wall.

Impressed, the Secretary looked at the Green Beret general and said, "Wow. Okay, General, show me how the Green Berets can do that better."

"I wouldn't say better, sir. Just different," the general replied.

They walked together over to a third wall. The general nodded to the Green Beret sergeant everyone knew as Trip.

Older and leaner than the hulking Ranger and SEAL, Trip sized up the wall, running a dozen calculations in his head. He then walked over to a construction worker standing off to the side, and said, "Hey, buddy, I need you to do me a favor." Trip pointed to a nearby small bulldozer and had a brief conversation with the man. The construction worker nodded and smiled—and then mounted the bulldozer and hit a single load-bearing beam. The entire wall collapsed. Trip offered his thanks to the driver, said he would honor the case of beer he had promised after work, and smiled back in satisfaction at the general and the Secretary. He hadn't broken a sweat.

"Mr. Secretary, if you want super-troopers to do bad things to bad guys, the Rangers and SEALs are the best in the world," said the general. "Add in the Air Force special tactics squadrons, and they are all part of our specially selected, trained, and equipped Special Operations Forces community, commonly called SOF. The Green Berets are unique in operating by, with, and through others—our allies. They specialize in local cultures, are required to learn languages, embed with local forces, and train them to take care of our enemies for us."

The Secretary, a former businessman, smiled. "I get it now, General. Thank you."

The story gets to the heart of what makes Green Berets different. Being a Green Beret requires a different way of thinking and leading. Just as Trip had no authority to order a civilian construction worker to drive a bulldozer into a wall, Green Berets don't have the authority to boss militia leaders or foreign army officers around. We work with people far outside our chain of command, often people whose values and commitments are very different from ours. We must influence, cajole, and convince them that their interests and America's interests are aligned. It takes a level of maturity and autonomy unlike any other mission. That's why our training is much longer and focuses on the psychological every bit as much as the physical. When it all comes together, a twelve-man team of Green Berets can train a battalion of six hundred local soldiers.

The Green Beret may be a master influencer, but make no mistake—their physical toughness is also exceptional. Even to attend the Qualification Course, a Green Beret candidate must successfully complete the three-week Special Forces Assessment and Selection (SFAS). It is exactly the sort of brutal physical and psychological crucible one would expect, consisting of long runs, grueling marches, and psychological testing. To become one of the most elite soldiers in the world, you have to apply just to apply. Just to gain entry to the tryout, I had to achieve the maximum score on the standard physical fitness test for eighteen-year-olds. That meant being able to run two miles in under twelve minutes and complete eighty push-ups and sit-ups in two minutes each in addition to pull-ups and a swim test. Most important, I spent long days on backcountry trails with a sixty-pound rucksack, hardening my feet. Sadly, my feet are naturally baby soft, and I had to deliberately (and painfully) harden them. I worked up to eighteen-mile ruck marches (and thick calluses) before I thought I was ready. My Special Forces selection course started with 430 candidates from all corners of the Army. Only 92 were standing at the end, gaining the coveted admission to the Q Course, where even more candidates would fall by the wayside.

The first phase is small-unit infantry tactics similar to Ranger School, followed by specialty training as a weapons specialist, an engineer, a communications specialist, or a medic. Next is language training and survival, evasion, resistance, and escape (or SERE) training. The time it takes to complete all this varies depending on your specialty skills and language. A weapons specialist who learns Spanish might get through the training in twelve months. On the other hand, a medic who is required to learn how to sew up gunshot wounds in the emergency department of inner-city hospitals and then goes on to learn Arabic could find himself in training for over two years. By contrast, Ranger school is two months, and Navy SEAL BUD/S training is six months.

For many Americans, their introduction to Green Berets came with the 1968 John Wayne movie of the same name. *The Green Berets* was a window into this new way of waging unconventional war and advancing national interests. As Colonel Mike Kirby, John Wayne plays a master of guerilla warfare. His character understands the vital importance of establishing common interests with the locals. Kirby builds rapport with village chiefs and his South Vietnamese military counterparts. While the Green Berets did not need a legendary Hollywood tough guy to give them legitimacy, the film did an excellent job of explaining a little about *what* they do—and *why* it is so important.

At the time the Duke made his movie about us, the Green

Berets had been around for only a few years. The first Special Forces unit was created in 1952 as a response to the changing dynamics of war. Russia and eventually China had growing nuclear arsenals. The kind of mass industrial warfare we'd seen in the Second World War was still possible, but military planners on both sides feared any victory by the armies of the other would only lead to nuclear warfare and global destruction. Some officials saw the beginning of an alternative pathway— that the contest between Soviet-led Communism and the West would play out through proxy wars in the developing world, all over the globe. The Special Forces would help local "freedom fighters" battle Communist dictatorships—or conversely, help allied militaries fight against Soviet-backed insurgencies. Our motto summed up our mission: *De Oppresso Liber*, "To Free the Oppressed."

John F. Kennedy was the first President to understand the new warfare paradigm. He became a champion of the Special Forces as they struggled for a seat at the table within a resistant Pentagon bureaucracy. Senior generals, many of whom were already uncomfortable with the unconventional role of the Special Forces, objected to the attempts by this elite new outfit to wear a signature addition to the uniform: the green beret. One of our early colonels had a classmate working directly for President Kennedy in the White House. These old friends worked around the Pentagon brass to arrange for JFK to visit Fort Bragg and meet with the resident Special Forces.

Defying the orders of the generals, the unit wore its unauthorized headgear, which the President loved, later remarking, "The 'green beret' is . . . becoming a symbol of excellence, a badge of courage, a mark of distinction in the fight for freedom." President Kennedy and these early Special Forces leaders knew that victory was no longer a question of who held the most advantageous battlefield terrain, nearly as much as it was who held hearts and minds in faraway countries and distant villages.

To lead this kind of soldier is the task of leadership elevated to the nth degree. This is why the Army requires both officers and the enlisted to first lead in the conventional Army before even being allowed to try out for the Green Berets. My first unit was a tank platoon in the Third Infantry Division. There, I learned to care for, motivate, and lead American soldiers. But those fellow Americans obviously had a common language, common points of reference, and a common political framework to inform their actions and their decisions.

The Green Beret does not have the luxury of working with those who share his values, his culture, much less his language. Having successfully commanded his fellow Americans, he now needs to learn how to persuade and lead people with radically different worldviews. When I was in training, I was reminded that a Green Beret might come from Anytown USA, but he will be required to understand how things work in Kandahar, in rural Colombia, or in Africa's Sahel. The senior medic on my first team, Brian Duffy, sought to exceed every requirement of technical, tactical, and physical tasks that it takes to be an elite warrior. But he also studied history, Islam, and constitutional law. He knew he had to rise above his own cultural frameworks and his built-in biases to be able to connect with our local partners.

The encounter with the G Chief that opens this chapter was part of a hyperrealistic exercise. It was deadly serious preparation for what I would face overseas as a Green Beret. The physical stress was real: I was negotiating over a prisoner's life while I was sleep-deprived, exhausted, and very hungry. I knew in the back of my mind that all of this was an exercise. At the same time, the G Chief was using all his fierce talents to remind me that someday, I'd meet men like him, and it wouldn't be in the North Carolina backcountry. It would be somewhere far more remote, and a mistake could cost American lives, starting with my own.

Back when I was a captain, my teams embedded in a small village in the Tagab Valley in eastern Afghanistan along the border. It was nestled in a low river valley sandwiched between a wall of mountains, not far from Kabul as the crow flies. A shallow stream fed a series of villages and farms where Pashtun women, blanketed head to toe in blue burkas, walked a tortuous path of trails between stone-walled fields, over hard rock down to a muddy riverbank in order to bring in fresh water back to the village. The area was a gateway from the terrorist sanctuaries in Pakistan to Bagram Airfield. The tribe was known to have affiliated with al-Qaeda years earlier—so we invested a lot of time and attention in changing that fact on the ground.

The chief was a wizened old elder named Rahimullah. He had dodged grazing fire from Soviet helicopters and then joined the resistance against the Taliban regime. In between the Soviet occupation and the Taliban takeover, he fought for a warlord who had repeatedly switched sides between the Taliban and the government. But Rahimullah had long put aside his rifle—and he cared little for politics outside his village. He was neither a friend to America nor an enemy. Rather, the chief was a man who wanted several new wells, a footbridge over the river that swelled every spring, and for the local police chief to leave him alone.

What America wanted of him was just as simple. We wanted the chief to report Taliban fighters in the area. We wanted him to prevent the young men of his village from joining their forces and instead sign up with the Afghan National Army. We wanted open communication and fresh intelligence, and in turn, we were willing to dig him a new well, target the Taliban fighters who approached his village, and build him a new bridge.

Rahimullah was typical of the types we worked with when it is in the greater American interest to do so. As a Green Beret, I was not a social worker; I was a warrior diplomat. I had no illusions that I could change a local tribal leader or police chief into model legislators. I could, however, find a way to get him to act in our interests—and to see where our interests and his intersected. Our presence meant a local G Chief—either a host nation military or tribal militia leader—gained at least partial access to the most powerful intelligence apparatus and air force in the world. It also meant medical support, logistics, and planning.

A G Chief didn't have to be a tribal leader in the mountains of Afghanistan or jungles of Africa. They also could be a general in a partnered army or even the monarch of an allied country. As the commander on the ground, I often worked with the colonels, while my Green Berets built relationships and influence with the captains, lieutenants, and sergeants. My bosses worked with the generals and up the chain to key leaders, such as the Philippine and Colombian Ministers of Defense and the President of Afghanistan.

Since World War II, my Green Beret forebears embedded with the Montagnard tribespeople, putting the Viet Cong on the defensive. They halted the tide of Communism in the hills of El Salvador by professionalizing their army. In the 1990s, Green Berets trained the Colombian military to defeat the brutal and wily socialist FARC, a narco-fueled insurgency. Weeks after 9/11, they rode horses across the Hindu Kush with Afghan tribesmen to overthrow the Taliban regime. They've hiked the jungles of the Congo in search of the notorious warlord Joseph Kony. Most recently, over a period of just a few years, Green Berets professionalized the Ukrainian army to stand toe-to-toe with a hugely superior Russian invasion force. In places you've heard of, and places you haven't, Green Berets continue to win hearts, minds, and firefights—always at great risk and often to strategic effect with the investment of relatively few U.S. soldiers on the ground. That return on investment and risk requires a soldier with an elite level of mental and emotional intelligence to be able to communicate effectively, empathize, and negotiate and to know when to initiate conflict—and when to defuse it.

The opening scene of *The Green Berets* features two sergeants briefing members of the media skeptical of the U.S. involvement in the Vietnam War. One journalist points out that the South Vietnamese government had yet to live up to its promise to craft a constitution. The lead Green Beret, Master Sergeant Muldoon, reminds the reporter (and us in the audience) that the original thirteen colonies took eleven years of debate and deliberation before crafting a constitution. Muldoon also points out the heavy amount of Soviet and Chinese Communist support for North Vietnam. Cultivating allies and building representative democracy is laborious, almost always dangerous, and requires patience on the part of the governments who invest in this vital work.

The traits that stem from the mindset of the Green Beret—restraint, adaptability, resilience, determination, and bottom-up leadership—have served me well in business and in politics. In any new business, there must be a mentality of finding a way to yes, especially as an entrepreneur with everything on the line.

The same has applied to my congressional career. Understanding the various tribes and their agendas has not been that different from understanding the political factions in Congress and across the nation. Each of them has a G Chief that I must understand, take on board, and navigate to achieve a desired end state just as we did in the Special Forces Qualification Course and across Africa and the Middle East. I'm only half joking when I say that sometimes, understanding the motivations and machinations in Washington, DC, is harder than working with tribal leaders in the Middle East.

Because I have served in so many difficult places around the world, I have a clear vision of what America is and what she is called to be. Those experiences abroad have strongly reinforced my belief in the principles of limited government, individual liberty, personal responsibility, free markets, equal opportunity, and a strong national defense. I am often confounded and, frankly, angered by what I see as growing contempt for American exceptionalism and American virtues. It is a result of a generation of neo-Marxists who decided in the 1960s and '70s to stop attacking American institutions from the outside with kidnappings and bombings but rather infiltrate and influence them from the inside. They started with academia and have produced acolytes in the media, Hollywood, sports, and now the grand prize, corporate America. They have influenced an entire generation to believe that the United States is a republic dominated by a capitalist patriarchy that is inherently racist, misogynist, and colonialist at its core. Because these traits are "systemic," American institutions must be torn down to the base and rebuilt in a more "equitable" system. Of course, these academics ignore the millions of people the United States has liberated through multiple world wars, its own Civil War to end slavery, the increasingly equal opportunity and upward mobility provided to its citizens of all races and religions, and the phenomenal wealth generated globally by the liberal world order underwritten by American leadership since World War II. By no means is it a perfect country, but I thank God every time I land back here after traveling abroad.

Green Berets are taught to negotiate with the ideological, even fanatical, that have a worldview completely different from mine. I cannot choose my colleagues in Congress any more than I could handpick the tribal leaders whom I was sent to persuade. We have no choice but to use our skills and training that are fundamental to the Green Berets found in this book to craft solutions that move our mission and our nation forward. Like in our training and on missions, there is no quitting on this great nation.

In the story that begins this book, when I told the G Chief I could not let him execute his prisoner, he told me that if I didn't like his plans, I could just walk away. If I had, I would have failed the course, and if it had been a real situation abroad I would have been complicit in a murder. Green Berets don't walk away from a crisis. Likewise, there is no walking away from the crises that confront this country, no matter how difficult, intractable, and maddening they seem. The qualities that make the Green Beret indispensable abroad are the qualities we need more than ever at home.

2

RESTRAINT

Uruzgan isn't the middle of nowhere, but it's close. The Taliban had turned this rugged, arid south-central Afghan province into a central staging area for their operations. From Uruzgan, they could launch attacks southeast on Kandahar (Afghanistan's second-largest city) or the Ring Road, the only major road in the country. It's a hell of a place to fight a war: a place where some of the struggle is combat, and more of it is a contest of persuasion of Uruzgan's various tribes. In a counterinsurgency, the latter matters most.

That's why the Green Berets were there. Influence and persuasion are our job.

Three other Green Berets plus myself were embedded with about twenty soldiers from the United Arab Emirates, themselves partnered with several platoons of Afghan National Army soldiers. On this particular day, we were all part of an even larger coalition operation, conducting overwatch on a valley as a combined American and Australian force cleared out Taliban from the district in Operation Perth.

As we conducted our security operations, the ordinary ebb and flow of life in Uruzgan Province continued. Farmers worked their fields. Truckloads of laborers passed by. Men on foot trekked to destinations unknown. Women, more or less hidden away in the foreigners' presence, would sometimes be seen working at domestic tasks. Children often came out, some friendly and curious, others keeping a wary distance.

Our mission was to block the northern entrance to the valley to prevent the Taliban from attacking the rear of the Australian task force. As soon as we guided our UAE and Afghan vehicles into position, my medic, then on his second tour, said, "Sir, anytime we are static in one position for too long, we are eventually going to get hit." My concern was a suicide vest or vehicle car bomb coming into our checkpoint. As we went about our work—stopping every passing vehicle, searching them, taking photos of them for records and analysis—my concern grew. With every passing minute, the likelihood of a Taliban attack grew.

We'd been in position for barely two hours when we heard the distinctive whistle and thud of a mortar round impacting two hundred yards in front of us.

The first round hurt no one—thank God—but we knew what was coming. Somewhere out there was a spotter, calling in our exact location to the Taliban firing the mortars. We couldn't flee for cover; the Aussies needed us to hold the line. That left one option: find the spotter and kill him.

Our two snipers—an Australian and an Emirati, both

consummate professionals—scanned the landscape. They found the spotter in moments and radioed in the location. On my order, the snipers would open fire, and the spotter would be dead.

Normally, I had no trouble giving this order. This time was different. The snipers told me the spotter was a small boy, no more than twelve years old.

This child stood on a ridgeline with binoculars and a walkie-talkie. He was perfectly silhouetted for a shot. Our snipers watched him for a bit, just to be sure. The boy peered through the binoculars at us, raised the walkie-talkie, spoke, and moments later, another mortar round landed nearby—much closer than the last one.

This small boy was almost certainly the spotter for the Taliban. Left alone, he would get one of my fellow soldiers—American, Emirati, Australian, Afghan—wounded or killed. Our two snipers watched, and after the next mortar round came even closer to our position, the request came through the net. They wanted permission to shoot the child.

I received the request and knew I had to decide. The snipers would not miss, and the round would probably cut the boy in half. It would be a justified call, a terrible decision undertaken out of necessity rather than malice or callousness.

Another mortar round landed. The snipers were screaming, *"Sir, let me take the shot!"* The Emirati sniper was emphatic but civil. The Australian sniper, with his rifle perched on a tripod across the hood of the Humvee, unleashed a string of four-letter words, and felt free to question my manhood.

It's a hell of a workday when your manhood rests upon the decision to kill a child.

As an American soldier, I was bound by some things my enemy was not: a moral code, for one, that I'll defend as superior to anything the average Talib will bring to bear; and also, codified rules of warfare that guided every action and decision. Civilians actively aiding combatants on the battlefield were fair game, whether it was bringing the Taliban fighters water or ammunition. Once they engaged in assisting the enemy's attack on coalition forces, we could defend ourselves under our rules of engagement—even unarmed. The gray area became intent. What if the woman or child was forced into that aid rather than giving it willingly? In this case, what if the unarmed boy was simply observing? I was, however, pretty sure that the present situation was different. The binoculars and walkie-talkie the boy was using were de facto weapons: instruments meant to kill my men and our allies. If I ordered the shot, I would have a strong defense.

In the back of my mind, I knew it was possible I might have to mount that defense in court. This was the sort of situation in which soldiers risked prosecution. Former First Lieutenant Clint Lorance, for example, was sentenced to twenty years in prison over charges stemming from a split-second decision to open fire on three Afghan men riding a motorcycle toward his platoon. The incident occurred days after his platoon had been hit at the same checkpoint and the previous platoon leader badly wounded. He was finally pardoned by President Trump in 2019, but only after serving years behind bars.

Maybe, though, my manhood rested upon something else. Maybe it rested upon *restraint*. I knew what we could do according to the rules of engagement. I knew what I was being urged to do. But this is where a Green Beret, familiar with the ways Green Berets are meant to think, asks the unasked question: *What if we don't take action?* Some of the struggle is combat, and more of it is persuasion. What got us to satisfy my duty to keep my soldiers safe—and also got us to thwart the enemy's objective, which was to exploit this child, dead or alive?

We could leave our position and go somewhere more defensible, and presumably be less exposed to this child and his mortar team. But we'd been ordered to hold this line: and I knew that if we moved, the chances were high that Taliban fighters would move through the gap we'd opened, to kill Americans and Afghans alike. I wasn't going to do that. Further, there were only so many places to go in the relatively narrow valley. We would soon be under mortar fire again.

The Taliban, like the canny and experienced insurgents they are, created a decision-making vise. Either I moved our forces, which delivered them the tactical advantage they wanted—or I order the child killed, which delivered them the propaganda advantage they wanted. The Taliban had a long history of parading the bodies of civilians killed as accidental collateral damage in this brutal war as evidence of American imperialism and anti-Muslim hate. They often videoed the bodies for distribution across international jihadi websites to further their misinformation campaign and help their recruiting.

All of these thoughts flashed through my mind in a matter of seconds. I had to decide *something*. My snipers were screaming. The Afghan soldiers were starting to panic. Another mortar round landed, even closer. What's next, team leader?

Uruzgan Province was not even close to the first time Americans at war were compelled to confront—and execute—on the principle of restraint. Look back, across American history, at episodes where restraint worked—and let's think about why.

The end of the Civil War, April 1865, is a good place to start.

Robert E. Lee's Army of Northern Virginia straggled out of fallen Richmond and Petersburg, redoubts they had held, entrenched, for the preceding ten months. Despite huge losses, the Confederates retained their capacity to fight, presenting an extraordinary operational and tactical danger to the Union Army. General Ulysses S. Grant found his Union forces mauled again and again by the retreating Confederates. Grant and Lee both understood that strategic initiative and momentum had passed decisively to Grant—but both understood that the road to peace was still long and bloody.

The toll of the American Civil War was perhaps around three-quarters of a million Americans dead, and countless more wounded, missing, and captured. If the American Revolution was the defining moment of our republic, then the American Civil War was a defining disaster. And for the side determined to preserve the Union at any cost, the principal cause of so much of that immense suffering was the Army of Northern Virginia.

After a final fight at Appomattox Court House on April 9, General Lee sent word to General Grant that he wished to learn the terms of surrender. To the minds of many in the North, the Union had spilled too much blood for there to be an easy truce. General Grant had it in his power to make the peace whatever he wished. He could have imposed brutal terms. That would have been both popular and understandable.

Instead, Grant allowed Lee to choose the place of his own surrender. He allowed the men of the Army of Northern Virginia to return to their homes, with their horses and mules. He allowed the officers of the Army of Northern Virginia to retain their sidearms and possessions, and guaranteed the officers and men of the Confederate forces immunity from prosecution. Grant even directed his quartermaster to provide food to the hungry soldiers of the defeated side. With these early steps, Grant set the country on its long course of national healing.

As General Lee left the Appomattox Court House, Grant's entourage and the assembled spectators began to cheer. After four years of horrific war, it was over, they had won, and they had every right to cheer. Grant stopped them. Later in life, he recalled the moment: "The Confederates were now our countrymen, and we did not want to exult over their downfall."

This wasn't just Grant's generosity. In North Carolina, General William Tecumseh Sherman received the surrender of an even larger Confederate army, General Joseph Johnston's Army of Tennessee. The terms Sherman gave Johnston were even more generous than those Grant gave Lee. The two generals became friends, and Johnston was a pallbearer at Sherman's funeral.

Some historians think this was all a terrible mistake. They think the South got off too easy, and the result was an era of racist oppression that saw Black Americans denied their own full rights until a full century after the war they helped win. They are not wrong: Reconstruction was inconsistent and abandoned too early. Racist segregation, often brutally enforced, lasted for another hundred years as a result. We have spent the last sixty years working hard to overcome that stain, and in some respects, we still have further to go.

Nevertheless, the restraint shown by the Union to surrendering Confederates has been largely vindicated by history. So often, a brutal peace guarantees a "war after the war." Had the Confederates been punished more viciously, it might easily have guaranteed an ongoing and bloody Southern insurgency. We know Grant feared that possibility, and some of Lee's subordinates urged the surrendering general to consider it. To his great credit, Lee refused to lead a new phase of the Civil War, writing to Confederate President Jefferson Davis in an attempt to dissuade him from the idea. "A partisan war may be continued," he wrote, "and hostilities protracted, causing individual suffering and the devastation of the country, but I see no prospect by that means of achieving a separate independence."

It's impossible to quantify the generosity shown by Grant and Sherman to their defeated counterparts. But we do know what *didn't* happen—years of horrific guerilla warfare across the South—and we know what did. What happened is the restraint of the victors and the stability that restraint created.

Today, we are fortunate to not have civil strife of the 1860s variety marring our society. But the riots in the wake of the death of George Floyd showed that race relations can still be a powder keg in America. Our politics and national conversation around the issue cannot be zero-sum. In my time in Congress, I've seen that firsthand: politicians whose first concern ought to be the good of the country are gripped instead by a compulsion to demonstrate how uncompromising they are in the face of the threat posed by the other side. There are ways to be principled in your positions but find common ground as fellow Americans. I can't help thinking that the restraint of a Grant or a Lincoln, "with malice toward none, with charity to all," is just what America needs—then and now.

Restraint continued to be a key element of our policy into the twentieth century.

In Korea, the American-led United Nations forces defending the peninsula regained the initiative after a wave of early setbacks. At great cost, we battered Seoul—and effectively gutted the Chinese forces roughly along the line of the old border between north and south. At the U.S. Eighth Army headquarters, there was serious discussion of pressing forward into North Korea and establishing a defensible stop line. North

Korea would be reduced to a rump state, mostly barren and mountainous, stripped of most of its population and its major cities.

As you know, that's not what happened. The Truman White House rightly decided that the strategic goal in Korea was containment, not conquest. The West was not prepared for a Third World War, not prepared for a land war in China, and not prepared for the intervention of the Soviet Union. The USSR had recently acquired the atomic bomb. Escalation in pursuit of victory is a dangerous game. The enemy gets a vote—and had cast it a few times in this war already—and no one knew how the Chinese and Russians would vote next.

Restraint bought the free world time to do what it most needed to do. Because Korea's war does not become a world war, NATO has the opportunity to stand up, the West has the opportunity to rebuild West Germany, and America has the opportunity to establish its network of alliances for mutual defense around the world. Four decades later, the foundation laid with the time bought paid off, as the Soviet empire fell, a victim both of itself and of the united free world that faced it down.

Restraint is vindicated again.

Restraint isn't only an American virtue. In October 1962, one Soviet submarine officer saved the world from nuclear war. Vasily Arkhipov had already had an extraordinary career in the Soviet navy. Two summers prior, he found himself executive officer of the infamous submarine K-19, whose crewmen sacrificed themselves to save the boat from a reactor meltdown. Now, he was the executive officer of submarine B-59, bound for Cuba—which was under an American blockade during the Cuban missile crisis. An American destroyer detected B-59 and began dropping depth charges, intending to force the submarine to surface and identify itself. Under the waves, though, B-59's command crew believed that war had broken out and the American ship was attacking with the intent to sink the sub. The captain and the Soviet political officer wanted to hit back—hard.

B-59 had nuclear-tipped torpedoes aboard. One launch would wipe out the American flotilla on the surface and buy the submarine its escape. The Soviet captain ordered the launch. The political officer gave his concurrence. It remained only for the boat's executive officer, Vasily Arkhipov, to agree. The use of nuclear weapons, according to Soviet Navy regulations, required the concurrence of all three.

Arkhipov did not agree. The captain of B-59 erupts in anger. American depth charges were dropping, and the captain is determined to retaliate. One can only imagine the pressure on Arkhipov, especially knowing the consequences back in the Soviet Union for an officer who disobeyed an order. Arkhipov still does not agree and stands firm.

Because of the executive officer's refusal to launch the nuclear torpedo, B-59 was compelled to surface. There, they learned that the Americans were not mounting a lethal attack—and the submarine was able to communicate with Moscow, which informed them that war had not broken out. Had B-59 launched a nuclear strike against the United States Navy, of course, nuclear war would have erupted from the Cuban missile crisis.

The *restraint* of one man, Vasily Arkhipov, saved the planet from destruction. Arkhipov wasn't a general or a president; he was the deputy commander of a submarine, fending off the pleas and anger of his fellow officers. Restraint in deciding terms of surrender is one thing. Restraint under fire with nuclear war at stake is another.

In September 1983, the Soviet Union downed a Korean civilian jetliner, killing hundreds of innocent travelers, including a member of Congress. Already-high tension between the two superpowers grows higher. The Soviets convince themselves that President Ronald Reagan will launch a surprise nuclear attack. To protect themselves from what they are sure is coming, they launch Operation RYAN: a comprehensive effort to detect, by various means, the launch of a U.S. first strike.

Operation RYAN includes a satellite early-warning network, monitored by Soviet air-defense personnel. On the morning of September 26, 1983, Stanislav Petrov is on duty— and he receives an alert that a satellite has picked up the launch of a single missile, from the United States, toward the Soviet Union. Petrov's duty is clear: he must notify his superiors, who will pass the information up the chain of command. That chain of command has perhaps half an hour or less to react.

Petrov knows that once he alerts his superiors to the

inbound-strike notice, the near-certain response will be a full-force nuclear counterattack. The young officer hesitates. Why, he asks himself, would the Americans attack the Soviet Union with only a single missile? That makes no sense. He recalls his doubts as to the technical reliability of the satellite early-warning system. He decides to wait. If further confirmation of launch is received, he will alert the chain of command, and thermonuclear war will ensue. But not yet. Not quite yet.

No confirmation is received. The Soviet satellite, Petrov discovers, had misinterpreted sunlight glinting off clouds as a missile launch.

Two decades apart, the restraint of two men saved the world and prevented the Cold War from going hot.

In the first Gulf War, President George H. W. Bush decided not to go on to Baghdad after liberating Kuwait. His generals achieved the objectives President Bush and his team set out before the war and didn't let the ease with which they defeated the Iraqi army allow them to get greedy. He was questioned and criticized at the time and in the decade to follow. In retrospect, that restraint looks incredibly wise. For once in modern American history, we won both the war and the peace.

This all brings us back to one hot day in Afghanistan with two snipers demanding that I allow them to shoot a small boy. The stakes weren't quite as high as nuclear war. But I knew that if I didn't give the order, a mortar round could kill one (or many more) of my soldiers. I wasn't thinking about Petrov, or Grant, or Truman. I had learned their stories at VMI, and perhaps they were somewhere in my subconscious.

I was thinking of my men and of this child. I was thinking of my duty—and what it meant to be in this moment as a Christian and as a father.

From months of near-continuous combat with the Taliban, I also knew what was happening. The Taliban, untroubled by any sense of morality or decency, would often demand that local families supply one of their children to undertake tasks like this. Sometimes the children would be mortar spotters. Sometimes they would be pressed into service as ammunition bearers. Sometimes they would be compelled to act as suicide bombers. If the families refused, the Taliban would simply kill their child, and sometimes them, too. If the families complied and their child died in combat, then the Taliban would exploit the propaganda angle: *Look, the Americans have killed an Afghan child!*

"Fire a warning shot and splash him," I said.

The snipers glared at me for a moment and then complied. A round pinged in near the boy: a deliberate miss. Then another. The frightened boy was pelted—splashed—with rocks and debris as sniper rounds came in at his feet.

"Get the message," I said silently. He did. The boy disappeared over the ridgeline in a terrified scramble. The mortar rounds stopped.

But if he had come back, I'd made up my mind. I was going to give the order for the kill shot. Thankfully, I never had to.

The boy came back into view—but not as a spotter. He

raced downhill toward a small village in the distance. I decided to follow him in my Humvee, along with a UAE and Afghan vehicle. Upon arrival in the nearby village, the malik, or head elder, was already waiting for us with a group of older men. He knew what was coming. One of the Afghan sergeants demanded that all the village elders assemble. When the group gathered, he yelled at them, "Why are you helping the Talibs attack us? We are here, sons and soldiers of the new Afghanistan, fighting for a better life for your families and children. The Talibs will only take us backward!"

One of the elders stepped forward. He was indignant and not at all cowed by the berating from a soldier. "The Talibs came yesterday in five trucks full of mujahideen," he said, "They said the infidel Americans are coming to attack our homes, our mosques. They will destroy our poppy crops and take some of our women. The Talib commander said that we must resist!"

I glanced back at one of my operators manning the machine gun in the turret of my Humvee. We locked eyes, and I knew we were thinking the same thing. This confrontation could go south fast: and any one of these villagers—or all of them—could be Taliban themselves. We were also wondering if those five trucks of Taliban fighters were nearby.

Another elder stepped forward in the semicircle that formed around us. "The Talibs demanded each family give up their eldest son to help them fight you. We have no choice. We have no heavy weapons. One family refused their demands."

The elder pointed to a man with his head down, standing near a cart with a body lying on it, wrapped in a white sheet. "They hanged him. They hanged his boy."

I didn't need the translation.

This was the life-and-death dilemma of the villagers. They lived it every day. They lived it before we came, they lived it while we were there—and they would live it when we were gone.

I looked up and thanked God I hadn't given the order to kill another young son.

Restraint, holding back, has served America well, tactically and strategically, many times throughout our history. This time, it served me well—and saved a young boy's life. The dilemma I faced was replicated over and over again in Afghanistan, in Iraq, in Syria, in Yemen, in the African Sahel, and in every other American theater of war throughout history. Every soldier ends up making their own call, and I don't sit in judgment of them. These decisions are the haunting ones—especially when the call is to shoot. Young Americans make these decisions and are then expected to live with them for the rest of their lives. It's a recipe for disillusionment, PTSD—and in the worst case, without the social and mental-health support they deserve, veteran suicide.

I was exceptionally lucky to have arrived at a situation I could live with. That wasn't due to my own exceptional decision-making. I was fortunate in a host of ways: the boy chose to run, and the villagers chose to talk to us. But the outcome easily could have been very different. What if the boy had come back and called in a fatal round on one of my soldiers before my snipers could get him? At some point, I would have been sitting in the living room of my fallen soldier's parents and explaining to them that I had chosen the life of that boy over their own son's. That Afghan boy wasn't entrusted to me, but their son was. Maybe they'd forgive me. But I wouldn't forgive myself.

These are the calls a leader makes. A Green Beret specializes in living in the gray zones where these dilemmas are inevitable. Shooting a Russian tank or downing a Chinese aircraft in a conventional combat environment is a fairly black-and-white mission. Defending a village against an insurgency that just might be run by some of the insurgents is significantly more challenging. Persuading an influential elder to dissuade his community's young men from jihad is not a straightforward task. Empowering local militia to stand up to a ruthless guerilla enemy is not a job with simple, quickly measurable outcomes. The definitions of success and failure may vary from day to day or may be barely discernible. All we know is this: the Green Beret is expected to make the toughest calls and be one hundred percent accountable for them.

The incident with the boy calling in that mortar fire wasn't the first such experience I'd had. A few months earlier, we had an incident where a Taliban fighter took cover behind a woman in a burka while he fired on our perimeter. We'd seen this before, and we knew that often enough, the women were willing cover for the Taliban lurking behind them. Nevertheless, I ordered my men not to take the shot. What if the woman was

unwilling? Was a human life a price worth paying for that level
of uncertainty?

Or—this is the one level deeper we must go—what if
she *was* willing and noted that the Americans left her alive?
What does that restraint teach her? What does it stir up inside
those Taliban fighters who used her life as cover for their own?
Maybe it means nothing and is interpreted as Western weakness. That's a possibility. Maybe, though, it starts her thinking
about the difference between us and them. The same circum-
stance applied to the village that sent its young boy to help the
Taliban kill us. We showed them forgiveness—exactly the opposite of what the Taliban would do if the roles were reversed.
We couldn't change what the village had done—but we could
affect what it would do in the future. These things are cumula-
tive. In sparing the woman, in sparing the boy, in sparing the
village, we didn't just answer to our own moral code: we set
ourselves apart from the enemy who regularly kills civilians, by
doing something they would never do. In showing restraint, we
stepped off the violence-escalation ladder.

The lesson here applies well beyond the battlefield. Turn
away from Afghanistan at war and look at America today. Normal Americans—which is to say, nonideological people with
ordinary jobs and lives, who do not live constantly online—
hate our current atmosphere. They hate cancel culture. They
hate everything becoming politicized—from kneeling during
the national anthem at football games to beer companies div-
ing into contentious social issues. When one side acts, the other

must hit back, compelling another counterattack. Many people feel increasingly trapped by these negative spirals. Because so few are willing to do it, the leader who demonstrates *restraint* and steps off that escalation ladder is doing something both radically countercultural and genuinely attractive. We are in a situation where, because intensification is nearly everywhere, *restraint* becomes a real source of power.

This lesson came home for me in my first campaign. When then Congressman Ron DeSantis decided to run for governor of Florida, I announced my intent to run for his congressional seat. I had been considering it for a few years since he ran to be senator, but dropped out. My business with my partners was finally taking off after years of struggle. We had received a buy-in from a private equity firm so we could start paying ourselves a good salary. I was so proud of what my partners and I had built from scratch, and it was a little nuts to walk away at this point. After I discussed it all with my family, they knew my heart was in public service. I needed to get back into the fight. This congressional seat had opened up near where I grew up in Jacksonville and also had in it the same small town, Umatilla, where my wife, Julia, grew up. What were the odds? It was a sign. So, I decided to take a swing. I knew there would be tough competition; I had never held a local office and had no idea what I was doing. The idea that a kid with blue-collar roots could be a U.S. congressman was insane. And the millions of dollars my consultants told me I would have to raise sounded like mission impossible. It was intimidating as hell.

But good Green Berets absorb their environment, map out the key objectives, and surround themselves with good people to help execute. Ultimately, I didn't want to regret *not* trying. Plus, a statistic kept gnawing at me—the record-low number of veterans serving in Congress.

In the late 1970s, over 75 percent of the House and Senate had previously served in the military. Forty years later, the percentage of veterans in Congress had declined to 15 percent. I thought that record decline went a long way toward explaining the record amount of dysfunction in Washington, DC. It's not that, as veterans, we agree on all issues. Of course we don't. But if we were willing to fight and die together on a ship, on a plane, or in a foxhole, we can figure out how to come together to move the country forward. Further, there is a different perspective on American exceptionalism when you have served all over the world and seen how good we have it here. And finally, there is a commonality of being mission focused and accomplishing an objective. I've found in business and in combat, failure is not an option, and we must have a mindset to accomplish things bigger than ourselves. We need more of this mindset in our politics. The thought of being a representative for the republic I had been willing to die for was humbling and exciting. I also thought with my policy, business, and combat leadership experience, I could be effective and went for it.

It took me a while to get comfortable with it, but we ran more heavily on my military rather than policy or business experience. My team was convinced that in a time of divisiveness, voters would gravitate to my ability to lead, to unify, and to stand strong for traditional American values. I said repeatedly on the campaign trail across central Florida, "I will fight for you in Washington just as hard as I fought for you in combat." It was not just a slogan. I meant it with every fiber of my being.

But sure enough, several months into the campaign, the hits started coming. A letter began circulating among the Republican clubs questioning my service—and even accusing me of stolen valor. The letter suggested that there was no way, by my mid-forties, that I could have served over twenty years in the U.S. Army Special Forces, served in the White House, and helped build an award-winning, veteran-run business that eventually employed four hundred people. Further, the letter questioned the awarding of four Bronze Star medals. Soon the letter appeared online. I started getting calls from local influencers who had publicly supported me but now had questions.

I was pissed. I knew who was behind it. I wanted to hit back and explain to these haters that I was in the National Guard for all those years and had to have a "day job." In my case, those day jobs were in the Pentagon, the White House, and, later, building a business that trained our military and provided expert analysts that tracked down "bad guy" money all over the world, among other things. I was determined to nip this nonsense in the bud. Someone fires at me, I want to return fire. How dare they directly question my integrity! A number of my family and friends felt the same way, outraged on my behalf. It was my biggest fear about getting into politics coming true—some false accusation forever etched in concrete on the internet. I felt justified in my anger, and when everything in our modern society reinforces and promotes hitting back, I was ready to launch.

Fortunately, some cooler heads on my team stepped in, especially my wife, Julia. She was herself a combat veteran with tours in Afghanistan and Iraq, had her PhD in resiliency, and served as the State Department's diplomat to negotiate the release of American hostages held around the world. She stopped me before I could unload on social media and to local journalists. My campaign advisors pointed out that I had extensive details of my service already out in public. My book *Warrior Diplomat* had been in print for years, so my fellow veterans would have called out any type of stolen valor a long time ago. My advisors reminded me that issuing a statement, hitting back, or even questioning the motivations of those leveling these accusations would only pour more fuel on the fire and call attention to it. It would also make me look defensive. In other words, restraint and holding fire were the better way to go.

It was a basic lesson, one that I already knew from personal experience and from my classes in military history: not every attack merits a counterattack. In our contemporary political culture, it's very hard to show restraint when your very character is maligned. It is painful to be lied about and to have your loved ones hear and see those lies forever online. Yet even as my blood boiled, in the spirit of bottom-up leadership, I listened to my team. As we discussed the best way to respond, I recalled all the times in combat that the enemy fired on my soldiers and I ordered them to hold back because of civilians in the vicinity, not wanting to reveal our position, or some other compelling factor.

Restraint isn't natural for most of us. It is a learned skill that is rooted in humility—both increasingly rare virtues in modern society. From the aftermath of the Civil War to the moment the Cold War nearly turned hot, and from my own small role in deciding the fate of a small boy in Afghanistan to my hard-fought race to become a United States congressman, I've seen the value of restraint. Restraint saves lives, it wins hearts and minds, and it preserves relationships with family and friends.

Green Berets are warriors. We do not hesitate to use lethal force when there is no other option. But we know that sometimes, there are other, smarter options. I am committed to doing all I can to make sure that Americans understand and appreciate the very undervalued option of restraint.

3

DISCIPLINE

I'd seen fights before, but never one like this. A sergeant and a second lieutenant were in a full-on, out-for-blood brawl with each other in the middle of the swamp phase of the U.S. Army's Ranger School. Those of us watching were so spent that for the longest time, we just stood and stared. We understood why these two men were beating the crap out of each other and why it mattered so much. One of the soldiers believed that the other had stolen, and eaten, his last remaining MRE chocolate-covered brownie bar.

That sounds like a pretty stupid reason for a fistfight to someone well fed and comfortable. These two men weren't, and neither were we. The idea that the accused would have eaten the brownie bar made sense. The possibility that the accuser had simply lost his mind also made sense. In either case, there was a breakdown of basic human judgment. Reasoning and cognition had all gone out the window. This was just primal rage.

This was Ranger School, and we were learning a lot about

human nature. We were finding the best and worst of ourselves.

The thing about all training in Special Operations Forces is that it isn't designed just to weed out the unwilling or the unable. It's designed to test the absolute limits of character and endurance. Most people think Ranger School testing is primarily for the Army's benefit, so that it can discover the few men worthy of a Ranger tab. That's only partly true. The lessons learned in the crucible of Ranger School are for the aspiring Ranger. What will all that deprivation, suffering, and hunger do to a person? Who will they become? What will be left of them when they are at the very end of their mental and physical rope?

The thing about Ranger School is that it asks a basic question: How long will discipline last? The sergeant and the lieutenant pummeling each other over the brownie bar were both good soldiers. I had seen them in the field executing ambushes and patrols very well. But something had finally snapped in them that we all understood.

The problem in America today is that far too many of our fellow citizens have broken down as well. Not from arduous Ranger training but from a mix of social and cultural factors that have left them unmotivated, ungrateful, suspicious, and, above all, undisciplined. I don't want or expect most young people to endure or experience what I have. I do very much want to help our young people rediscover the power and purpose of discipline.

We still teach psychology students about the Stanford marshmallow experiment. The brainchild of Walter Mischel—a survivor of the Nazis—the marshmallow experiment became the classic study of the human ability to delay gratification. The researchers would place a marshmallow in front of a child and then leave the room—but not before telling the kid that if they were able to resist eating the marshmallow for a given period, they'd get a second marshmallow. Some kids ate the treat the second the researchers left; others held out, waiting patiently to double their marshmallows. The researchers were interested in what the factors were that led certain children to delay gratification and others to forget about a reward they could not see. The immediate results of the experiments were in *how* delayed gratification was achieved.

The more interesting results came only later. Across the many years after the experiments, the researchers followed up with the children—those who showed the ability to delay gratification and those who did not. Something remarkable emerged as the children grew up. The ones who possessed the ability to defer the greater reward to a later time ended up having superior outcomes in life versus those who did not. Educational status, social status, health status, and so on—all were better among the delayed-gratification group.

The Stanford marshmallow experiment took the teachings most of us heard as children—"Slow and steady wins the race" or "The early bird gets the worm"—and proved them right. To our grandparents, the marshmallow experiment might be one great big "I told you so." Discipline and self-control, even in the smallest things, pay huge dividends.

Discipline *matters*.

Discipline matters not just as a tactic for specific situations but as an ethic for a life well lived. It is often the difference between success and defeat, or between flourishing and failure to thrive. This was the basic lesson that our superiors at the Virginia Military Institute tried to impart to us with their regimen of seemingly endless and sometimes pointless minutiae of discipline-focused demands. I remember one of those tasks in particular: the daily bed-making.

The barracks at VMI were, to put it nicely, antiquated. My room for my junior year was Stonewall Jackson's classroom 140 years earlier and hadn't changed a bit. Our Civil War–era rooms were so small that when the beds were laid out, there was almost no floor space on which to walk around. I still vividly recall, nearly three decades later, how we put the beds away in a strictly prescribed manner. We stripped the wool blankets and folded them in a specific way. We rolled the thin mattresses like cigars and lashed them tightly. Then we folded up the legs of the heavy wooden bed frames and leaned them against the wall so we could have a room to use. There were three to four men per room, so it was tight. As cadets, we did this *every day* for our four years there.

The point was not really the floor space. The point was the discipline. The daily necessity of a cooperative task, done to a set standard, for the benefit of yourself and others was the real purpose of the thing. If we had spacious rooms as cadets, the institute would have had us do something else.

There is another aspect of discipline here. If the Stanford experiment showed the value of delayed gratification as a disciplinary *approach*, then the VMI experience hammered home the value of forming habits as a disciplinary *mechanism*. This is not a new insight. Retired Admiral William McRaven has built an entire cottage industry on the tenets of his bestselling book *Make Your Bed*. Philosophy majors might recall that some 2,500 years ago, Aristotle argued that "we are what we do repeatedly." Excellence, he said, is just the result of the right habits. Action shapes belief more than vice versa, and belief flows into character.

Character is often thought of as the source of discipline, but the reality is there is a feedback loop between the two. Character informs discipline, and discipline undergirds character. Human nature is shaped by habit, by pressure, and by discipline. In Ranger School, I got an up-close-and-personal look at how pressure both shapes and tests character. The Rangers test human limits in the most basic way possible: hunger.

It's worth revisiting just what sort of physical hell Ranger School puts you through, in the name of testing your qualities as a leader. I've written already about the extreme sleep deprivation: the denial of rest, with many twenty-four-hour periods featuring perhaps thirty minutes, or on luxurious days a full hour, of sleep. Add onto that the constant movement, the endless tactical scenarios in swamps and mountains, and the never-ending carrying of heavy packs plus rifles. All this means that the body requires a truly immense caloric intake to sustain itself. The average Ranger School student is expending, according to an Army study, about 4,500–6,500 calories per day.

The average Ranger School student *gets* about 800–1,000 calories per day. The rule of thumb for us was five Meals Ready-to-Eat—the famous MREs familiar to soldiers everywhere—for every five days. It's a tough regimen, especially if you've never experienced real hunger before. I don't mean the hunger that comes before an ordinary mealtime or while on a typical weight-loss diet: I mean *profound* hunger, the sort of hunger that clouds thought and overrides judgment, a hunger that can totally consume a man unless he possesses the prerequisite of discipline.

One of the findings in the Stanford marshmallow experiment was that delayed gratification was easier for the child subjects if the lesser reward was out of sight and therefore out of mind. If you tell a child, "You can have one marshmallow now, or two in ten minutes," but you don't *show* them any marshmallows, they're more likely to restrain themselves than if you place a single marshmallow right in front of them. Ranger School's well-honed method struck directly at that human weakness: we were not given an MRE every day and a half. We were given *all five MREs* up front for the whole five-day period and told to carry them with us. Like a kid in agony staring at a marshmallow that he desperately wanted, every hunger-racked man carried instant relief in his rucksack. As his body rapidly consumed itself—in the literal sense, I dropped from about 175 pounds to about 145 while on the Ranger course—his mind would continually remind him that he had *more food, right now.*

In circumstances like that, the ordinary chatter of quiet, tempting thoughts quickly rises into a chorus.

Some men would do okay for a day or so, and then desperately eat all their MREs in a single go. The indiscipline of their approach—including my own, as well—led them to greater suffering on the back end. Early reward translated to greater pain.

The good news was that we would inevitably have the opportunity for resupply. In five days, five more MREs were coming. The bad news was that *everything* was tactical at Ranger School, including receiving more food. So, having come to the end of a particular stretch without food—most of us having eaten our fifth and final MRE two to three days back—we were given orders. The Ranger instructor walked up, dip protruding from his lip, a big, thick walking stick swinging lightly in his right hand. He pointed the stick at a soldier a few feet down from me. "Hey, stud, you're up. You're the platoon leader for the next mission. Resupply. Don't screw this up, or all your buddies will hate your ass forever."

I listened as the instructor gave the new platoon leader the coordinates for the drop zone to receive the helicopter resupply. I could already taste the MRE spaghetti meal.

The particular clearing just happened to be on the opposite side of both a rushing stream *and* a mountain. I looked at my watch. The hit time was *very* soon. So, we had to move quickly to get to where we needed to be. I didn't envy the newly minted second lieutenant who was in charge at that point, because his platoon of Ranger candidates was less than ideal. We were all in the throes of extreme hunger, to the point of pulling leaves off trees to chew, just to mimic the motions of eating. Mental acuity was low, and morale was lower. Adding to the difficulty, we couldn't just get in a line and walk—we had to proceed tactically, as if the enemy were near and could appear at any moment. When progress was slow and halting, it was no surprise. When some of the students got carried away by the rushing stream and had to make their way back to the group— halting all progress until they did—it was also no surprise. We just knew we were losing precious time.

The constant ribbing from the instructors didn't help. It wasn't meant to. The instructors would whisper to themselves just loud enough for us to overhear, "I wonder if the supply sergeant threw that extra box of Snickers on the bird," they'd say, laughing at themselves—and us. The jokes never seemed to get old.

"Jackasses," my battle buddy murmured under his breath.

We finally got to the point where we could sense relief at hand. We could hear the Black Hawk, circling at the appointed place, awaiting a signal from our platoon leader to drop its supply of precious food. No signal, and there would be no drop. Better no supplies than risking the supply drop falling into enemy hands.

The sun was setting, but we knew we were so, so close. Our platoon leader stopped to check his map, more than once. All the while, the sound of the helicopter circled in the distance.

We could not find the clearing. Another map check. Another hasty movement. Another sound of circling rotors. So near. And yet—

The rotors circled again, and then we heard the most terrible sound imaginable. The noise faded away. The Black Hawk was gone—and with it, our resupply. It hit us just how bad things were and how much worse things were about to get. Five more days: now, with no food at all.

"Hope you Rangers had the discipline to keep some spare chow. You're gonna learn the hard way to plan for contingencies." The instructor turned and grabbed the next candidate for the next mission.

I had something. Even though I had gone through my MREs as fast as everyone else, I hadn't ever eaten the whole thing—even with my hunger pulling at me. There were little packs of Skittles in the MREs, and I saved them. I dropped them into my cargo pockets and moved on. There we were, listening to that resupply bird fade into the distance, and I remembered that I had the most precious thing there. I had a small pack of Skittles.

I decided to eat a single Skittle for every five hundred meters we walked. Every time I slipped one from my pocket and ate it, there was an explosion of flavor, sweetness—and morale. A single Skittle was a reward, a promise, a tiny but precious comfort. We walked and we walked, and each time, I summoned the will and the strength to get another five hundred meters.

At one point, we stopped to set up fighting positions, and I took a moment to slip out another Skittle. I looked over to the adjacent fighting post—and I saw two of my fellow Ranger students staring back at me. Everyone at this point had a faraway, exhausted look, except for these two men. They were very much in the moment, intent upon the bright purple Skittle in my hand. I stared back and put it in my mouth. We regarded one another wordlessly for a moment, and I wondered whether they were going to come over and fight me for the rest of them.

Finally, one of them spoke up. "Where's some for us?" he hissed.

"You tell me. Where *are* yours?"

"Share some, man." The voice was appealing to our common bond. It was also the voice of someone who had made sloppy decisions and was asking me to pay the price.

"No way," I replied. "I saved these up. This is the only thing keeping me going. I don't remember you offering to share yours when you scarfed them down."

I turned away, still wondering if they were going to come and try to take them. Eventually, feeling guilty, I turned around and tossed one over to one guy and then the other. They both closed their eyes as they sucked on the little ball of sugar, savoring it. And then the son of a bitch had a nerve to press me for another one. "Kiss off," I hissed.

When you're graded in Ranger School, you get two sets of assessments. One is from the training instructors on how well you led your various missions. The other is from your peers, who rate how you did by them. It's important, because the Army is as much about duty to peers and subordinates as it is duty to superiors. For the final evaluation to graduate the Florida swamp phase and the entire school, the head instructor called me in to his office.

"All of your peers give you top marks, Ranger Waltz," the master sergeant said, flipping through my file.

I was exhausted and starving but now suddenly feeling great.

"All except two," he continued. "They basically wrote in their peer eval that you are a self-serving son of a bitch who doesn't help your squad mates."

Now I was fuming. I thought, barely containing my anger, *If those two assholes cost me my Ranger tab . . .*

I explained to the sergeant what happened. I pointed out that I had the discipline to prepare for a situation like missing our resupply, and those lazy bastards didn't. "I had a responsibility to keep myself in the fight, and I did it," I explained. The master sergeant leaned back in the chair and left me standing at attention, wondering my fate as he slowly put in a dip.

"It says in your file here that you describe yourself as a Christian. And you describe your leadership style as that of a servant leader." He looked up from the file.

"That's correct, Sergeant," I replied.

"Let me ask you this. In that situation, what would Jesus have done?" he asked.

The question was like a punch in the gut. "He probably would have given them the whole bag," I said.

"Servant leaders share the spoils of their discipline, right?" the sergeant said in an even tone. "If you have the discipline to keep yourself squared away, then you use it to set the example for others and help your fellow Rangers when they get weak and stumble. Leaders eat last. Especially Ranger officers."

"Yes, Sergeant. You are correct," I replied.

"Damn right I'm correct!" the sergeant said as he shot up from his desk and came within inches of my face. "Thank you for letting me know that. Sergeants are always correct!"

Now I was convinced I'd blown it. Damn. The sergeant stood inches in front of me, almost nose to nose. My adrenaline was pumping, but I decided to stay quiet and not try to explain my way out of this. That little bit of discipline paid off.

After a long, painful pause that seemed to last hours, he backed away. "I'm going to let you graduate, Ranger Waltz," he said as the smell of his tobacco breath wafted over me. "You're going to wear that Ranger tab on your uniform the rest of your career. But everyone who sees it will expect more of you as a leader. They will expect you to be better, more disciplined, more squared away than your peers, your soldiers, even your superiors who didn't have the guts to go through Ranger School."

I was stunned. "Roger that, Sergeant. One hundred percent and then some," was all I could get out.

"What you just went through to earn the tab was the easy part. Now the hard part comes—living up to it. Don't embarrass me, Lieutenant. And don't embarrass the regiment. Now get out."

I walked outside and took in a deep breath of swampy Florida air. And smiled.

We got to experience a different sort of discipline later, in the Special Forces Qualification Course. If Ranger School gave us the test of discipline in what was ultimately a highly regimented experience, then the Q Course tested you with wide-open and unpredictable field problems. It made a point of challenging our thinking and planning in ways that went way beyond the light-infantry tactics of Ranger School, especially in the final graduation exercise known as Robin Sage.

One of the basic but really important parts to every Green Beret mission was the PACE plan. (No one loves acronyms quite like the Army.) PACE stood for *primary, alternate, contingency, and emergency*. In effect, it signified the need for *three* backup courses of action when the first one goes wrong. The operating assumption was that the first *would* go wrong. For a force designed to literally go to the ends of the earth and operate with very little backup or support, the PACE plan was a matter of life and death.

One of the realities of being a Green Beret is that you will mostly carry *everything* with you, and so it was in the Q Course.

Being doubled over with weight and walking miles through the wilderness compelled you to think about what, exactly, you were carrying—and to make tradeoffs when you could. Every candidate fought for the things they needed for their specialty, and it was my job along with my senior team sergeant to make compromises. The weapons guys always wanted more ammo and grenades. The medic, more water, medical supplies, and so on. For the Robin Sage culmination exercise, we had to go meet a guerilla chief, or G Chief, who, I knew, might as easily kill us as welcome us. We were also carrying about 120 pounds of gear and supplies each. The packs were so heavy that none of us could stand up by ourselves. I had an idea on lightening the load a bit, while giving us something to gain favor with the guerillas.

I went to our commo sergeant, who had all the heavy-as-hell radios and batteries, and told him to ditch a number of the batteries. They were exceptionally heavy, but he was not relieved—he was furious.

"Hey, sir, we can't do a damn thing without those batteries. We may as well ditch the radios, too, and use smoke signals," he said with all the sarcasm he could muster.

"We have to cut weight, man. We'll keep enough batteries to operate all the radios but also take a hand crank to recharge them rather than taking a bunch of heavy spares." The commo sergeant protested strenuously, for understandable reasons, but I made the call. Instead, we packed bags of rice and beans as a gift to build rapport with the G Chief.

We rucked way out into the wilderness for days on end with our still brutally heavy packs, avoided detection, and eventually successfully met with our assigned band guerillas in "Pineland." They brought us to their chief.

"What can you do for me and my resistance?" he asked, getting right down to business. "My men are being hunted by this evil regime. Their families are in hiding. We have many mouths to feed, my men are poorly equipped, and we are having trouble hitting back."

I smiled as I presented him the rice and beans we had lugged up and down hill after hill to get there. I also put a box of machine gun ammunition at his feet. "My Green Berets are the best of the best. We will train your men to be the toughest soldiers in Pineland. We can use our radios to call in for resupply and more ammunition. Most important, if my superiors approve, we can call for help from the United States Air Force."

He smiled and nodded to one of his men. My team was welcomed into the guerillas encampment that we called their G-base, and I was pleased with my strategy and myself. As dusk fell, I ordered one of our commo sergeants and another soldier to head to a nearby hilltop—with both our primary and alternate radios—to make contact with higher headquarters and let them know of our success. It was such a routine task, I failed to plan it out properly.

Our two men with our two radios went out—and promptly got captured. Suddenly, thanks to my lack of planning, we not only lost the men but also the radios and the key to their cryptography. Because they were captured, our higher head-quarters sent a message to our contingency radios to stop using them because the codes were compromised. In a blink of an eye, we were down to just one emergency radio and a couple of batteries plus a hand crank. It was a colossal screwup. My first thought was, *I'm going to fail the course and never get my beret.* I'd blown right through the primary, the alternate, and the contingency. I was down to the *E* in PACE. Matters got worse when the higher headquarters called out to all the other teams embedded with their guerilla forces and told them they couldn't use their radios anymore, either, because *mine* had been captured and compromised. I now faced the prospect of having blown it for everyone else—a situation that, in the real world, could have genuinely terrible consequences.

The G Chief was immediately in my face, saying, "You're worthless to me and my resistance now. If you can't call for supplies for us and air strikes on the enemy, I don't need you." I broke into a cold sweat. A flash of panic crossed my mind. Then I took a deep breath and explained our backup plan in an even, confident tone. He told me I had one hour to prove we could still communicate or we had to leave.

Thankfully, the emergency radio still worked, and we had al-ternate frequencies for these situations. I will never forget the I-told-you-so stink eye from my communications sergeants. So, there I was, up all night every single night of this already gru-eling and stressful final exercise, hand-cranking our last usable radio to recharge the two batteries we had left. Fortunately, that last radio stayed with us the whole way through.

Training is exactly where to make these mistakes. Things will go wrong, but it's always useful to discover why they went wrong—and learn a lesson you can use in combat, when the stakes are higher still. PACE wasn't just a system designed to help soldiers respond to things going wrong. It was a test of how disciplined you'd stay after you'd made a vital mistake. Would you panic? Would you give up? Would you double down on the error? Or would you do *the next right thing*, mastering your emotions and your fears? The Army wanted to know the answer to these questions. More important, the Army wanted you to know the answers for yourself.

One of the reasons I went through so much training—Infantry Advanced Course, Ranger School, the Q Course, the whole VMI experience—is the credibility I saw these courses bestow upon people I looked up to in my career. My mentor at VMI was Green Beret Sergeant Major Bill Goodson. When he walked into the room, all of his patches and medals screamed, "Listen to this man. Take him seriously. He has earned your respect." I'm always interested to observe which earned credentials attract the greatest respect in society. Some people like to seek counsel from Ivy League graduates with degrees, or they look to celebrities. I seek it from people who have been through the toughest tests of discipline and character I know.

We live in a culture that trains us to expect instant results. Our smartphones have shortened the time between desire and gratification, whether it involves finding dinner, a date, or a ride. Discipline has never been easy, but it is harder now. Too often, we give up on a long-term pursuit because the benefits accrued are so marginal and compound only gradually over time. Someone who begins a weight-loss regimen—tracking their food, perhaps, or walking around the block—may see results exceedingly slowly, across a time horizon that seems too far away to matter. They give up and look for a pill or an injection instead, something to shorten the gap between the effort and the result. The hard truth is that most just want the result with little effort at all.

In our deeply partisan political era, it takes discipline to stay in dialogue with people with whom you disagree so profoundly. It's easier to hang out with your own team or preach to the choir on cable news and social media. But of course, if you do that, no one gets persuaded, and few ideas are challenged. Sometimes, committee work in Congress is about the discipline to hold fast to your convictions while still searching for some common ground. I am one of 535 members of what is a closely divided Congress. The only wholly controllable element in my work is myself. That's true in Congress, and it's true in business, and it's true in Ranger School. It's true in your life, too. Discipline provides a mastery over the one thing you can and must master.

Discipline matters as much in politics as it does in business and in being a Green Beret. In Special Operations, it takes a unique kind of maturity to know when to have the discipline to stick with the plan—and when to pivot to meet the moment. In my first campaign running for the congressional seat Ron DeSantis vacated to run for governor, the Democrats threw everything they had at me. It was an open seat in a wave Democratic year—the first midterm election after Donald Trump was elected. Not only did they think they could flip the Florida governor's race with progressive Democrat Andrew Gillum, but they thought it was an opportunity to flip the DeSantis congressional seat as well.

In the final stretch of my first campaign, just three weeks before Election Day, I got a phone call from my campaign consultant. "Mike, this is the type of call we dread making in this business." I took a deep breath. I knew it wasn't a scandal (at least not a truthful one), but whatever it was, it sounded bad. "Michael Bloomberg just dropped two-point-five-million dollars into attack ads against you—and positives for your opponent. I have never seen this much money dumped in a congressional race this close to the election before. Three weeks out, that's very highly concentrated firepower. I don't know if this is going to bury you or just get lost in the noise with so many other campaigns also pouring money into the same media markets."

Nancy Soderberg, my Democratic opponent, had been an impressive fundraiser on her own. She'd gotten considerable help from the Soros family, Nancy Pelosi's super PAC, and a host of other outside groups. Now she had Mike Bloomberg?

I paused before answering. I had shaken down every family

member and friend I ever met for campaign contributions already. "Well, I can't match them at the money game, so we'll just beat them on the ground," I told my consultant. "We will have to outwork them." I hung up the phone and knocked on the next door. By Election Day, my team of amazing volunteers and I ultimately knocked on 210,000 doors and made 240,000 phone calls. We personally touched every Republican and independent in the district multiple times.

The Bloomberg machine put over $41 million into twenty-four congressional races that election—and won twenty-one of them. We were one of three Republicans to survive that onslaught in a lean Republican district, in a Democratic wave year, when the GOP lost over forty seats in the House.

I believe we won because we had the discipline to keep marching, to stick to the plan. I even took a bag of Skittles and ate a single one after every successful encounter on a voter's front porch.

On the day before the election, I had one more door to go to hit my goal for the day. I had one more Skittle sitting in my console. I was exhausted, the sun was setting, and I felt like I had been door-knocking, calling voters, and calling donors for half my adult life. I was ready to go home and lift it up to God. Fortunately, I had the discipline to do one more door and hit my goal.

As I walked up, I noticed a small shrine in the front yard: a headstone sitting next to a flagpole. An older woman opened the door as I approached.

"Ma'am, my name is Mike Waltz, I'm running to be your congressman after serving over twenty years as a Green Beret—"

"I know who you are," she interrupted. "I've seen those commercials—more negative ones against you than positive for you, I might add."

"Those nasty negative ads aren't true," I said, smiling.

"I would expect nothing less from a Green Beret," she replied. She saw me looking at her memorial.

"It's my son, James. James Markwell, Second Ranger Battalion. Killed in action in Panama. He was killed during his jump into Rio Hato Airfield."

I was taken aback. "That jump is legendary, ma'am. The Rangers led the way that day. Your son died so that other people can be free."

She nodded, we both started tearing up, and she stepped forward and gave me a hug.

I needed a moment to compose myself. "Ma'am I'd like to earn your vote, if you have a minute."

"You already did, Colonel. You're a little conservative for me. But if you have the same discipline in Congress you had to have had to graduate VMI, be a Ranger, and be a Green Beret, you'll be a fine congressman."

Many people knew my biography. Very few knew what those milestones meant. Sandy Rouse—James Markwell's mom—did.

I gave her another hug and thanked her. As I walked away, Sandy said, "I know you will be worthy of my son's sacrifice.

Don't lose your soul up there in Washington. It takes discipline to always do the right thing."

It was the second time she'd used that word. *Discipline.* It was the code her son had lived by, and she knew that it was an indispensable quality to strong leadership.

Emotion and gratitude coursing through me, I climbed back into my car, took the last Skittle, and popped it into my mouth. "Okay, God," I said. "Mission accomplished. It's up to You now."

4

BOTTOM-UP LEADERSHIP

I'll never forget my very first encounter with the Green Berets. It was the late 1990s, and I was a young armor officer deployed out to Kuwait with a company of tanks. In the aftermath of the First Gulf War in the late '90s, there was a lot of activity in that theater; Iraq's Saddam Hussein was still menacing the region, deploying chemical weapons against the Kurds, massacring entire groups of his own people, and threatening global energy supplies.

For my platoon of M1A1 Abrams tankers, being there meant a lot of routine in *a lot* of heat. Desert temperatures regularly soared to 110 degrees Fahrenheit, and it was no joke working, and staying battle ready, in those conditions. We lived in tents and tanks, and our days didn't vary much. The scenery didn't vary much, either. Apart from its capital, Kuwait is almost entirely featureless desert, and we were posted up on its northern edge near the Iraqi border.

One day, we saw some Humvees barreling toward us from that trackless horizon—from the direction of the border. They weren't Iraqis: it was a squad's worth of Americans, back in from scouting out the frontier. It was quickly clear that they were United States Army soldiers, but they were *nothing* like the ones I knew. They wore thick mustaches common with Middle Eastern men and nonstandard uniforms, had machine guns poking out from every corner of their vehicles, carried a variety of small arms, and carried themselves in a way that was simultaneously informal and disciplined.

The team of Green Berets pulled up to our tank and asked if we had a mechanic with us that could take a look at one of their Humvees. I chatted with the team leader, a captain who had been in the Army a few years longer than I had. I asked him, "Are you guys out here alone?"

With his sunglasses propped on his head of slicked-back hair, he replied, "Pretty much. We do a week at a time with the border guards before heading back to KC [Kuwait City] to refit, and then back out again."

I knew they weren't heading back to a small tent city like ours in the middle of the desert. They were headed for an air-conditioned hotel in Kuwait City. And in a few days, based on their mission analysis of which Kuwaiti units needed their help the most, they would be going out again to a different part of the border.

"Where is your next higher command?" I asked. "How do they give you orders out here?"

The captain stroked the thick black mustache that he had grown, in the spirit of the Kuwaiti soldiers he was advising.

"No, brother, it doesn't work like that with us. My team tells higher what *we* think needs to be done out there to keep an eye on the Iraqis, and they get us the resources to get the mission done. My higher headquarters is in Qatar."

"Really? You just tell them what you want to do?" I asked.

"Not me so much, man. My sergeants who are embedded with the Kuwaitis. They tell me, and I tell my superiors," he explained. "Don't get me wrong, we have rules of engagement. We have a good understanding of the big picture from the general in charge and where we fit into it. They told us to build a relationship and to partner with Kuwaiti border guards, train them to get better, report back to my HQ our assessment of the Kuwaiti capabilities, and monitor what the Iraqi Army is up to. But they don't micromanage how we do it. My bosses know my team is best suited to figure out how to get 'er done. If I didn't get another speck of instruction from them the rest of the tour, then I would be fine because I know my commanders' intent. Big-boy rules out there."

He pointed toward the border with Iraq.

"Now, my Kuwaiti counterparts, on the other hand," he continued, "have to ask permission two levels up their chain of command to take a leak. Teaching these guys to shoot more accurately is the easy part. Teaching them how to operate independently and stay one step ahead of the enemy is far harder. Reminds me of my days in the conventional army—no offense," he said, smiling.

"What happens if Iraqi tanks decide to take a shot at you

guys?" I asked. "It would take us hours to reinforce you if something happens." I looked over at their unarmored vehicles with soft tops, full of water and ammo.

"Yeah, we factor that in," replied the captain. "Move fast, be hard to hit, and always, always make sure one of our radios can get in touch with the Air Force if we need them to come save our ass."

This is my kind of soldiering, I thought. Give me my mission and let me go do it. Then I'll tell my higher headquarters the resources I need to be successful.

I saw the cool professionalism of the Green Berets there in the blazing Kuwaiti desert, and there was something immediately attractive about it. In the 1990s, in a post–Cold War era of downsizing, cutting costs, and peacekeeping, these men *looked* and *acted* like warriors. I wanted to be one.

There is a (probably apocryphal) story told by the nineteenth-century German General Helmuth von Moltke the Elder. A colonel was called before his superior general officer for a reprimand. The colonel had made an error on the battlefield, and now he was to account for it. His defense was simple: "I was only following orders."

The general replied, "His Majesty promoted you to colonel because he believed you would know when *not* to blindly obey his orders! He promoted you because he believed you could *think*!"

Moltke told the story to illuminate the difference between his army and the armies of other nations. In every other army, the principle of total subordination reigned. A subordinate was to blindly follow the orders of his superior, and so it went on up the chain. Importantly, a subordinate was not at liberty to act until he received orders. But in Moltke's German war machine, a soldier was also expected to *understand* the orders he was given and to grasp the context in which they were issued. Armed with an understanding of the larger mission, he had a duty to act to advance that mission, even in the absence of orders—and sometimes contrary to them. He could never allow his obedience to override his obligation to *think critically*.

The English term for what Moltke was talking about is *mission command*. The Germans under Moltke were good at it, but historically, the United States military has been better than anyone else at mission command. Perhaps it was the rugged individualism of the American frontiersmen that made the U.S. military inherently suitable for more independent-minded operations. You don't get patriot partisans conducting guerilla warfare in the South Carolina backcountry during the American Revolution, Texas Rangers riding the frontier in the conflict with Mexico, or long-range patrols in Vietnam's Central Highlands without a strong culture that trusts its soldiers right down to the lowest levels—to think, to know, and to do.

It's in the Green Berets that you see mission command perfected. Even if the U.S. military at large is pretty good at the ethos, it remains a hierarchical, top-down, rule-bound, large organization. In the Green Berets, we turn that upside down. We have a job to do, and it doesn't always go by the book. In fact, we're trained to fight, and win, *where there is no book*. I prefer a simpler term to mission command, a term that explains itself: *bottom-up leadership*.

Bottom-up leadership was at the core of what I found so compelling about those Green Berets in the desert. Bottom-up leadership meant that they were unusually empowered—which meant their selection and training were unusually intense to produce the quality of soldier that could have such autonomy on strategic missions. The end product of that process is a soldier, and a leader, that is qualified and ready to do great things in extremely isolated circumstances, far away from any other American units.

Read any of the accounts of modern American war from the past twenty years. Pick up stories of combat such as Jocko Willink's recollections of his time leading SEALs in Iraq in *Extreme Ownership*. His SEAL platoons conducted incredibly heroic sniper overwatch and direct-action missions in complex urban terrain in Iraq against a deadly entrenched insurgency. The lessons he draws from these experiences will benefit millions of Americans for a generation. Note one consistent thing about the operations he recounts: there are *plenty* of whatever military resources are needed to get the job done. There are so many American personnel on hand in and around the Iraqi cities in which his SEAL platoons are operating that friendly fire becomes a constant danger. If a unit is in trouble or pinned down, there are tanks or armored vehicles nearby as backup. If there is a particularly difficult problem—say, the enemy is in a bunker or reinforced position that small arms won't breach—there are literally stacks of air support in the sky readily at hand to put bombs on target. If a teammate is wounded, evacuation and care is close by.

I have tremendous admiration for Jocko, his story, and his heroic task force. But my combat deployments were a very different experience and emphasized somewhat different skill sets. In 2006, I found myself in the Kajaki District of Afghanistan's Taliban-infested Helmand Province. When I arrived, we had only *fifty* Americans in a province that covered more than twenty thousand square miles. Those fifty Americans naturally included Green Berets, because it was the Green Berets—my teammates and I—who were embedded in tribal militias and partnered with local military units. We were trained to do what needed to be done far away from easy help and ready aid. Years later, during the Afghanistan surge in 2011, there was a full twenty thousand Marines: still not enough to pacify the region. In retrospect, more American soldiers was not better. Fewer American soldiers with the resources and training to empower the locals to fight their own war was the way to go.

In places that remote, bottom-up leadership is the only way to survive.

My men had authority to take matters into their own hands—and we operated "by, with, and through" surrogates whenever possible such as the United Arab Emirates Special Operations Task Force, local militias, and the Afghan National Army.

On more than one occasion, I was the only American in the room as my UAE Special Operations counterparts made a case to a large gathering of tribal leaders we knew to be sympathetic to the Taliban. No one noticed me. With tanned face, beard, and sand-colored turban, and identical uniform to the UAE soldiers, I was doing what Green Berets are trained to do—blend in.

On this day, the UAE captain was impassioned. "The Taliban are leading you astray," he thundered. "They are *not* the authority on Islam. The Taliban 'mullahs' are *not* true religious leaders. Most of them cannot even read Arabic!" The captain threw his hands up in the air in mock exasperation. Several of the elders laughed. Every Muslim knew the Koran was an Arabic text, so to be an authority on Islam, one had to be literate in Arabic. I watched the faces of several young men cradling AK-47s in their laps. They wore dark eyeliner, black turbans, and dyed reddish-black beards typical of Taliban fighters. Their faces softened. Several even cracked a smile.

"Look at the great Islamic cities of Istanbul, Jakarta, Jeddah, and Dubai," the UAE captain continued. "You can have a better life for your children, including your daughters, and still be good, strong Muslims." I saw the elders nodding. He took his appeal a step further, to the endorsement of the United States: "The Americans and the Europeans are here to be your friends. Do not believe the propaganda that they're here to occupy your land, or to take from you, or to make you Christians. Look at what America did after World War II for Japan.

Look at what they did for Germany. America is a country that aids its former enemies, helps them become prosperous, and does not plunder or take from them. For the sake of your families, you should support them, and all of the nations like mine that are here to help Afghanistan. And most important, you should stop fighting your own Afghan brothers in your army!"

The captain grabbed the arm of the Afghan Army lieutenant standing next to him for emphasis. Several elders in the front row enthusiastically stood and grasped the lieutenant's hands in both of theirs. This endorsement of the coalition effort in Afghanistan and America's good intentions, coupled with the questioning of the Taliban religious credentials, was a one-two punch coming from an Arab and Afghan. I quietly stood against the back wall thinking that this was gold. It would have a greater effect on undermining the Taliban than a whole American infantry battalion.

Unlike me and the other Westerners, our UAE counterparts could deliver a powerful message that hit center mass to the values and aspirations of the ordinary Afghan tribesman.

I could dress to blend into the background, but I would always be an American Christian. Green Berets are not Hollywood actors. We cannot pretend to be what we are not. We work with our partners to achieve our mission, and we incentivize them to do what needs doing, because there are things only they can do.

We supported the UAE and Afghan platoons as they engaged village after village, tribe after tribe, in the most hard-core

Taliban areas of Afghanistan. We turned whole villages to our side without firing a shot. Violence in this area dropped noticeably. In one village, the malik standing outside the mosque took his scythe that was typically used to extract opium paste from the poppy bulbs and broke it over his knee. He pledged to turn his tribe away from the poison of the poppy.

It was relatively easy to bomb a tank or hunt down an individual. It was far harder to kill an idea. But it could be done, with the right messenger who delivered it with authority and credibility. The success we enjoyed with the UAE and the Afghan population was bottom-up messaging at its best. The incredible fact about this bottom-up approach? We had tremendous return on investment with only *four* of us Green Berets on the scene. It was three sergeants and me, embedded with several dozen UAE personnel with their own command structure. What did we do for them? We did some advising— and we provided a lot. We were the UAE task force's link to the full range of American military power and resources. We could call in U.S. Air Force assets as needed. We would summon medevacs. We could request equipment and gear. If the UAE forces were our lifeline to the people of Helmand, then we were the UAE forces' lifeline to the incredible military might of the United States.

This is the reverse of the traditional approach. The "normal way" might look like the broader American military apparatus commanding the Green Berets, and the Green Berets commanding our local partners. But that isn't how we worked.

Bottom-up leadership meant that we were there with our partners to enable them, and the great machinery of the United
States Armed Forces in Afghanistan was there to serve *us*.

All of this was to help the people of Afghanistan achieve
some semblance of stability and so that their country was no longer a breeding ground for international terrorism like it was before 9/11. Beyond that, we didn't dictate how the Afghans should
live. We weren't trying to turn Helmand into Switzerland. I
often say that my time with the UAE soldiers was the closest I'll
ever come to Lawrence of Arabia. Like Lawrence—whose book
Seven Pillars of Wisdom is a must-read for every Green Beret—I
was sent forth into an alien land, to empower and sustain its
people against our common enemy. We never forgot we were
strangers in a strange land, but even in the most distant places,
after years of studying and embedding in a local culture, we
were Americans first. And all our strategic intent and initiative
was directed toward advancing American interests.

Because I was empowered by that bottom-up ethos, as a
mere captain—I came up with the strategic concept to convince the UAE command to build an air base just north of
the Kajaki Dam in southwestern Afghanistan. Kajaki is the
only truly modern dam in Afghanistan, built by the United
States as part of a 1950s-era development-aid project. It gen-
erates power for the country's second-largest city, Kandahar.
From the dam, there is relatively easy access to a string of
riverside settlements, the north end of an agricultural plain,
and the great Ring Road that encircles most of central

Afghanistan. Looking at the dam and its position, I realized that there was an opportunity in that very spot. A permanent air base, there, with UAE and perhaps Jordanian forces, could have yielded tremendous gains for the coalition in the heart of Taliban country. An added potential benefit? It was not far from Afghanistan's border with Iran.

In four weeks, I worked through the concept with the leadership of the UAE task force, helped them as they briefed their Ministry of Defense back in Abu Dhabi, won the approval of my higher headquarters, and sought the concurrence of the provincial governor and the commander of the Afghan National Army unit. Of course, I met some resistance from various majors and colonels who thought I was punching way above my rank. Fortunately, I circumvented the staff officers (and their rigid belief that all decisions flow from the top down) and made my case directly to the Special Operations commander for the theater. He approved, and I was off and running.

Once again, I found myself as the only American in the room, doing my best to blend in while my interpreter whispered in my ear so I could follow the conversation between the Helmand governor and the UAE colonel as they brokered a deal for the land for the UAE air base. I was sure my teeth would be permanently brown from so much tea, but it finally seemed like we had a deal.

"I spoke to President Karzai on this matter this morning," the governor announced at the end of the hours-long meeting.

"From the authority of my office and the Presidential Palace, it is done. I will ensure you have the land available for this air base with no problems. The people of Helmand Province will be delighted to have our Arab brothers standing with us. With your help, we will build the next Dubai in Afghanistan!" The governor smiled broadly as he stood to shake hands with the UAE colonel. The governor got the credit, and the UAE got the lead role—but I had set things in motion. Not just with the idea, the clearance, and the coordination with my own chain of command: I had also worked to ensure that leadership back in Washington, DC, was communicating and coordinating with their UAE counterparts at the ministry level that I was doing what the Green Berets had been sent to do. And as a young conservative, I smiled to myself that the American taxpayer wouldn't pay a dime.

The approval in hand, the UAE's Ministry of Defense sent out two colonels—an air base commander, as well as an engineering commander with a survey team. That's how we ended up, one bright day in Helmand, in a convoy headed toward the dam to finalize the site of the air base—and how we ended up in a four-kilometer-long ambush.

"PKM on the berm, nine o'clock!" yelled my turret gunner, alerting everyone to a Taliban machine gun to our left. Seconds after tracers from the machine gun flew over the vehicle, an RPG streaked across the front of the hood of our Humvee and exploded against the cliff to my right.

"Hard left!" I yelled to my driver. "Charge the ambush!" The Humvee swung left off the road and toward the machine gun and RPG position in a maneuver we had practiced dozens of times. When caught in a near ambush, the only thing you can do is hit back—hard. My Humvee, another American vehicle, and several UAE armored cars charged the enemy, destroying the Taliban position and killing several fighters. Our shock-and-awe response momentarily stunned the initial line of Taliban fighters firing from behind a dirt berm. Behind the berm was a series of irrigation canals leading from the Helmand River toward the road we were traveling. They served as makeshift trench lines, interspersed with walled mud-brick compounds that became small forts.

All hell broke loose as we realized we had kicked over a massive hornet's nest of dozens of fighters. The rooftops of several nearby mud huts lit up with muzzle flashes, and volleys of RPGs streaked toward us.

"Mortars!" one of my teammates yelled over the radio just as I heard the *ka-thump* of their impact behind us. We stood toe-to-toe, exchanging an incredible volume of fire for what seemed like a lifetime. Adrenaline exploded through me. I was amped and thoroughly pissed off. I was sick and tired of being on the receiving end of Taliban IEDs and ambushes only to break contact and let them live another day to hit us again. They were going to pay for this one. They were not going to stop this new air base. I was ready to charge the Taliban line on the berm and kill every last one of them.

Fortunately, some bottom-up sanity kicked in when one of my sergeants calmly but firmly yelled over to me. "Hey, sir, just a suggestion, but we need to get the hell out of here, right damn now!"

To punctuate his point, an enemy bullet smacked against the armored door I was using as cover, and another mortar round exploded behind us. "Roger that. Let's roll!"

As we fought our way back to the road, I heard, "I'm hit!" from the back of the vehicle. I turned around and saw my medic slumped over in the open, flatbed of the Humvee. He was trying to pick up his rifle with one hand to keep firing while cradling his right arm. I immediately crawled between my turret gunner's legs to the back to help. An enemy round had taken a chunk out of his forearm and struck his armored chest plate, causing the bullet to fragment and slice through the femoral artery in his left leg. He needed immediate aid. Without it, he'd bleed out and die in less than five minutes.

Fortunately for him, our medic had saved his own life long before we embarked on the mission. In the Kajaki District, he knew we were hours from any reinforcements even by helicopter. We'd have to care for any combat injuries ourselves, within the "golden hour" that often makes the difference between life and death. That's why my medic had insisted on training the team on advanced combat-lifesaving skills, to a level well beyond the basic class. Everyone on the team bitched and complained because of all the other time-consuming training we also had to do. But our medic demanded it. He exhibited bottom-up leadership—and it saved his life.

There's multitasking, and then there's Green Beret multi-tasking. I compressed my medic's injury with one knee while returning fire from the back of a bouncing Humvee truck bed, the entire area slick with blood. At the same time, with two different radios fixed to my gear and the hand mike for a third stretched to the back of the Humvee, I directed everyone to get off the road so we could get far enough away from the ambush zone to call for an air strike and a medevac. On top of it all, I did my best to advise and direct my UAE counterparts, who were themselves taking wounded from the ambush.

"RPG!" our turret gunner yelled. The driver swerved hard to avoid the incoming rocket, and the last thing I remember was a flash as it hit the rocky cliff to the right of the road we were traveling. I woke up face down on the bed of the Humvee. I was pretty sure I had only been out a few minutes and got back to making sure my medic didn't bleed out, putting more rounds on the enemy, and getting our convoy off that damn road. It was extreme rural warfare. The nearest coalition forces were hours away. No one was anywhere near us to help. There was no quick-reaction force. The whole mission was in pursuit of building a strategic air base that I had briefed all the way up my chain of command. Success could mean a strategic game changer in the war. Failure meant our entire force would be overrun and killed. We were on our own and I took full responsibility.

Bottom-up leadership is all about knowing when *not* to blindly follow the rules. And even though my second medic and I eventually stabilized our wounded man, I needed to break some rules to save his life.

The infamous "Black Hawk down" incident in Somalia in 1993 became a book, a movie, and a case study. Helicopters are large, slow, and thin-skinned targets. If shot down, it is often with catastrophic loss. Mindful of that painful legacy, our choppers in Afghanistan were ordered to avoid approaching a landing zone if it is under fire, or "hot." And this landing zone—where my medic was wounded—was definitely hot.

The UAE platoons and my two Humvees found an opening in the cliff that ran along the right side of the road. We moved up on to an elevated knoll and circled the wagons. The medevac helicopter was on its way, but, given the nearest base was over an hour away, I knew we had to stabilize the wounded while putting ourselves in a position to defend against further attacks. I heard my communications sergeant talking to the pilot as I helped my second medic continue to dress the wounds.

The chopper called in: "Are you taking small arms or any other type of incoming on the landing zone? Confirm the LZ is not under fire. Is it green for pickup?"

"We are still receiving—" my communications sergeant began to answer, until I threw a water bottle at him. He spun around and cursed me, but he also released the mike and stopped transmitting.

"Tell them it's all clear," I yelled, "or they won't land!"

Just then, a short burst of automatic-weapon fire rang out from the direction of the ambush site. We both instinctively flinched and looked at the direction of the fire. The sergeant looked back at me and paused; comparing my order against what he knew to be standard operating procedure. He nodded and squeezed the handset: "All clear, I repeat, all clear on the LZ."

We both knew it was a lie, and a serious one: telling the Black Hawk helicopter to come on in with rounds in the air risked a damaged aircraft at best, or worse, a lost aircraft—or still worse, lost lives. But it was the kind of tough call it was my job to make. I knew the pilots themselves had no problem taking the risks necessary to get our guys out, but they had to check the box with their superiors in their aviation chain of command. As a Green Beret, I wasn't going to check with mine. Our medic's situation was stabilizing but could quickly deteriorate. He was sucking on a morphine lollipop with a sliced femoral artery that could cause him to bleed out in minutes if the two tourniquets I had put on his leg failed.

My obligation to my wounded medic outstripped my obligation to the rules on safe helicopter landings. *I'll be damned if he's going to die on my watch*, I thought.

The medevac helicopter came, landed, and loaded my medic and other wounded aboard. As it took off, another string of Taliban machine-gun tracers climbed the sky after it. The bird banked hard, and we all returned fire. My heart was in my throat at the thought of losing the four lives that were crewing that helicopter, because of my determination to save my medic.

Anger flared in me. I was sick and tired of being on the receiving end of Taliban ambushes. I crafted a plan with the UAE commander to counterattack the Taliban position. Half of our force would suppress the attackers by firing on their ambush position while the other half would secure the bridge near the Kajaki Dam.

As I began briefing my men on the plan, my communications sergeant walked up with the satellite phone. He handed it to me and told me it was the Special Operations Command with responsibility over all of Afghanistan. I grabbed the phone and informed the operations officer on the line of our status and my intent to press the attack.

The officer, Major Scott Mann—who nearly two decades later would form Task Force Pineapple to evacuate our Afghan allies during Biden's debacle of a withdrawal—was blunt: "Mike, your plan sounds like some good aggressive Green Beret shit, especially since there's only six of you left. But let me tell you what you're going to do. You're going to abort this mission and return to base."

I protested.

"Look, Mike," Scott said. "Half the Taliban army is waiting on you on the other side of that bridge. We have intercepts of a dozen commanders spinning up their boys to come after you. They've got heavy machine guns, mortars, the works."

"Nothing the U.S. Air Force can't take care of," I said. I wasn't letting go of my plan.

Scott sighed. "Mike, I'll be straight with you, brother. The network is lit up with the Talib shitheads talking about over-running you guys. We got a hit from inside Pakistan of a Taliban commander offering a bounty for a captured American. And a bonus bounty for one with a beard," he said, referring to Green Berets, who were known to grow beards like their Afghan counterparts. "They know they've got you surrounded and they smell blood. It's going to take every air asset I have just to bust you out of there, much less help you fight deeper into that rat's nest. Besides losing you and your men, we can't lose an entire coalition element. The Crown Prince of the UAE will be on the phone to the President. The diplomatic fallout will be devastating, and the propaganda victory for the jihadi world will be huge. You know this. You need to take a deep breath and think this through, brother."

I didn't say anything.

"Mike," Scott continued, "the next call you get from me, I'm going to have a B-1 bomber, an A-10, and two Preds ready to light up the group of Taliban trying to block your escape. When night falls, I'm adding in an AC-130 Gunship. It's going to look like *Apocalypse* fucking *Now* out there. You guys punch through that hole and live to fight another day."

I stood there holding the satellite phone to my ear, looking at the horizon in the direction of the future UAE air base. We were so damn close. I saw several of my men repairing our shot-up vehicles and changing boxes of ammo. They looked de-termined, but I could tell they were listening to my every word.

As much as I wanted to kick the shit out of the Taliban, I knew I had to set my emotion aside, detach from the situation, and listen to a reasonable and broader perspective. Sometimes grassroots, bottom-up leadership is too close to the problem. Leaders can start viewing the situation through a soda straw. The soldier, or salesman, or politician closest to the problem, who has the most detail at their fingertips, should be the default leader to make decisions, but we also have to realize that sometimes that leader can't see the bigger picture. I had to take a step back. My higher headquarters had the wide-angle lens, and I knew it.

Looking back on it, it's notable that Scott Mann, as the operations officer for the entire theater, didn't give me a direct order to just shut up and blindly follow. He easily could have, but that wasn't the way of the Green Beret. Instead, he took the time to walk me through the situation. He explained the why of the better course of action. He shared with me what he knew and I didn't know. In the heat of combat, I needed to be reminded. A key element of bottom-up leadership is knowing that there is a time to work around the rules and push your agenda up the chain, and there's a time to fall in line and follow orders.

Green Berets are older than the average special operators. Part of the reason is that every Green Beret first spends several years in the Army at large. It is also because the Army understands that a soldier past his early twenties is likely to have a bit more maturity and wisdom—and a greater capacity for the combination of strength and humility—that are critical for bottom-up leadership. That maturity doesn't just show up in our decision-making. It also expresses itself in a culture that prizes admitting mistakes and learning battlefield lessons. The key aspect of each mission is the After-Action Review, or AAR. If an operator makes a mistake on a mission and holds back during the AAR, his teammates will call him out in a heartbeat. If you want to be entrusted to lead, you need to demonstrate your willingness to be ruthlessly accountable.

Bottom-up leadership doesn't mean you have a blank check to always do things your way. It requires an acceptance of considerable risk—because sometimes things go wrong. One dramatic and tragic example of this came in the October 2017 ambush at Tongo Tongo, in the extreme outlands of Niger—a country deep in the vast Sahel region of Africa. An ISIS attack upon a Nigerien force, in which several of my fellow Green Berets were killed, highlighted the isolation and remoteness of our work. For them, there was no quick-reaction force nearby, no indirect-fire support available, and no air support within minutes. It is part of the job, and we know it—and sometimes we pay the price for it.

The Green Berets on the scene did their best to exercise bottom-up leadership. The captain leading the team repeatedly informed his higher command, located hundreds of miles away in another country, that the Nigerien soldiers were not ready for the extended mission they were being ordered to conduct. The team was first ordered to divert from their standard patrol to stage as a quick-reaction force for another group of U.S. Special Operations Forces that was going to conduct a helicopter raid against a known leader of ISIS. The team leader, listening to his very experienced sergeants, exercised bottom-up leadership and protested that the Nigerien platoon lacked enough water and supplies for such an extended time in the African bush. The Nigeriens were tired, morale was low, and discipline was lacking. The lieutenant colonel in charge overrode the team's objections and ordered the Green Beret captain to proceed anyway, as the ISIS commander was suspected of holding an American aid worker hostage.

When the leader of the Nigerien platoon elected to stop to rest in a village en route, he refused the Green Berets' counsel against it. When the Green Berets sensed that the village elders were seeking to delay the force's departure, the Nigerien platoon leader failed to listen to that counsel as well.

Sure enough, the village leadership sold all of them out to ISIS, buying time with their delay for the ISIS fighters to get into an ambush position. Some one hundred ISIS fighters surprised the convoy of light pickup trucks with machine guns and AK-47s as they left the village. Four Green Berets and four Nigerien soldiers were ultimately killed, and two Green Berets, including the team leader, were wounded before French aircraft finally arrived on the scene for close air support.

The Green Berets on the scene on that terrible day did everything correctly: they communicated with candor with their higher echelons, they executed the mission ordered to

their utmost regardless of their misgivings, and they adhered
faithfully to the principle of putting partner forces up front and
in the lead. When we talk about the Green Beret principles of *by*,
with, and *through* local allies, we have to remember the tremendous risk inherent in the approach. Those same locals can easily
let you down with bad decisions or betray you—sometimes with
fatal results, as at Tongo Tongo.

The investigation, conducted by a military apparatus under intense media and political scrutiny, focused on finding
fault. This precautionary mindset seeks to eliminate risk, and
that works well in zero-defect environments like commercial
aviation—but not irregular warfare. Green Berets operate in
an environment filled with flawed human beings who are often
trying to kill one another—and you. Eliminating any possibility of tactical failure means seriously reducing the possibility
of strategic success.

After Tongo Tongo, the Defense Department went all in on
the precautionary mindset, removing authority from soldiers
on the scene and punishing entirely reasonable judgment calls
of the type Green Berets exist to make. Bottom-up leadership
was cast aside in favor of traditional command and control, with
an emphasis on *control*. It was a tremendous mistake and has
limited the effectiveness of our Special Operations just as terrorist groups are exploding and China's influence is expanding.

This tragic episode illuminates why bottom-up leadership
is so rare. It's risky. It has to be done well. Leaders must be pre-

pared to shoulder the consequences if their subordinates fail. Subordinate leaders must understand the overall mission *and* be empowered to figure out how to achieve the objectives necessary for mission success. They must understand *why* they are putting the lives of their unit on the line to achieve the mission.

In Helmand, the higher echelon countermanded my desire to press the fight after the ambush and build that damn air base. In Tongo Tongo, headquarters forced a mission on a team that had strongly advised against it. In Afghanistan, at one key moment, my superiors saw the situation more clearly than I did, and they rejected my counsel. In Niger, the commanders could not see the status of the partner force as well as the Green Berets on the ground, but they still overrode the team's advice and insight. The key to leadership is understanding who has the best grasp of the overall mission at any given moment. In Helmand, the higher echelon had it. In Tongo Tongo, they did not.

Critics of bottom-up leadership point out that it's risky, that there are not enough controls and guardrails to allow soldiers to chart their own path. The risks are real, but the arguments for heeding them are reminiscent of arguments against basic democratic principles. Something I have come to understand over the course of my career is that the genius of the American experiment and the Green Beret mindset are the same: you have to let the people lead.

I've done my best to emulate this bottom-up mentality throughout my military career as well as in business and in Congress. As CEO of a rapidly growing company, I ended every staff meeting with questions: "What do you need from me? What decisions do I need to make or guidance do you need? Is there anything stuck on my desk or in my inbox?" Above all: "How can we best apply our limited resources?" The trick to scaling the business was to keep it feeling small and decision-making nimble even as it expanded to several hundred employees. To that end, I borrowed a doctrine from the Navy that they used for their fleets in the centuries before radio and satellites allowed for real-time changes to guidance to a fleet on the other side of the world. Before the twentieth century, a ship captain was given broad guidance and told to accomplish the mission, "unless otherwise directed." For example, keep the merchant lanes between New England and France open, unless otherwise directed. Patrol the Caribbean for pirates, unless otherwise directed. Conduct a show of force with the Great White Fleet to intimidate the Japanese government into entering a trade agreement, unless otherwise directed. In an era when a faster ship would literally have to be sent to catch up with the other ships to deliver a message, it placed a lot of autonomy and responsibility on the ship captains to understand the strategic intent of their leadership, understand the rules of naval warfare, and have the judgment to know when a change necessitated that the ship captains seek additional guidance from headquarters. I did my best as a CEO to emulate this approach with our team of program managers in multiple states and countries. I gave them a relatively short list of strategic items that would need my input and told them everything else could be decided at their level. They knew the deliverables in our contracts with our customers, understood our corporate culture, and had their budget for expenses. Unless otherwise directed, go for it.

I've tried to do the same as a member of Congress. Our most successful leaders surround themselves with true professionals and empower them to lead from below. Ronald Reagan chose experts in their fields like Brent Scowcroft, Colin Powell, James Baker, George Shultz, and Caspar Weinberger, and he let them make real decisions. I've attracted a great team on my congressional staff, given them the broad guidance and general direction they need, and let them go after it. Whether in the Green Berets, business, or Congress, I've told my teams that a jockey can always pull back the reins—but he can't push them forward. I would always want to have to hold back a group of thoroughbreds rather than try to push a group of mediocre performers. We've been very effective to the point that one of my senior legislative staffers, who's worked for multiple members over his twenty-four years on Capitol Hill, told me that he had passed more into law during his several years with me than his previous twenty. That pronoun is worth emphasizing: *he* and the team did it. I just empowered them to do it.

Listening, empowering, trusting, accepting risk as well as responsibility: that's at the heart of bottom-up leadership. It's the most effective way to lead—and just as important, it's the American way to get things done.

5

ADAPTABILITY

The Australian commander had a heavy accent. Sometimes, listening to him, I had to silently repeat his words to myself. The men under his command were only a little easier to understand.

I stood next to him, listening to his three sniper teams calling in at their regularly scheduled communications windows. A bank of radios sat on a table in front of me, two Aussie soldiers manning them. I was at the Australian forward operating base in Uruzgan Province, one of the remotest regions in one of the most remote countries in the world.

"No activity on target site Alpha. All men, weapons, equipment are green, over."

The Australians were hunting Mullah Abdul Bari, a notorious Taliban commander. Bari was the leader of an IED-making cell and had led several ambushes against the Australians. He had infamously tortured two Afghan police officers and broadcast it live on the radio as they begged for their lives.

"I have three four-man teams covering the three known bed-down locations for this shithead," explained the Australian commander, "a sniper and spotter, plus two pulling security. Every few hours, the two-man teams switch so the others can get a few hours of rest."

I asked how long his teams had been out there looking for Bari.

"Too long, mate."

The Australian snipers lying in their hide sites were suffering in the brutal heat of an Afghan summer, under the constant threat of being exposed or compromised. I thought of the Operation Red Wings disaster that happened just before we arrived in theater, where a sniper observer team of Navy SEALs was compromised by a goat herder wandering into their position. Following the rules of warfare, the SEALs chose not to kill him and let him go, whereupon he immediately alerted a Taliban commander, who gathered a force that killed three of the four SEALs. The Taliban also shot down a U.S. helicopter sent to rescue the SEALs with sixteen Rangers on board. Only one SEAL, Marcus Luttrell, survived the firefight due to the generosity and fortitude of a local elder who protected him. It was one of the worst disasters of the war and formed the basis of the book and movie *Lone Survivor*.

As I stood listening to the sniper teams calling in their status, I saw the potential for it happening again. Right in front of us.

I was there because the Australians requested that my Special Forces team and our partnered UAE platoons serve as a quick-reaction force in case their teams were compromised. Waiting around on the Aussie commandos to get their shot on Mullah Bari or going to rescue the snipers if they got in trouble wasn't exactly what I had in mind for winning the war in this part of Afghanistan.

Years later, we had Predator drones overhead, constantly monitoring various Taliban commanders' locations until it was time to strike with a missile launched from its wing. But at this point in the war, there were only a few drones in theater, and they were rarely available.

"There has got to be a better way," I said to my team sergeant standing next to me.

The mission dragged on fruitlessly for days longer. I didn't doubt the Australians' competence or courage, but it was time to bring some Green Beret innovation to the problem.

My team and I came up with a plan. We decided to put together a MEDCAP—basically a public health clinic—in a village near one of the targeted compounds. A little public health goes a long way in regions like these, where basic pharmaceuticals and care are unavailable. We pulled together some doctors, nurses, and clinicians from the health ministry, as well as some nongovernmental organizations (NGOs). I arranged to have the next resupply bird from Bagram Airfield bring several large cases of medical supplies and drugs. Our UAE partners shipped in humanitarian supplies. We put the word out on local radio that the Afghan government was sponsoring the clinic. Anyone who wished to come for basic care could.

It didn't take long for a line of villagers to form down the main dirt road leading to our clinic. People arrived with every ailment one could imagine: dental, intestinal, ophthalmological, arthritic, infectious, and more. We saw things that had been cured in the developed world for decades. Often, all the doctors and my medics could do was give pain relievers like Tylenol and throat lozenges. In other cases, a pulled tooth or some basic antibiotics worked to relieve at least a little suffering.

We set up a holding room between the entrance to the makeshift clinic and treatment room, where one of my intelligence sergeants photographed and fingerprinted each individual as they stepped inside. None of my men wore their uniforms, but rather wore the standard clothes of western NGOs: cargo pants and lightweight button-down shirts with the sleeves rolled up. Each had a pistol tucked in a concealed holster. No rifles were visible. It was a risky approach right in the middle of Taliban country—but the intel sergeant on my team thought it could pay off.

One elder was so pleased that we provided some pain relief to his grandson that he whispered a warning to one of my men that a very brutal Taliban leader was in the area. Sure enough, a few moments later, a grizzled older man with a red-tinted black beard stepped into the holding room. As soon as we pointed the camera at him, he wheeled around and quickly walked back out.

The intelligence sergeant holding the camera instinctively stepped forward to chase him out the door, but another one of my operators grabbed his arm. "Remember the plan," he said.

The instinct was to arrest him on the spot. But the Green Beret approach is *by*, *with*, and *through* others. We had discussed this contingency even before we'd set up the clinic.

The man shuffled briskly down the dirt road to a waiting Toyota pickup truck.

Rather than chase him down, I called the Uruzgan police chief, who had several trucks of his most trusted officers on standby. They intercepted the truck and the man with the red-tinted beard. Less than an hour later, I stood beside the police chief, looking at Mullah Bari and his driver lying face down in the bed of the police pickup, hoods over their heads, flex-cuffs securing their hands behind their backs.

I called the Australian commander to let him know the good news. He wasn't thrilled that Bari was in the hands of the Afghan police rather than dead at the hands of his snipers. "Captain, you know how corrupt the police are. One way or another, this bloke will bribe his way out or just be let go," he protested.

"The police chief says he will handle it with Afghan justice," I replied. "I'm not going to ask exactly what he means. But no matter what, we won't be seeing Bari on the streets again. We need it to be the Afghan government who gets the credit for bringing this bastard down."

By adapting our operation away from the traditional scout-sniper model, to luring our enemy in with a medical clinic, we achieved multiple objectives. We built goodwill, treated local villagers who desperately needed care, and reinforced the power and prestige of the local authorities whom we were trying to support. The police chief was once again viewed as the top dog in the province. The Australian commandos did not get their kill—and I have to be honest, I did have a little pride in telling them that we had succeeded doing things the Green Beret way.

We pushed the good news story on local radio and through our network of elders. My unit and my men were never mentioned at all. We were never there. Perhaps most important, we didn't have a repeat of *Lone Survivor*, with an Australian sniper observer team getting compromised and wiped out.

This is what success looks like for Green Berets.

We bent some rules in the process to adapt to the situation. It was my job to accept that risk and, if things went sour, take the blame.

In the unconventional battlefield, and often in the business world, and certainly in politics, *adaptation is survival.* It seems obvious, but when it comes to large systems—bureaucracies, states, societies—death seems easier than adaptation. History is littered with systems that died because they failed to adapt to changing circumstances, from the Soviet Union to the Aztec Empire, to a corporation like Kodak, which infamously abandoned its early digital camera product.

Institutions that can adapt without compromising high standards and professional rigor are the ones that succeed. Those that don't will fade into history. Adaptation is the Green Berets' specialty.

As with so many other life lessons, I got my first taste of

creatively adapting within a system of strict rules at Virginia Military Institute. VMI had a long list of rules: cadets were forbidden to have civilian clothes, phones, televisions, pets, and most other comforts. It was intentionally very spartan. So, while conforming to the directives on the uniform of the day, marching in formation to each meal, and so on, we found innovative ways around the rules. My roommates and I discovered that previous cadets had knocked a hole in the wall behind our mirror—and there, we hung our civilian clothing on the nineteenth-century pipes inside the walls. A neighboring cadet who was an engineering major fashioned a refrigerator out of an old box speaker, and we even managed to hide a small bed in which slept our (very much forbidden) pet cat, Kitty, behind a row of books. We bent those rules while never, ever breaking the one rule that mattered above all others: our honor code.

It is difficult to explain the inherent value in this tightrope walk between rules that can be bent or broken and rules that must always be honored. Being caught and accepting the consequences is part of the training. So is enjoying the secret thrill of success. The honor code, however, was very different. With honor code violations, we watched in sadness at those who disgraced themselves. A loud, distinct drumroll roused us from our racks in the middle of the night, and the entire corps gathered in the darkness facing the inner courtyard of the old barracks. There, the honor court marched in, read the name of the cadet who had lied, cheated, or stolen, and announced that they were forever stricken from the rolls. It was at VMI that I learned small infractions, like violating our standard operating procedures to catch a Taliban scumbag, were worth the risk. But it was also at VMI that I learned violating certain ironclad rules, like the Geneva Convention or our honor code, were red lines never to be crossed.

Adaptability in our tactics is what caught Mullah Bari and it's going to take some strategic adaptation in how we fight the broader war on Islamic extremism. In addition to torturing police officers, Bari was so irate at the idea of girls getting education that he would have his fighters spray girls' schools with automatic-weapons fire—while the terrified girls were inside. Bari and the rest of the Taliban believed in an extreme and brutal interpretation of Islam, one that appalled the Muslims I fought alongside. From the Afghan National Army soldiers to my United Arab Emirates special operators, they were disgusted by the Taliban's treatment of women, Shia Muslims, and anyone else who didn't share their puritanical outlook.

In America today, we have numerous professors on the far left who complain about the "patriarchy," a society where men hold the predominance of power and women are marginalized. They have no idea what real patriarchy is. I've seen it brutally enforced in Taliban-ruled Afghanistan, and it is cruel beyond measure. The Taliban hostility toward women's education was a subset of their fundamental belief that women are simply not fully human.

The Islamic extremist jihad, like most insurgencies or rebellions, is ultimately a war on two fronts: it is a battle of ideas, and it is a battle to out-adapt the enemy in order to exploit their weaknesses. It is a contest of systems, and the system that wins is the one with the greatest flexibility. These two dynamics—the war of ideas and the battle to outwit your opponent—applies whether it's Hamas attacking Israel or ISIS inspiring attacks across Europe and the United States. One of the Islamic extremists' top vulnerabilities is its mistreatment of women.

It all came home for me when dealing with the Mangal tribal elder Ghafoorzai. His tribe are a subset of the Pashtuns, arguably the dominant ethnicity in Afghanistan and the traditional base of the Taliban. The Mangal live mostly in the eastern provinces along the border with Pakistan, in one of the most historically violent areas of a violent country. This region has seen countless conflicts, from the time of the British Raj to the Soviet invasion and occupation, to the twenty-year American war in Afghanistan. The Mangal were in the middle of all of it.

In the fight between the Taliban and the allied coalition, the Mangal worked hard to stay on the sidelines. But if you want to be left alone in a tough neighborhood, you have to be armed to the teeth. The Mangal did exactly that, developing a powerful tribal militia that was easily as well armed as the Taliban—and nearly as well armed as our own partner forces in the Afghan National Army. Their primary moneymaker for the tribe was in the pine nut harvest that they controlled. Pine nuts were a big business in central Asia. The Mangal cultivated, harvested, and exported them to Pakistan for distribution globally.

We were eager to build a relationship with the Mangal. They were interested as well, but cautious. As Ghafoorzai told me often, he was deeply worried that sooner or later, the Americans would leave. And when they did, the Taliban would come seeking retribution. I spent a great deal of time with this elder and came to know him not just as a potential ally but as a genuinely wise man despite the fact that he was illiterate. I wanted Ghafoorzai and his well-armed militia fighting on our side rather than sitting on the fence—and I definitely didn't want them partnering with the Taliban.

In meeting after meeting, we sat and talked for hours, drinking more chai tea than I could shake a stick at. We talked about family, his tribe, the long, painful history of Afghanistan, and life in America. After several meetings, he mentioned that he had a "secret weapon"—one that would destroy the Taliban.

The first few times he mentioned it, the hair on the back of my neck stood up. I worried he had some cache of Stingers from the 1980s or special Iranian-made IEDs.

"You've got to find out what the hell it is, sir," my senior sergeant said to me after one of the meetings. "CIA and our HQ have gotta know. If we keep working with this guy and he's got some kind of contraband or WMD, it's all our asses."

The next time Ghafoorzai mentioned the secret weapon, I put my foot down.

"Sahib, sir, respectfully," I said in a firm voice, "we cannot continue our relationship unless you show me this weapon."

As he listened to the translator, Ghafoorzai furrowed his

brow. "Commander Mike, it is harmless. You can be sure there is no harm to you or your fellow Americans."

"No, sir, I must see it," I replied. "My superiors will not allow my men to train and provide money to your tribe unless we know everything about this weapon."

The elder nodded. He could see that I wasn't going to be put off further. He leaned back a bit and studied the ceiling. After a long pause, Ghafoorzai spoke. "Okay, Commander Mike."

He motioned to one of his lieutenants, and they spoke in hushed, urgent Pashto. The lieutenant left, and I heard a commotion in the next room. I glanced back at my sergeant sitting near the door. His rifle was in his lap. I slid my hand down by my side to have it near my pistol. The commotion grew louder and nearer, and I looked up—and there were the secret weapons.

In walked Ghafoorzai's two daughters. They walked in confidently and stood next to their father, pride etched on their faces. It was extraordinary in this ultraconservative province in Afghanistan to ever see a woman outside of a burka. They dressed in ordinary (but elegant) Afghan women's clothing, faces uncovered, hair flowing freely down their backs. I knew immediately what this meant. I was being given a great trust, and a great honor, to see—and more important, to meet—these young women.

"The secret weapons," said the elder, smiling.

I was stunned and speechless. I was also incredibly relieved.

"These women, and many Afghan daughters like them,

must be educated!" Ghafoorzai said, smacking his hands together in a loud clap for emphasis. "Educated women will run
our universities, our government ministries, our radio, and television. They will move Afghanistan away from corrupt warlords
and their wars. They will be our army that will win the battle
for the mind," he said tapping the side of his head. "Success for
women like this strikes a mortal blow at the heart of the Taliban's extremism!" The elder pounded his chest over his heart
with his fist; I heard the raw emotion in his voice.

This elder, their father, had been smuggling his daughters
in and out of India for years—to and from the Afghan hinter-
lands—so they could attend university.

One of his daughters was training for law. The other was
studying medicine.

"These strong women will do more damage to the Taliban
than a hundred of your tanks and bombers!" said the elder,
now beaming with pride. "Educated girls are like a missile firing
right into the heart of the extremists," said Ghafoorzai.

I was floored. Not just to see these educated, gifted women—
but to see the elder's insight into the broader systemic vulnerabilities of the enemy. He knew that an educated class of women was
a powerful, unconventional weapon in the war of ideas against
Islamic extremism. They would drive change in the war on
terrorism more in the long run than any military effort possibly
could.

These days, after the unconscionable debacle of the U.S.
withdrawal from Afghanistan, we see the Taliban returning

to the dark era of brutal women's repression. No longer can a young girl be educated beyond sixth grade or even leave the house without a man. Ghafoorzai was right. The extremists are petrified of the power of women.

This isn't just an issue in Afghanistan. In neighboring Iran, the regime of the ayatollahs is also fearful of the immense power of educated women. For years, Iranian women are the ones who have resisted them, despite brutal and murderous oppression. We see it in Pakistan as well, where Nobel laureate Malala Yousafzai was shot in the head by local extremists for campaigning for girls' education. Mercifully, she survived and has become a global voice for women's rights. In Malala's case, as with the daughters of Ghafoorzai, she was encouraged and educated by a father who believed in her potential—and was willing to risk everything to realize it. Malala famously said, "The thing the extremists fear the most is a girl with a book."

People often ask me what victory will look like in the war on terror after decades of conflict. "We can't kill our way to victory," a journalist once challenged me.

"You're right," I said. "We have to think about it differently. We have to be more adaptable."

"Victory against Islamic extremism will look like women marching in the streets of Kabul, Tehran, and Gaza," I explained. "Victory will mean the jihadists have lost their credibility and therefore their grip on fear. We will fight the tactical fight and neutralize the radicalized young men that would attack us and our allies. But the long war is to successfully discredit the fanatical ideology that inspires them. It's about winning the war of ideas, and the brutalization of women by radical Islam is a key battleground."

Just a few decades ago, Communist-inspired terrorist groups were a tremendous threat. They are all but gone today—not because we wiped out every last one of their fighters but because these groups can no longer recruit. The ideology has been discredited, thanks in no small part to the way we adapted to combat and expose Communism's fundamental lies and failures. In the same way, we must undermine the legitimacy and credibility of Islamic extremism. That will take adaptation, innovation, and commitment.

As a member of Congress, I cofounded the House Women, Peace, and Security Caucus. I wanted to ensure we were incorporating the soft power of girls' education and women's empowerment into our strategies and resource decisions. In every speaking engagement I take on terrorism, I make the same point: in societies around the world where girls are educated and women are empowered, the extremists are not; when women thrive in business, society, and politics, the extremists fail.

Ghafoorzai had the best reason to side with us; a future for his beloved daughters. But even a father's love wasn't enough to overcome his fear that the United States would eventually abandon our Afghan allies to face the fury of a vengeful Taliban. I spent a lot of time advancing the proposition that America was a good partner, and an enduring one. I described our relationship with the South Koreans, pointing out we had stationed nearly thirty thousand troops there for decades as that government transitioned from a dictatorship to a thriving economy and democracy. I told him about the Marshall Plan, about how America helped its former enemies in Europe, and about the fifty thousand troops in Japan since World War II.

Eventually, the years' worth of relationship building paid off. Ghafoorzai agreed that the Mangal would commit his tribal militia to the fight.

We planned a formal ceremony, up in the Khost Mountains, effectively announcing that the Mangal were siding with us. Ghafoorzai planned to commit his well-armed militia and his prestige to the fight against the Taliban—and we would gain a tremendous ally in a region of Afghanistan of genuine strategic importance to the enemy. It was the sort of payoff that the Green Berets exist to generate. I was proud to be part of it.

Then, just days before the ceremony, Barack Obama made his fateful announcement on his strategy in Afghanistan at West Point.

It was December 2009, the disastrous results of his policies had yet to be felt—the rise of ISIS in Iraq in the wake of a full U.S. withdrawal, the loss of credibility with unenforced redlines in Syria, the feckless response to Russia's taking of Crimea or China's taking of the South China Sea, and finally the empowerment the Iranian regime with the Iran nuclear deal.

In his address on the Afghanistan war, President Obama said:

As Commander-in-Chief, I have determined that it is in our vital national interest to send an additional 30,000 U.S. troops to Afghanistan. After 18 months, our troops will begin to come home. These are the resources that we need to seize the initiative, while building the Afghan capacity that can allow for a responsible transition of our forces out of Afghanistan.

My men and I watched the speech in my operations center in Khost. We were excited at the announcement of reinforcements—but to also hear in the same breath from the President a timeline on their withdrawal was a gut punch. We were floored. One of my warrant officers said, "This is like FDR announcing that we've successfully taken the beaches of Normandy on D-Day—and telling the Germans we'll be gone by Christmas no matter what."

He was right. All President Obama had done was let the Taliban know that they just needed to wait us out for the next eighteen months. When we next traveled into the mountains to see Ghafoorzai, the warmth and connection were entirely gone, as if shut off by a switch. There was no food, no tea, no invitation to sit. We were made to stand and wait until the elder appeared. I could see it in his face: his fears about the Americans had been realized, and he was both angry and sad.

"Commander Mike," he announced without formalities or even courtesies, "I cannot work with you anymore. This deal, this relationship is over. Your President has told the world you're going to abandon us. The Taliban will have a gun to my family's head, if not tomorrow, then eighteen months from now when you leave."

In a land that has no national television, no internet, spotty radio coverage, and a largely illiterate population, the Mangal tribe had gotten word of President Obama's speech. Bad news travels fast. I tried to explain that the President was only withdrawing the reinforcements in eighteen months, but the Green Berets would stay. The nuance was lost on him.

As my sergeants and I walked dejectedly back to our vehicles for the long trek back to our base, Ghafoorzai followed me outside and stopped me. "Commander Mike, you take this back to your leaders in Washington," he said. "Until your children and grandchildren are prepared to stand shoulder to shoulder with my children against terrorism, you will fail here. It will take a generation to defeat their extremist ideas. We who are putting the lives of our entire families on the line to fight them, must know you are with us."

He knew, in that moment, that America would fail in Afghanistan—and he wanted me to communicate the fact back to the policymakers in Washington. I didn't want to believe him, because I knew our capacity to adapt. We had tools in the war of ideas, such as the elder's "secret weapons," and other elements of soft power. We could evolve to a smaller Special Forces–led advisory role to the Afghan Army, like we did for many years in Colombia to help them defeat the FARC narcoinsurgency. There was the option of keeping a small presence at Bagram Airfield to provide intelligence, air support, and logistics. There were reasons to keep the air base that was right on China's doorstep. There were (and are) trillions worth of untapped critical mineral reserves to generate economic development in Afghanistan and fuel our modern economy.

To my regret, Ghafoorzai was right, and I was wrong. We were rigid and linear in our strategy of focusing on troop numbers, and as the tribal leader rightly feared, we would eventually abandon all pretense of support for our Afghan allies in the fight against terrorism. In December 2009, Ghafoorzai could foresee the shameful Biden withdrawal of August 2021. The Taliban could foresee it, too.

All we could do was continue to apply the Green Beret approach for adaptation to the tactical and operational levels and hope that improved tactics on the ground filtered up to the strategic decision-making in Washington. It wasn't just the Afghan units we sought to influence but our European NATO allies as well.

At one point, my team was ordered to advise and assist the French Special Operations Task Force operating along the southeastern border region of Afghanistan and Pakistan. I was given this additional mission with no additional resources or people: my headquarters told me to figure it out. I understood the bigger picture by this point: the Pentagon was making decisions with the misguided notion that the Taliban and al-Qaeda were largely defeated and that the conflict was trending more toward a Bosnia-style stabilization and peacekeeping mission. We were going to withdraw eventually regardless. With this reality in mind, I decided to implement some bottom-up leadership and consulted with the highly experienced sergeants on my team. They recommended we peel away just one of our best Green Berets to assign to the French headquarters. It's all we had to spare.

"You're sending *one* sergeant to advise an entire French task force?" my higher-headquarters operations officer said incredulously over the satellite phone. "Is this guy Jason Bourne?"

"Hey, sir, you know we are really spread thin out here," I replied. "Sending one guy to the French leaves us with just three operators to assist the UAE task force as they try to establish multiple bases in theater. The rest of my men are spread out among embedded with the Czech, Polish, and Canadian task forces."

Doctrinally, we should have had a full twelve-man Special Forces team per allied task force. Instead, we had just my one team advising and liaising with multiple task forces across multiple provinces in southern Afghanistan. It was just a dozen Green Berets, but they were having a serious operational impact. In order to do so, they most definitely had to adapt and overcome.

"The French operators can fight," I continued. "Their soldiers don't need our help to shoot, move, and communicate. This sergeant is one of my smartest, and he can help the French commander with air support, intelligence assets, and drones.

Plus, he can keep an eye on what the French are up to and report back. I trust my guys. They would not set this mission up to fail."

"Roger that," replied the operations officer. "You guys know best. But if things go bad, the complaint goes like a heat-seeking missile from the French commander on the ground back to Paris, over to the Pentagon, and then down on us like a four-star ton of bricks. That one sergeant had better be damn good!"

This type of mission is where it all came together. My team was perfectly capable of kicking in doors and putting two rounds into a bad guy's forehead. But this is where maturity, experience, and years of training came together. Twelve Green Berets, led by one lowly captain, shaping and influencing an entire theater.

I wasn't instructed by my higher headquarters what to tell the UAE or French or Czech special forces teams to do. We had no authority to order our allies about. We could only advise and influence. I gathered recommendations from my experienced sergeants, made some decisions on where we should focus and could take risk, and passed them up my chain. To their credit, they listened. It was a bottom-up process—and showed the adaptable mindset of every Green Beret up the chain of command.

We didn't always find the mentality of bottom-up leadership with our allies, though. Months later, my headquarters was growing very frustrated in their relationship with the French task force. The Taliban were moving aggressively into the French area of operation, putting numerous villages under their control and flowing weapons and fighters over the border into southern Afghanistan from their sanctuaries in Pakistan. The American command was frustrated. They just could not get the French to engage. I flew out to their base near Pakistan's famed Torkham gate to see for myself what the hell was going on.

Here's what I saw. The individual French soldier was fantastic. They were aggressive, competent, candid—everything you could want in a warrior. French soldiers in Afghanistan were ready and willing to come to grips with the Taliban, kick their asses, and win. The problem was that French politicians in Paris were determined to avoid exactly that.

When I caught up with Tom, my sergeant at the French base, he was clearly frustrated.

"I present these guys intelligence target packages on local Taliban commanders, and they sit on their hands. They think about it for a day or two. They talk to Paris and their lawyers about interpretations of rules of engagement. They never say no, per se, but rather analyze some more and make all kinds of demands. First, they want a quick-reaction force from the Afghans, then they want Predators overhead, and then they want helicopters nearby," Tom continued, clearly venting and getting angrier and more animated as he spoke.

"Of course, I can't get them all of those damn assets every time they want to go out of the wire. And they know it. Every time I come through with some new demand, they move the goalpost. So eventually, they send out a patrol . . . in the opposite direction of the enemy . . . just so they can say they did something! We use intelligence to find the enemy. They use the same intelligence to *avoid* the enemy. Their leadership is terrified of accidentally killing a civilian or losing one of their guys in a firefight. That will make headlines in France, and the officers will lose their careers."

Tom threw his hands up in the air. "But," he continued, "the biggest problem is that I have no juice, no *wasta*"—the Arabic term referring to influence—"with the commander." Tom told me the French officers were "old school." That meant they wouldn't listen to him, a "lowly sergeant." The results-oriented Green Beret culture meant that sergeants were expected to give advice and insight to officers. That wasn't the way the French worked.

And then they got a new commander in the field. A whole new cadre of French officers arrived—and they hadn't met Tom yet. That gave me an idea.

"What if I made you an officer? A battlefield promotion, so to speak."

He grinned. "I always liked how you think, sir. We both know you don't have the authority for that, and we could get in a lot of trouble." He thought for a second and smiled. "Does it come with the extra pay?"

"Nope," I said. "All you get is a little extra juice you need to get the job done."

Just before we were to meet the new French commander

and his team, we walked over to the tractor trailer that served as a makeshift uniform store at Bagram Airfield. I grabbed a set of captain's bars and walked with Tom around back. Right then and there, we had a mini ceremony as I pinned the bars on his collar.

"I'll take the heat if anyone makes a stink about it," I reassured him. "My job is to get you what you need to get the mission accomplished."

Captain Tom wasn't able to solve all problems and turn things around overnight. But he was able to shift the way they operated in a subtle but important way. Whenever Tom shared U.S.-generated intelligence on Taliban locations with the French commander, he suggested partnering with the local Afghan Army unit and encouraging the Afghans to take the lead in engaging the Taliban with the French in support. The Afghan Army company commander, younger and ready to prove himself to the coalition forces, was eager to be invited into the planning process. Tom convinced the French commander that he could send the French forces on patrols near the targeted area so that they could act as a quick-reaction force for the Afghans whenever they made contact with the Taliban. In this way, the French commander wasn't ordering his men into the teeth of the insurgency but rather simply patrolling in an area that had the added benefit of coming to the aid of the Afghan Army in self-defense.

One small shift in approach—one adaptation—solved multiple problems. First, it gave the Afghan National Army confidence to engage in more offensive operations, with the French special forces nearby and ready to react. Second, the Afghan people saw their own military taking on the Taliban rather than the coalition. Third, any risk-averse officials in Paris who did not want their forces chancing casualties with aggressive operations would have a hard time chastising the French commander for assisting the Afghan military.

Finally, the partnership and trust that was established between the French and Afghan military was a lasting legacy for Tom. Green Berets always aim to work themselves out of a job, and by the end of our tour, the coordination between the Afghan Army and French command had grown strong enough that Tom's replacement could step back and simply coordinate intelligence and air support. This was only possible because Tom understood the strategic intent. I had exercised bottom-up leadership and listened to my sergeants about who to put in the job—and I listened to Tom about the obstacles he was facing. Then I wasn't afraid to bend the rules to get the job done and take the possible heat for doing so. I had no authority to pin captain's bars on Tom's uniform, but it was the right—and necessary—thing to do.

In Afghanistan as in so many other theaters, Green Berets proved themselves as adaptable as they were courageous. But for all our unique skills, we cannot create grand strategy. We cannot fund our national defense. Now that I am in Congress, serving on the Armed Services Committee that oversees the entire defense budget, I am relentless about pushing a massive department to adapt to future threats. This is especially true in the case of a threat as devious and dangerous as the Iranian regime. For over forty years, Iran's Islamic Revolutionary Guard Corps (IRGC) and its external arm, the Quds Force, have used many of the traits of the Green Berets to terrorize the Middle East. The Iranian regime knows it will never win an arms race with its wealthy Gulf Arab neighbors like Saudi Arabia and the UAE while under decades-long economic sanctions. The IRGC understand they cannot compete head-to-head with the vibrant technological powerhouse that the Israeli military has become.

Instead, the IRGC has adapted, taking a page from the manuals of the Green Berets, ironically. They started developing proxy forces on the cheap all over the region—Hezbollah in Lebanon and Syria, Hamas in Gaza, the Houthis in Yemen, and the Shiite militias in Iraq. The Quds Force operate with a similar mission to Green Berets; embed with, arm, and train "resistance" forces. But in this case, instead of fighting to defend democracy, they are violently resisting the liberal global world order led by the United States and America's allies in the region—Israel and the Gulf Sunni Arab states. The Quds Force and their militias have no problem employing asymmetrical warfare to circumvent traditional military advantages in tanks, planes, and ships. They have no issue using the brutal tools of terrorism: hostage taking, bombings, and massive amounts of cheap rockets. They couple this with new warfare like cyberattacks and small disposable drones. The regime has been all too happy to trade the lives of its proxies in the battlefields of Gaza, Lebanon, and Iraq for the lives of Israelis and Americans.

It wasn't until President Trump took the bold and necessary step of taking out, in a targeted strike, the head of the IRGC Quds Force, Qasem Soleimani, that costs were imposed on Iran itself and deterrence was restored. After months of Iran attacking shipping; shooting down our drones; threatening Saudi energy supplies and storming our embassy, the President decided he had to escalate to de-escalate. As always, bullies don't stop until they're punched in the nose. After firing a harmless round of missiles at our base in response to the Soleimani operation, relative calm was restored. Our willingness to take out their top people—plus the maximum pressure campaign shutting down oil exports—effectively dried up Iran's available cash for funding terrorist militias like Hezbollah and Hamas.

Even as it fights these bloody proxy wars, the Iranian regime has continued its march toward an operational nuclear missile. The mullahs know that once Iran has the protection of a nuclear umbrella, it will have even more license to spread terror with far less threat of retaliation on Iran itself. The failure to grasp this has been the underlying (and incredibly dangerous) policy flaw of both the Biden and Obama administrations. Every time Western sanctions cause the economic situation to deteriorate to the point where the regime's survival is threatened (and it can no longer pay its proxies), Iran offers to slow down its enrichment capability to leverage more cash into its coffers. They've supplemented this strategy by taking Americans hostage in Tehran and leveraging their release for billions. Multiple administrations have been outfoxed, not appreciating that the appeasement approach means that money flows right through Tehran to Moscow for advanced weapons and out to terrorist proxy groups. Our reckless refusal to stand up to Iran has meant those proxy groups are ever-better armed and trained for what Ayatollah Khamenei calls a "ring of fire" around Israel to be used at a time of his choosing.

My consistent question to the Pentagon and State Department has been "How are we adapting to the IRGC?" In my experience, the thing the regime cares about most is its own grip on power and its money. As is so often the case, what the regime fears most is an uprising from its own people. The more we have the regime focused internally, the less energy and resources they have to muck around externally. From both a human rights and geopolitical standpoint, we should be aiding the groups that are brutally oppressed inside Iran, like the Kurds, the Baloch, and the Arabs. The Obama administration missed a huge opportunity to support the massive protests during the Green Movement in 2009. When nationwide protests erupted when Iranian police killed teenager Mahsa Amini in September 2022 for refusing to wear a headscarf, the Biden team should have made her a household name worldwide—particularly as thousands of schoolgirls stood heroically in the streets against Iran's thug-like internal security services.

Young Amini was of Kurdish origin, an area that traditionally has resisted the regime over the years. Yet, when a leader of the Iranian Kurds came to Washington, he literally could not get a single meeting at the State Department or with the administration. I met with him, of course, and heard of the brutality and torture being meted out to these children and their families. He begged for my help to keep the protests alive. For months, the regime was on its back foot because of how widely the unrest had spread. My office worked with local nonprofits to get Starlink base terminals and other means of communication like encrypted apps to the groups, but it was a drop in the bucket compared with what we could have done with an organized program. The unofficial word I received back from the State Department was that engaging with these groups— even with informal meetings at a low level—would upset the fragile nuclear talks underway with Iran. We were so rigid in our appeasement strategy that we missed opportunity after opportunity.

By contrast, the Israeli military has decades of experience punching above their weight. Israel is a small nation that has faced outsize threats from the moment it came into being. As a result, the Israel Defense Forces has set the standard for adaptability. Special forces from all over the world seek Israeli counsel on everything from hostage rescue to integrating new technologies into their operations. They deployed daring covert programs to target and slow down key elements of Iran's nuclear program and became masters at offensive cyber to keep their adversaries on their back foot. The Israelis, bold in the application of diplomacy, teach bottom-up leadership and infuse a culture of speaking truth to power up their chain of command. As a result, they have defied the odds for decades, fighting and winning war after war while being surrounded on all sides by those who want to exterminate them. That mix of urgency and adaptability has much to teach us.

Adaptation is survival. We see it again and again throughout American and world history. We saw it in granting an unauthorized battlefield promotion, giving a sergeant the *wasta* he needed to push an ally into the fight. We saw it with a father finding a way to educate his daughters in a fight against extremists. We saw it with our enemies like the Taliban who circumvented our IED jammers with trip wires. We saw it with Hamas's cynical use of human shields to maximize civilian deaths—and score propaganda victories. We see it with Israel deftly utilizing offensive cyber to hit Iran's nuclear program—after the Iranians had buried it so deep Israeli fighter jets no longer had the option to bomb it.

As a Green Beret and now an elected official, I know that if you aren't constantly adapting, your adversary will eventually figure out how to defeat you. The key is having the moral compass and judgment to know what rules to bend and what rules to never break. And as we adapt, we should always adapt toward a desired mission end state. Sometimes it is tactical—like hosting a makeshift health clinic to capture Mullah Abdul

Bari. Sometimes it is strategic, say, to win the war of ideas on Islamist extremism. Either way, adaptability with commitment is the key. In my case, that commitment will always be to the Constitution, the Americans I represent, and my family.

6

LOYALTY

The Humvee in front of us eased down an embankment into a wadi—a dry riverbed—in central Uruzgan Province. As it reached the bottom and accelerated up the other side, my interpreter, Spartacus, started yelling into the radio, "Stop! Stop! Stop! IED!"

My heart was instantly in my throat. *Where the hell was it?* I looked frantically for the bomb. The Humvee in front of us was perfectly straddling an old Russian anti-tank mine. Its exhaust blew the rocks and sand off the top of the device. Designed to destroy a tank, the mine would easily obliterate the lightly armored vehicle in front of us, along with the three men in it. Just as the Humvee hit the gas to get away, my Humvee started sliding down the embankment toward it. By the grace of God, my driver avoided rolling directly over the mine, but we were not out of danger. We braced for some nearby Taliban fighter to remotely detonate it right underneath us.

"They are trying to blow it up!" Spartacus yelled. Sitting in the back seat of our Humvee, he held a walkie-talkie in his hand that he used to scan known Taliban frequencies to listen in on their chatter. "Some shithead Talib is being ordered to blow us up! It sounds like he is looking down on us from a high-up position." Spartacus peered out the window, gazing up.

"Light up that ridgeline!" I yelled over the team's radio frequency. A few seconds later, a mix of machine guns and grenade launchers from the convoy began peppering a rock outcropping a few hundred yards to the right.

"He's telling his commander that the Americans are shooting at him and that the IED is not exploding," reported Spartacus. "It sounds like he is trying to escape."

Eventually, we cleared the vehicles away from the mine, and one of my brave engineers walked into the wadi alone with a block of C-4 explosive, placed it on the mine, and blew it in place.

"Shit. Thank you, Allah," Spartacus said under his breath. "Taliban bastards." His sixth sense for what they were likely to do had paid off again. Had Spartacus not seen it, either the vehicle in front of us or ours would likely have been blown to pieces.

In addition to his virtues as a soldier and a fan of American pop culture, Spartacus had an uncanny ability to detect IEDs. In a time when the IED was the principal Taliban weapon, he was a lifesaver.

Spartacus was not his real name, of course. He was a small, wiry, tough, and very young man, straight out of rural Pashtunistan. Spartacus may have been as far as you could get from the States, but he loved America. America, for him, was two big things, and he was devoted to both.

First, it was our pop culture: the movies, the television shows, and the music. He had an insatiable appetite for American music and would listen to everything we had—especially rap. Everything he learned about America was exciting to a young man accustomed to the dull, dusty, brown-and-green palette of the Afghan countryside. The idea of America was insanely compelling, the place where he believed he *must* be, someday, if only he could find his way there. There was no path for him, though—until the war came, and Spartacus found his way: working with the Green Berets.

The second thing that America meant to Spartacus was *us*: the soldiers who came to fight the Taliban and, in the eyes of Spartacus, defeat the forces that sought to deny him his own dream. Spartacus couldn't go to America, but in just about the most wonderful turn of fate possible to him, America came to Spartacus. Given the chance to join up and fight alongside the Green Berets, he seized the moment.

We got to know Spartacus pretty well—and we all came to like and respect him tremendously. He was more than just an interpreter. He was a cultural advisor and had great insight into what motivated your average young Taliban fighter. Counterinsurgency—the core work of the Green Beret—takes place in the gray areas of human motivation and action. Both our survival and our success depend on one key high-stakes decision: discerning who to trust. Every assessment technique we had told us this was a man we could trust. We nicknamed him Spartacus because of his enthusiastic aggressiveness in taking on the Taliban. He had learned English by watching movies and listening to rap music, so every other word was a four-letter curse word. Over time, he got to the point where at least half of his profanities made sense. *Shit fucker Taliban gangsters* was a favorite phrase.

Everyone who served in Afghanistan was well aware of the persistent problem of what was called "green-on-blue" violence. Usually without warning, Afghan partners would abruptly turn on coalition forces, attacking and often killing them. Sometimes it happened because of some sort of radicalization trigger: for example, an Afghan concluding, through exposure or third-party narrative, that the Americans or Europeans with whom he worked did not respect Islam. Sometimes it happened because the killer was a Taliban agent, either having joined to serve as one, or having become one in the interim. Some of them could be very patient indeed, only betraying us after months or even years of what we thought was loyal cooperation.

Even strict vetting was never quite enough to weed out the ones determined to betray: the double agent suicide bomber in the 2009 Forward Operating Base Chapman attack, for example, was vouched for by both the CIA and Jordanian intelligence. I was just down the street when the sound of the explosion snapped our heads around just in time to see the plume of smoke rising from inside the CIA base. A Jordanian doctor had convinced both Jordanian and U.S. intelligence that he knew the location of Ayman al-Zawahiri, the number two leader of al-Qaeda. After months of vetting, he was brought to the base in secrecy for an in-person meeting. As a sign of trust and to an abundance of caution to hide his identity, the CIA Chief of Base Jennifer Matthews decided not to have him searched by the Afghan gate guards. As the car carrying him pulled into a portion of the compound that had recently housed one of my teams of Green Berets, Jennifer and key members of her team lined up to great him. He exploded his suicide vest as he left the car and caused the largest number of CIA casualties since the Marine barracks bombing in Beirut in 1983. My medics helped treat the wounded. It was a colossal intelligence failure and huge win for the bad guys. For us, it was a brutal reminder of how tough it is to balance building trust with local allies with the need to always, always be on guard.

In the case of Spartacus and all our interpreters, the Taliban had figured out how valuable they were to us. The Taliban commanders knew our operations would grind to a halt without the interpreters because we would not be able to communicate with the locals, our sources, or the tribes. It would be like going to combat without radios. The Taliban also loathed the interpreters because they were powerful examples of proud Afghans who did not fall for the extremist narrative. Spartacus in particular hated the Taliban for their backwardness, their tyranny, and their cruelty; they hated him in return because he would not bend a knee to them.

Spartacus had family, of course, and he missed them when he was embedded with the special forces units. One day, he took leave and got on one of the buses that makes long odysseys through the Afghan countryside. Somehow, the Taliban knew that he had left the protection of an American base alone, and they knew exactly which bus he was on. Well beyond the base, the bus was stopped at a Taliban checkpoint, and Spartacus was dragged off.

The Taliban forced him back to his village, and when he arrived, hands zip-tied behind his back and in tears, his family was herded out to see him—and forced to watch as Spartacus was beheaded before their eyes. A young man who believed in the dream of America was killed before his loved ones by the enemies of that dream. It was an unspeakable end to a heroic life.

As Green Berets, we train for this uncertain moral terrain. We have to figure out who to trust and when. Spartacus proved himself worthy, and he was a friend and an ally and a moral beacon. But in this type of warfare, trust is a two-way street. We also *must show ourselves to be trustworthy*, because our counterparts are constantly making the same assessments and calculations we are. They watch us as much as we do them, and the stakes for all of us are life or death.

It is in this context that our relentless focus on mission

is not just a moral virtue but a practical one. Our prospective partners have to know we are in their country, among their people, bearing arms, to do exactly—and only—the things we say we are. And they have to know *we will see it through*. When we betray that purpose—for example, with a Presidential speech promising an eventual American retreat from Afghanistan—the consequences can be devastating. It is a very hard thing to see a sense of betrayal in the eyes of a man you've asked to trust you. I hope never to see it again. I am still angry—rightly so, I think—at an administration that didn't let us keep the promises we made.

When I found out about Spartacus, it was a punch in the gut. It felt like I had lost one of my own men. He was not an American, but he loved our country as he loved his own. This Afghan whom we could trust with our lives stands in stark contrast with an American soldier whom we absolutely could not trust: Sergeant Bowe Bergdahl. When I think of these two very different men, I am reminded of the tremendous value of loyalty—and the very high cost of its absence.

On June 30, 2009, I took command of my company of Green Berets, attached forces like dog handlers and FBI agents, and a platoon of SEALs in the border region with Pakistan. Coming from my previous assignment as counterterrorism advisor in the White House, before we were mobilized, I had an entire campaign plan I was eager to execute. I had helped write the strategy to both protect Afghanistan's upcoming elections and engage the tribes to get their militias in the fight against the Taliban and al-Qaeda. I was eager to now get to execute it.

All of those carefully crafted plans went up in smoke when we heard the call over the theater-wide satellite communications of a DUSTWUN, the acronym for *duty status—whereabouts unknown*. An American soldier was missing and possibly captured. Soon the order came down from the theater commander— then General Stanley McCrystal—to stop everything and shift to the search for the missing soldier. We quickly learned that Sergeant Bergdahl's remote outpost to the south of my base had not been attacked, so it was very unlikely he was captured. Then his unit reported that he had left his weapon, body armor, and other gear on his bunk and walked off the base into the local village in the dead of the night. Bottom line, he was a deserter. My intelligence sergeant told me that Bergdahl had apparently sent emails to his father denouncing America and what we were doing in Afghanistan and showing some sympathy with the Taliban. We were livid.

"This guy is a piece-of-shit traitor," my chief warrant officer said. "We should leave his ass and not lose a single American going to look for him."

My chief was right, and there was historical precedent for it. In 1965, Sergeant Charles Robert Jenkins defected to North Korea from his army post on the DMZ. He joined three other American soldiers in defecting. They were soon used by the regime in anti-American propaganda films. They were abused and treated harshly. But the U.S. government treated them for what they were—deserters. The Army didn't classify them as prisoners of war. We certainly didn't sacrifice the lives of fellow soldiers or trade some of the most valuable North Korean officials for them. In fact, when Jenkins surfaced decades later in Japan, he was immediately extradited and court-martialed. There was no politicized attempt to celebrate him as a "hero" or sweep his case under the rug. With Jenkins, there was no doubt about his disloyalty—and the consequences for it.

It would be different for Bowe Bergdahl. That difference still angers me.

Though we knew he had betrayed the very fiber of what it meant to be a soldier and our commitment to care for one another, we were ordered to pull out all the stops to find Bergdahl and prevent the Taliban from putting him beyond our reach in Pakistan. We were furious and frustrated, but we also all knew that his capture would be a massive propaganda victory for the Taliban, and soon they would be showcasing him on every jihadi website in the Middle East.

We had to do everything we could to keep him from being used by the enemy against us.

My sergeant gave me a grim overview of where we stood: "Sir, our intelligence sources are informing us that the Taliban have him and are moving him from safe house to safe house until they can get him across the Pakistani border. This is a race against time. They also know that we are throwing everything we have into finding him, and they are feeding false information to our informants in the hope that they can bait us into an ambush."

Day after day, our brothers in the conventional units manned static checkpoints on key roads leading to the border, searching every Afghan vehicle for Bergdahl. Almost every time they set up a checkpoint, they came under attack within hours. Meanwhile, our special forces chased down every lead—no matter how poorly it was vetted—and conducted countless raids night after night.

The problem was that the Taliban knew that we would spare little expense in trying to retrieve Bergdahl. I protested to my commander that we were taking colossal risks. If the Taliban thought we were desperate, they could play us easily.

My boss shot back, "Major Waltz, if there is a five percent chance Bergdahl is where our sources say he is, then we are going to launch on it. Every other mission should be stopped, and every asset we have is focused on finding Bergdahl. You know that if they can get him to Pakistan, our ability to retrieve him is pretty much gone."

That very night, my team in Ghazni Province launched a raid based on flimsy intel from a source we couldn't verify. All we knew is that there was a slim chance that the Taliban was hiding Bergdahl at the site. About an hour into the raid, while the team and its partnered Afghan police force were searching a very large compound, I heard a code word over the radio that made the hair on the back of my neck stand up. Every operator knew what that word meant: "Stop what you are doing and get the hell out now." The compound was a trap. Sitting in the center courtyard was a car rigged to explode. C-4 explosives lined the ceiling of another room in a way designed to collapse the building on the team inside. By the grace of God, the explosives didn't detonate, and my team and their police unit escaped.

I had been angry to begin with. Now, I was furious that we were taking such risks for this one soldier who had betrayed us.

The conventional units in our area were not so fortunate. Looking for Bergdahl, they took casualties. One of those casualties was Second Lieutenant Darryn Andrews of the Twenty-Fifth Infantry Division. He grew up in the rolling farmlands of Texas, and when he was old enough, he pursued his dream of soldiering with the United States Army. That's how a young man from the small town of Cameron, Texas, found himself on the other side of the world, in Afghanistan's rugged and dangerous Paktika Province. Darryn had a lot to live for: waiting back home for him was a beloved wife, a young son, and an unborn daughter. None of that caused him to hesitate on that fateful day when his platoon was hit by a Taliban ambush. An IED detonated, and a rocket-propelled grenade was fired at his men. Seeing the incoming round, Andrews tackled *three* of his fellow soldiers to protect them and take the blast himself. He died of his wounds.

Darryn Andrews gave his life searching for Bowe Bergdahl.

After weeks of sending teams on raids that amounted to wild-goose chases, my intel sergeant came to see me, a grim look on his face. "Sir, I have three sources now saying he's in Pakistan. He's gone. But I've got something that is going to really piss you off: my sources are reporting that Bergdahl is giving them all the information he can—how our mine-clearing teams work, how we detect IEDs, our patrol routes, and so on." The sergeant paused, his jaw working in anger. Then he continued, "What a piece of shit. This is an epic betrayal."

It was hard to disagree.

In the following years, I assumed that one of our Tier One units—Delta or SEAL Team 6—would eventually locate Bergdahl and snatch him out of Pakistan. I hoped they didn't. I was convinced he was a deserter and a traitor and didn't deserve more soldiers risking their lives to rescue him. Let him live with the people he chose, I thought.

Never in a million years did I think I would turn on the television one spring morning in 2014 to see Bergdahl's parents standing next to President Obama in the Rose Garden. Nor did I imagine Obama's National Security Advisor Susan Rice would go on the Sunday talk shows to proclaim that Bergdahl "served with honor and distinction."

Fox News anchor Bret Baier began texting me to come on his show and tell the world what I had told him upon return from my tour—that Bergdahl was no hero.

Two mentors of mine advised me not to do it. "Don't be the only babe in the woods raining on Obama's big moment bringing home a U.S. soldier. They'll come after you," one told me. They warned me that the IRS would come after my business if I spoke up. I was warned they could even come after my security clearance in the reserves. Ultimately, though, I had to do it. I had to call out this betrayal. Yellow ribbons were popping up all over the country to celebrate Bergdahl. This wasn't about one traitor getting a welcome he didn't deserve. It was about the lessons we were teaching. We were allowing disloyalty to be redefined as honorable. I could not stand that.

I was the first person to go on national television and say, "Time out, America: this guy is a traitor." It was a risk I took, but when I thought of Darryn Andrews and other soldiers I knew had died on missions searching for him, I knew that there was nothing anyone could do to me that would dissuade me from telling the truth. Fortunately for my business and military career, I found out quickly I wasn't alone. The internet exploded with outcry from soldiers who had been in Bergdahl's unit at the time he deserted, soon joined by the broader veteran community outraged at the Obama administration's attempt to take a victory lap. To this day, I'm convinced that Obama's team expected some rumbling from Congress about trading five hardened Taliban out of Guantánamo, but otherwise thought this would be a victorious moment for the administration for bringing a soldier home. In the aftermath, they figured his transgressions would have been swept under the rug.

If it weren't for the media spotlight that I—and others—shone on Bergdahl's betrayal, there would have been no recognition of the harm this reckless, selfish man had caused.

Darryn Andrews deserved to be honored, rather than the fool who cost the young Texan his life.

Years later, I testified before Congress next to Darryn's father on the Bergdahl trade. When asked by then Congressman Tom Cotton if he had anything to say to President Obama, Darren's father replied, "Where was the Rose Garden ceremony for my son? He selflessly gave his life for someone who betrayed him. Where is *his* celebration for serving with honor and distinction?"

It both pained and angered me that we had no good answer for this grieving father.

Eventually, Bergdahl was court-martialed, reduced in rank to private, and given a dishonorable discharge. Rather than a jail sentence for his desertion, though, the judge gave him time served for his time in Taliban captivity. Unfortunately, in July 2023, a federal judge vacated Bergdahl's conviction on a technicality. As of the writing of his book, the Justice Department is fighting to reinstate the court-martial conviction. I'll never forget the image of Bergdahl leaving the courtroom a free man. Bergdahl could walk. Following behind him in a wheelchair was Sergeant Mark Allen, who could no longer speak to his family or walk due to the gunshot wound to the head he'd taken from a Taliban sniper while searching for Bergdahl. Ten years later, he died of his wounds. Sergeant Allen, like Lieutenant Andrews, and like Spartacus, lived with honor and gave their lives for their teammates. They can no longer experience the joys of this world while Bowe Bergdahl walks free.

Bergdahl's story matters. His return, achieved in exchange for five hardened Taliban prisoners at Guantánamo Bay, was heralded as a difficult choice demonstrating the lengths to which America will go to get back its own. It was a narrative that required Bergdahl to be, at worst, a naive and mentally unbalanced young man. It was a narrative that repackaged disloyalty as victimhood. Intentionally or not, the Obama administration was reinforcing one of the most destructive tendencies of the Left: the compulsion to make villains into victims. Disloyalty, even treason, becomes easier to excuse when you invent a sympathetic backstory about (take your pick) mental illness, childhood trauma, or systemic racism. Too often in our culture, we justify very serious moral failings by appealing to sympathy for the person who failed. Lots of people have had tough lives. Spartacus had a tough life, tougher than anything Bergdahl could have imagined. Spartacus stayed loyal.

Loyalty to nation, to family, and to principle—these aren't luxuries for people whose lives are already comfortable. They are necessary qualities for everyone. Disloyalty cannot be excused on the basis of youth, foolishness, ideology, or an unhappy childhood. What made the Bergdahl case so infuriating wasn't just that the Obama administration was letting a traitor off the hook. The real problem was the message it sent: "victimhood" cancels out everything else.

Some journalists have since tried to question whether any soldiers really died because of the search for Bowe Bergdahl. I have made it clear that everyone in eastern Afghanistan was ordered to support that search, directly and indirectly. So, unless a soldier tripped and hit his head on the way to the latrine, if they were killed or wounded in the months following Bergdahl's disappearance, then that death was related to the search. Secondly, what the journalists will never understand is the opportunity costs of his desertion to every other soldier in theater. Those soldiers may not have been directly involved in a search mission, but they didn't have the air support, intelligence, or logistics support they normally would have had because it was all diverted away from them to the Bergdahl search effort.

During his court-martial, Bergdahl said what he needed to say to avoid a long prison sentence. He explained that he was tortured, and I don't doubt that. However, we know he voluntarily gave away information—as much intelligence as any private had—until he was no longer useful. It's important to understand the accounts of his treatment during captivity are primarily sourced from him. The fact that his captivity was harsh (not surprising given he was in the hands of some of the worst people on the planet) doesn't excuse the consequences of his actions on his fellow soldiers, nor that he voluntarily deserted his post. The bottom line is that Bergdahl now has the luxury of living out his life—a luxury that those that were killed and wounded as a result of his actions will never have. For that reason, I have no sympathy for him.

Spartacus did not live to have his loyalty to America rewarded with the chance to immigrate here. It is a tragedy, not only because his death was so cruel but because we need more

Americans like him. I see the spirit of Spartacus in the millions of immigrants who literally risk their lives and give up everything for a chance to live the American dream, whether it's a group of Cubans who pile into an overcrowded, rickety raft to drift into an unknown fate—or parents so desperate they give their children to smugglers. In their hearts, these desperate people know that America may not be a perfect nation, but it is certainly the most exceptional on earth. If America was as bad as Bowe Bergdahl claimed, tens of millions wouldn't risk everything to be here.

How do we create a society that rewards and celebrates men and women like Spartacus? How do we recover the moral compass to call the Bowe Bergdahls of the world what they are—traitors, rather than victims? We need to proclaim a hard but vital truth: our culture of victimhood and grievance inculcates disloyalty. We need to teach again the essential virtue of coming together for a cause. The first sentence of the Ranger Creed reads, "Never shall I fail my comrades." The motto of our nation reads *E Pluribus Unum*: "Out of many, one." That creed and that motto point to the fact that our success always hinges on our commitment to one another.

Not every American will be a Ranger—but every American deserves the opportunity to bond with others in service of a common goal. Every American needs to find the cause and the comrades whom they will not fail. Every American deserves the chance to discover the sense of purpose and fulfillment that can only come through loyalty to something greater than themselves.

7

RESILIENCE

The dictionary defines *resilience* as "the capacity to withstand or to recover quickly from difficulties." The shorthand definition: "toughness."

Dictionaries define resilience. Men like Staff Sergeant Andre Murnane embody it.

The Taliban rocket teams often missed. Sometimes, though, they got lucky. One afternoon, a Taliban rocket hit a stack of artillery ammunition on his base facing the Pakistani border. The massive explosion blew Andre off his feet and gave him a severe concussion. He was medevacked in serious condition, and we did not expect him back anytime soon.

A week or so later, my sergeant major called me after visiting Andre in the hospital. Andre's doctors wanted him to go back to the States for some recovery time, but he was demanding to stay, insisting on returning to his team. I asked the sergeant major if he thought Andre could still contribute to the mission without endangering his team. His nod was all I needed. Andre rejoined us.

Andre had been back barely a month when his team was ordered out to investigate a Taliban rocket launch site. As the team rounded the top of a small hill, the lead Afghan Army soldier froze. "IED!" he yelled. The explosives dog handler moved forward to investigate. Andre accompanied him, keeping a wary eye on the Pakistani military outpost looming on a hill several hundred meters away. He stepped around a large shrub to get a better look at the dog approaching the IED.

The explosion blew Andre ten feet into the air, backward and onto his butt. He had stepped on a pressure-plate IED, basically an improvised land mine, and his right foot was a smoking, bloody, jumbled mess. It was the sort of attack, and the kind of injury, that was all too common. We so rarely had an enemy we could fight.

Fortunately for Andre, his medic and teammates worked fast to keep him alive and stabilized, and he was in the hands of top-tier physicians within hours. Several surgeries and flights later, he was in Walter Reed Army Medical Center. He stayed there for a long time, enduring surgery after surgery. The doctors meant to save his right foot. It would be hobbled, it would be partially lame—but they were going to save it. And, Andre learned, once the surgeries were done, the Army would take care of him. A discharge and disability papers were on their way. I visited him during one of his hospital stays. Andre was defiant and frustrated. "I don't give a damn what they do with my foot, sir. Take the whole damn leg. Promise me you will help me get back to my team."

Andre hadn't come this far—enlisted, became a sergeant, triumphed over the Q Course, lived the pride of being a Green Beret, and gone to war—to hang it all up thanks to the Taliban's jury-rigged IEDs. He wasn't done soldiering. His brother Green Berets were still out there, still at war, and the mission was still unfinished.

Andre knew his shattered foot would never work, even if it was saved. He also knew that if they amputated his leg below the knee, he would be more able to do all the things he wanted to do with a lower-leg prosthetic. "Let's not talk about how I'm getting out of the Army," he repeatedly said to every doctor and officer that would listen. "Let's talk about how I'm staying in and getting back to my team."

He was told by the bureaucracy that there was nothing wrong or dishonorable about taking a discharge after a serious combat injury. That's entirely true. There isn't. No one could blame him, or thousands like him across the past generation of war, for taking that very reasonable option.

The benefits administrators at Walter Reed and in the Department of the Army didn't know what to do with him. Keeping Andre in the military was contrary to the professional reflexes of the physicians and the bureaucracy alike. The media, veterans' organizations, and the general public had been pounding on the military medical system in the years since 9/11 to provide our wounded soldiers benefits faster and in greater amounts that would compensate for their loss from their injuries.

By the time of Andre's injury, that system was a fine-tuned

machine along with hundreds of well-meaning veterans' charities that filled in where the government couldn't or wouldn't do the job. Staff Sergeant Andre Murnane literally turned down millions in a lifetime of monthly payments and charitable contributions. He didn't want any of it.

Eventually, to their credit, the bureaucrats listened to Andre's request. The soldier who was taken off the battlefield with a shattered leg and foot, in time, reentered it with an *artificial* leg and foot so that he could hit the physical standards necessary to become a Special Forces operator again. He didn't take the easy way out—fully honorable though it would have been.

Just nine months later, after having his foot amputated, Andre stood next to me on a flight line, fully rigged in his parachute, with a shit-eating grin on his face. It was a mix of pride and relief. "I don't know what was harder, sir—beating this injury or beating the Army's medical bureaucracy," he said.

"Andre," I said, "Let's jump out of this plane and show the world how a Green Beret beats both," I replied.

An hour later, Andre hit the ground and rolled in a textbook parachute landing fall with a prosthetic foot. The soldiers on the ground cheered as he jumped up and pumped his fist.

Two months later, he successfully completed the Army ten-miler, and the next spring, he joined his team for the Special Forces Advanced Urban Combat course. Andre Murnane went back to kicking ass in the war on terror, just as he wanted. And those of us who served with him got exactly the kind of brother in arms we all want beside us in combat.

This level of resiliency, of grit, starts in training. You don't just learn about others in the Special Forces Assessment and Selection and the follow-on Q Course. You learn about yourself, too. You learn that you have limits you didn't know about—and you learn that you can surpass those limits in ways you didn't expect. I had a minor experience of this myself, when I shredded my feet during the course and forced myself to keep going. It was not the medically advisable thing to do, but I did it. I'd been recycled once before, in Ranger School, and I wasn't about to go through it again.

Injured feet were the great equalizer in Special Forces selection. No matter how great a shape a candidate was in when they showed up, if their feet broke down on the long-range movements with a heavy rucksack, it was guaranteed misery—and, eventually, failure. Halfway through the weeks-long selection process, my feet were a bloody mess. No matter what I tried in terms of bandages or sock combinations, the blood blisters just kept getting worse. They were excruciatingly painful. A seam in the back of my boot felt like a hot knife grinding into my heel with every step. Finally, I had enough. I stopped on the side of a trail and pulled a roll of gray duct tape out of my pack. I slapped multiple layers of that tape on the worst bloody blister.

The duct tape cast around my foot held and got me through. But in my haste to stop the pain, I didn't quite think through the side effects. The tape on my foot sealed the blister and thereby created a perfect environment for the bacteria festering within it. Soon enough, I was afflicted with cellulitis—and even *more* agonizing pain. My foot swelled with the infection, and filled my boot as it did. The crease of the boot leather behind my toes now sliced into my swollen and infected foot with every step forward. Mere walking was agony—and we were conducting tactical marches almost constantly. I kept my mouth shut about the pain and did my best to adapt, eventually adopting a sort of crippled stride, stepping forward with my left foot and dragging the right one behind me.

I feared that if I took my boot off, I would never get it on again. On top of all that, I could feel my body weakening as the infection and its toxins circulated throughout my bloodstream.

During the group phase of the movement, when the team plopped down on the ground for a few blessed minutes of break, I caught up with them. I didn't stop, though. I kept going to get a head start. I knew the team would soon catch back up and pass me again, starting the cycle all over. I was resolved to suck it up, grind it out, pain and all—even though it meant zero rest.

I'll never forget what happened next.

I felt the heavy weight of my rucksack lift off my shoulders. I turned and saw my classmate, Sergeant Taha, taking it off me. He had seen my suffering and decided to carry my pack in addition to his. I was momentarily speechless. Taha was a lean, diminutive, and wiry soldier who was nearly swallowed up by the size and mass of his own ruck, and now he had mine, too.

"I feel like a shitbag," I said to him in a low voice. "Sorry, man. My feet are gone."

"I know you would do it for me," he said, and we walked forward together.

Sergeant Taha was a son of immigrants from Sudan. After 9/11, he decided to defend the country that had been so good to him and his parents. When that day came, he had just finished his master's in economics at UMass. He set aside that future, and its earnings, for the Special Forces. All that was admirable in itself, but to me, nothing was more admirable than his selflessness in taking my ruck. I wouldn't have made it to the end without him and was so grateful for his generosity and his resilience.

Years later, while visiting my VMI classmate Jamie Edge— KIA in Iraq in 2005—at Arlington National Cemetery, the image of a crescent moon etched into a tombstone jumped out at me from among the rows of crosses. I looked down, and to my shock, it read: *SSG Ayman A. Taha*. He was killed in action in Iraq while defusing a cache of explosives—giving absolutely everything to his country's cause.

I owe him a lot, but America owes him much more.

"You easily could have come down with sepsis and died out there," the Special Forces medical sergeant hissed at me in the clinic, after yanking my boot off my swollen foot. "All you did with this tape is trap the bacteria. Your lymph nodes are hard as a rock." I wasn't surprised. By then, I knew the infection was well past the foot. I was urinating blood. My toenails were black. A few of them peeled off with my disgusting sock. The medic proceeded to inject me with some lidocaine and started ripping off the jumbled cast of duct tape with little mercy.

All the pain, infectious blisters, and pissing blood were nothing compared with what happened once we exited the field. The colonel in charge of the final evaluation of officers told me I had shown myself to be a liability to my team. The observer cadre had noted other candidates helping me. They noted that I fell behind and caused breaks in their tactical formation. I had physically gutted it out, but for an officer who would one day be expected to lead these men, limping over the finish line was not good enough. The colonel told me I was out of the Special Forces selection. I would not go on to the Q Course.

It was a tremendous blow. But it wasn't the hardest part.

The true emotional and mental resilience wasn't in absorbing this gut punch to my pride and aspiration to become a Green Beret. It came to bear months later, in gathering up the fortitude to force myself to go through it all again. This time, my feet were ready. I was mentally prepared for what was coming. I made it, proceeded through the Q Course, and earned my green beret.

This is not Andre Murnane–level stuff—not even close. But a consistent thread among everyone who dons the green beret is a mental grit that can overcome almost any type of physical setback.

I learned even more about physical and mental resilience

from Captain Ken Dwyer. It started in the Q Course—but it didn't end there.

Dwyer was my battle buddy during the tactics phase of the Q Course. Meeting someone in the Q Course is seeing someone as they really are. Imagine, in your daily life, if you could see every work colleague already tested in cold, hunger, grief, and exhaustion. For the rest of your life, you'd know exactly who you could depend upon. I learned that Dwyer was a man you could count on and also learned that he was a man who was serious but did not take himself seriously. He was a straightforward guy, tactically competent, devoted to his wife, the Army, and the Miami Dolphins—and this in an era when loving the Dolphins was not always easy. Together, we endured the tactics phase of the Q Course. It wasn't the brutal sleep and food deprivation that we suffered in Ranger School, but it was no picnic, either. Once again, we found ourselves spooning in our fighting positions to keep warm. Dwyer was a natural leader and far more tactically competent in light-infantry tactics than I was.

The next time I saw Dwyer was years later, in 2006, at Walter Reed Army Medical Center. He had become a well-respected Special Forces leader. On his third combat tour, Dwyer's team of Green Berets and Afghan National Army soldiers were caught in a vicious ambush. Dwyer, according to his Silver Star citation, charged into the open to draw the enemy's fire away from his trapped comrades in a disabled vehicle.

He showed battlefield leadership in coordinating supporting fires while firing at the enemy himself.

In the middle of the fight, a dug-in Taliban force of over a hundred fighters rained fire down on Dwyer's convoy from above. His turret gunner, manning a grenade launcher, yelled for more ammo. Dwyer grabbed a box from the exposed flat-bed in the back of the Humvee, and as he extended his left arm to hand it to the gunner, a Taliban RPG sailed across the battlefield and exploded above him. The hot shrapnel hit the Air Force tactical air controller standing next to him and killed him instantly. A burning shard sliced Dwyer's left hand off and peppered his upper body. His next thought was being unable to see and angry that the Taliban just shot him in the face. Dwyer, a Christian, then felt some peace thinking he would start drifting off to heaven.

The sound of his beating heart let him know that he wasn't dead. *Okay*, he said to himself, *I'm not dead. I'm not going to heaven yet, so let's get back in this fight!* He forced himself to open his eyes. "I could tell my left eye was gone," he recounted years later. Dwyer focused his right eye and raised his left arm in front of his blood-soaked face. He was horrified to see nothing but two bones sticking out of the charred skin dangling around his wrist. Now he was back to being really pissed off and tried to raise his right arm and weapon to start returning fire, but his right arm wouldn't move.

Incredibly, Dwyer didn't lie there feeling sorry for himself saying, "Why me?" or start screaming for someone to come help him. His only thoughts were for his men and making himself productive to his team again in the thick of this fight for their lives. One of the Green Berets rolled him over, looked him over quickly, and said, "He's gone," and moved on to the next downed man. With shrapnel in his neck and throat, Dwyer could only squeak out, "I'm alive," in response. Fortunately, the team's highly trained medic wasn't far behind, did a more thorough check, and started putting tourniquets on Dwyer to stop the heavy bleeding from his right arm.

As the medic loaded Dwyer on the medevac helicopter, Dwyer looked up at him and whispered, "Don't let them take my good arm," before passing out. Hours later at the combat hospital, a trauma surgeon took one look at Dwyer's grayish-blue hand and, knowing the arm had been cut off from any blood flow for hours, decided to take it off.

As she grabbed the bone saw, the medic who had accompanied Dwyer into the operating room said firmly, "No, ma'am," and by the grace of God, he told her of Dwyer's last request. Here, the enlisted Green Beret medic stood between the officer surgeon and Dwyer's fate. "Find a way, ma'am." She set down the saw and started sewing up everything she could—often guessing along the way.

Ken Dwyer, in that moment, lost an eye, an arm, almost his other arm, and nearly his life.

He had refused to die. There was something in Dwyer's constitution that those of us who met him in the Q Course had already seen: resilience.

Bleeding, ripped apart, one eye gone, he *refused* to quit.

He refused all the way to the final defeat of the ambush as the Taliban fled into the hinterland to be hunted and to hunt again. He refused through the medevac. He refused through the surgeries, first to simply save his life and then to somewhat restore it. He refused until he found himself in the long and painful recovery, sewn up and stapled together there in the ward at Walter Reed—where I saw him again. I wanted to find out how he was doing. All Ken wanted to talk about was the Miami Dolphins.

Ken Dwyer's story has a postscript to it, just as Andre Murnane's does. SSG Murnane at least regained full function, albeit with an artificial foot. Dwyer never had that option. In the place of his lost arm was an artificial one, ending in a metal claw that could never possess the same function as a real hand. In the place of his lost eye was simply the very best glass eye of all time; one with a Special Forces crest emblazoned upon it along with our motto *De Oppresso Liber*. More important than what he lost, though, is what he retained. The young captain could easily have left the Army, taken a well-earned disability stipend, and lived a life of honor with service well done. But Ken *wasn't* done. He knew he had the wherewithal to overcome these physical setbacks and still contribute to the war on terror.

Ken Dwyer is now a full colonel in the U.S. Army and has completed a tour as the Deputy Commander of the Seventh Special Forces Group.

The tales of Andre Murnane and Ken Dwyer—soldiers and men I greatly admire—illustrate a quality central to the Green Beret ethos. We court and cultivate *resilience*, and not just in the sense of physical endurance. In the movies, when you see Special Forces operators, they appear superhuman. Intellectually, you know that The Rock or Liam Neeson can't really endure that kind of punishment or kill that many quite that easily, but in the back of your mind, you start to believe that there's something otherworldly about these men. They aren't quite real. What you miss out on most in those movies isn't just a realistic depiction of combat—what you miss is the story of resilience and how fundamentally necessary a virtue it is.

There are a lot of physically strong people out there. Resilience isn't about imperviousness to injury. It's not about being a Hollywood superhero. Resilience is a moral strength, a metric not just of endurance but of the *choice* to endure, to never, ever quit. It is the characteristic that sees a young man in his prime horribly injured—and yet fight his way *back* toward the battlefield.

The ordinary individual accepts the logic of the system and its rules. But men like Ken Dwyer and Andre Murnane fight that logic and *restore* themselves within their units and among fellow special operators. They aren't whole in body and never will be again, but they are whole in spirit. In a world where we soothe people who cannot seem to cope with everyday setbacks, that "wholeness of spirit" is the kind of resilience we need to inculcate.

The examples of this resilience come from a long line of American warriors. Three historical examples from Green Beret lore come to mind.

Resilience looks like Sergeants Gaetano "Tom" Rossi and Caesar Daraio.

Best known to history as "Axis Sally," Mildred Gillars delighted in sharing bad news with the Allies in World War II. Gillars broadcast a mix of Nazi propaganda and swing music to American troops. From her Berlin studio, she taunted English-speaking soldiers with the suggestion that their sweethearts back home were cheating. In an April 1944 broadcast, Gillars gleefully read the names of fifteen members of the OSS Italian Operational Group who had been captured and executed near La Spezia.

Every name on the list was Italian American. The operational group—known as OGs, or Donovan's Devils (after "Wild Bill" Donovan, founder of the Office of Strategic Services) was made up of first-generation immigrants, young men both skilled in special operations and knowledge of Italian language and culture. Their task was to create havoc for the Nazis—and later, to secure the peace by winning the hearts and minds of the locals.

From their isolated operating base in Corsica, Rossi and Daraio listened to Axis Sally read those names. They knew each one. A few months earlier, Rossi, Daraio, and the fifteen executed OGs had played a vital role in the Anzio landings. Infiltrating the central Italian countryside and gaining the trust of the locals, Donovan's Devils had provided vital intelligence on German army movements. As a result, the Allies knew exactly when and how the German counterattack would come. The Allies held the beach at Anzio, and the Devils arguably saved the Italian campaign.

As they heard Axis Sally cheerfully recount the execution at La Spezia, Rossi and Daraio knew they could be next. They did not waver. After the murders of their brothers in arms, Rossi and Daraio were deployed to the remote Apennine villages to equip, train, and encourage local Italian partisans. The partisans were anti-Fascist and anti-German, but they were not necessarily pro-American. Some partisan groups distrusted both the Allies and the Axis. The OGs had the nearly impossible task of directing an effective guerilla campaign with a suspicious and unreliable irregular local force.

Rossi and Daraio succeeded on both fronts. The trust they and their fellow OGs earned proved vital against the Germans and Italian Fascists, as well as in the peace that followed victory. Many partisan groups were reluctant to disarm once the Nazis were defeated. They had scores to settle with one another. With their intimate knowledge of the language and culture, Rossi and Daraio did no less than stop a potential civil war.

The OGs were just 5 percent of OSS personnel, but accounted for more than 20 percent of its casualties. Gaetano

"Tom" Rossi and Caesar Daraio used their Italian ancestry to serve *in* Italy *for* the United States.

That is mental and emotional resilience.

Resilience also looks like Rocky Versace.

When the Viet Cong ambushed a Green Beret patrol in the dense U Minh forest in 1963, the team reacted swiftly. In the scramble, an American medic slipped and broke his ankle. A lieutenant rushed to his side to render aid. Captain Humbert Roque "Rocky" Versace provided covering fire to both men, allowing the rest of the patrol and their South Vietnamese partners to escape. Versace was shot in the knee and the back but was still firing when he was clubbed from behind and taken prisoner.

The Viet Cong soon discovered that their captive spoke both excellent Vietnamese and French—in other words, that he was a Green Beret in full. He was also quite willing to fiercely debate politics with his captors. Versace's fellow prisoners regularly heard the captain berate the Viet Cong over their violations of the Geneva Convention, their treatment of POWs, and for the evils of Communism itself.

As their highest-ranking captive and a known Green Beret, Versace was subjected to exceptionally cruel interrogation and torture. His defiance and bravery infuriated the Viet Cong, and they ratcheted up the torment. He was put in irons and kept in a tiny hut that had been thatched to make the temperatures inside unbearable during the day. Even in his pain—the wounds from his capture and subsequent torture were untreated—the other Americans could hear him singing a mix of patriotic hymns and pop songs. Despite his agony, Versace would intersperse his songs with shouts of encouragement to the other prisoners.

When the exasperated Viet Cong gagged him, he left notes for his fellow captives in the latrine.

At one point, the guards tried to bribe Versace for intelligence, promising him better treatment. He was overheard replying that he would have to answer in the next life for what he did in this one. He told his captors he owed them name, rank, and serial number—and the rest he owed to God and to America. The brief attempt at bribery ceased, and the barbarity of his treatment grew still worse.

Despite his injuries, Captain Versace attempted to escape four times. On his final try, in a severely weakened state, he dragged himself through vegetation for miles. Once recaptured, the Viet Cong placed him on a starvation diet of a few ounces *per day* of rice and salt. Every time the gag was removed so he could eat his meager rations, Versace sang.

The Viet Cong finally had enough of a Green Beret they couldn't break. On September 26, 1965, they dragged him from his hut, led him into a clearing, and shot him. Versace could barely walk—yet he still sang "God Bless America" as he went to his death.

In 2002, President George W. Bush awarded Captain Versace a posthumous Medal of Honor. He is the only Vietnam Medal of Honor recipient whose remains have never been returned.

That is resilience.

Resilience also looks like Nick Rowe.

Early on the morning of April 21, 1989, Colonel James "Nick" Rowe was shot and killed in Quezon City, in the Philippines. His killers were operatives from the New People's Army, a violent Maoist insurgent group. At the time of his assassination, Colonel Rowe was working with both U.S. and Philippine intelligence to defeat the NPA and end its threat to Filipino democracy.

Nick Rowe had escaped death at the hands of the Communists before. In 1963, while serving as a Green Beret, Nick was captured by the Viet Cong. They would hold him for 1,903 days. Tortured, beaten, and starved—and under the constant threat of execution—Rowe remained resilient and defiant. After years of solitary confinement and endless interrogations, his captors became convinced he had nothing more to offer. On December 31, 1968, his captors dragged Rowe from his bamboo cage and told him that they were going to shoot him in the woods. As they marched him toward his death, by sheer chance, American helicopters flew overhead—drawing his captors' attention. Seizing the moment of distraction, Rowe overpowered his captors, broke free, and escaped.

Back home in South Texas, Rowe told reporters that he had already asked to go back to Vietnam. He knew his experience of surviving five years of Viet Cong brutality was invaluable, and he wanted to share that wisdom to help win the war.

The Army had different ideas. Rowe, who the bureaucracy figured had suffered enough, was assigned a desk job.

After several restless years in civilian life, Nick Rowe found his way back to active duty in 1981. He developed the survival, evasion, resistance, and escape (SERE) program and taught it to Green Berets at Fort Bragg, North Carolina. The SERE program contained the distilled wisdom of Rowe's hard-won experience. Over the decades, SERE has helped Americans captured in battle survive the impossible—and come home to their families. Determined not just to teach what he knew but to continue living it out, Rowe sought posts in conflict zones. That commitment brought him to the Philippines—and to his death.

Nick Rowe could have chosen a safe life, without shame or reproach, after his ordeal in Vietnam. Instead, he fought to go back.

That is resilience.

Resilience isn't just for those who wear the uniform. Sooner or later, we will all need it. It is one of the most important tools we can give to our children. Our public institutions once taught and emphasized that skill. They do not teach it anymore, and the consequence has been bitter, dangerous, and unmistakable.

The hard truth is that a life without resilience is a life guaranteed to be a life of anxiety, disappointment, and dependency.

Generation Z—those born after 1995—are diagnosed with

mental illnesses at staggeringly high rates. Antidepressant prescriptions for Americans under nineteen have risen nearly 40 percent in the past decade.[1] They battle addiction and despair. Here's a hard truth: most are suffering less from physiological afflictions than genuinely crippling character issues. It's hard to blame the young people alone. It was their elders who weakened societal institutions like churches and civic organizations, allowed kids to get hooked on social media in their formative years, and then—in the name of "stopping the spread" during the ill-advised pandemic lockdowns—separated them from their friends and teachers for more than a year. Is it any wonder, then, that we see not resilience but fragility and anxiety rampant among our youth? It is not enough to complain about "young people these days." The culture has failed them.

In addition to this lack of fortitude among our young people, there are much more alarming effects on our civic culture. America has been through plenty of tough times, but there seems to be universal agreement that we are in a particularly fraught and delicate moment. We have become incapable of discussing nearly any topic without hysteria and hyperbole. Anyone who disagrees is judged, demonized, and labeled a bad person. This fragility is what you get when you take away resilience, an inability to contend with dissenting views or even to

---

1 "More Teens are on Anti-Depressants, What Can Be Done?," *Dallas Morning News*, October 28, 2023.

tolerate their existence. Students feeling entitled to safe spaces or proving themselves unable to distinguish mere rhetoric from real violence are a result of the fragility and vulnerability inherent in today's youth. The bottom line is America needs to toughen up, but how?

Resilience, toughness, grit, and fortitude shouldn't be taught only in a classroom. It has to be lived. We must seek out and seize opportunities to put our future generations through crucibles and trials and then celebrate what comes out the other side. You can't give a lecture on what it's like to practice your butt off for a game, only to come up short and lose. You have to experience it. Whether that's spending Saturday mornings doing yard work or scrubbing toilets or a summer job in construction, life experiences where you will be tested, struggle, and have to deal with failure are invaluable. As much as kids hate to hear it, life isn't always exciting. To have the fulfilment you want, you'll need to persevere not just through setbacks but through boredom and tedium. *Not everything that must be done is fun to do.*

This truth was driven home to me when I was fifteen. I asked my mother for help buying a car. "Sure, son," she replied. "I'll ask your uncle to fix up an old Volkswagen—but only if you get a job and pay for the insurance." That got me moving. Within a week, I applied to every fast-food joint within a bike ride of where we lived. I landed a job at McDonald's making $3.05 an hour. Every morning, I woke up at 5:00 a.m. to be at the store by 5:45 and open by 6:00. After busting my butt over the famously greasy french fry stand—and hours of cleaning bathrooms—my first weekly paycheck was $98. I was totally dejected as I handed it over to my mother. Could I possibly keep doing this? I had made a promise, and so I sucked it up the rest of the summer. I doubled my wage to $6.50 an hour and picked up a second job working at an Albertsons grocery store at nights after school. I was stocking shelves and pushing milk carts, and I took another ten pounds off my already skinny frame.

I'll never forget the advice of the Albertsons manager, a grizzled old Vietnam War Navy veteran. He had dropped out of high school to enlist. One night, he put his hand on my shoulder and gave me a hard truth: "Michael, you have so much potential. So I'll tell you what—if you are still working here after you graduate and blow off going off to college, I'm going to kick your wannabe Army ass." That was a wake-up call and a gift. I learned how quickly my energy, time, and patience could be drained. I experienced the grind of manual labor and customer service, and I got a glimpse of my future without an education or skill. Though my initial incentive was a paycheck to pay for car insurance, I ended up learning about taxes, punctuality, and what it took to deliver customer satisfaction.

Most of all, I had a newfound empathy for my hardworking single mom.

Resilience is a man or woman working a job that wears them down, but they grind it out because they love their family.

It's a mother waking five times a night and going through her days weary, focused on caring for the child she adores. It's a high school student hitting the books when he'd rather scroll through videos on his iPhone, because he knows education is his path out of poverty. It's an entrepreneur refusing to take no for an answer and finding a way forward even as the rejections pile up.

Resilience helped me build our business. I rely on resilience now in politics. People don't always see things the way I wish they would. (Some say the same about me!) I work hard to convince and persuade and demonstrate, and sometimes I get results—but other times, what I think should happen doesn't happen. I learn the lesson of that setback and keep pushing.

To the extent we can teach resilience, it is good to start by rethinking the people we put on a pedestal. Who are our heroes? Are they narcissistic, fame-driven celebrities coping with character flaws with drugs and alcohol—or are they men and women who have lived a tough but honorable life?

It's a tall order, but a simple start is insisting that our educational institutions celebrate resilient heroes—and more important, stop incubating fragility. We cannot tolerate speech codes, safe spaces, and the endless worrying about microaggressions. *The hard truth is you cannot coddle a child into resilience.* You cannot build self-esteem through praise. You build resilience and self-worth through challenges and opportunities to serve and grow. This is why I've advocated for an expansion of junior ROTC in high schools, a return to rigorous physical education that has been cut from many school curriculums, and the requirement of volunteer hours to qualify for high school diplomas.

From my personal perspective, I have tried to transfer the lessons and mindset I've learned in combat as a Green Beret to my life in business and in politics. I've boiled these down to several key tenets.

One of the first tenets that is beaten into you in the military is that you are *reliant on a team* to accomplish the mission. Everyone has to pull their weight, or everyone fails. We need community—not government—to provide that vital support system. I am where I am because I had mentors and buddies. The kind of civic institutions that provide that support—churches, sports clubs, the Scouts—can do their work more effectively when we get government out of the way. Our young people need mentors and coaches who push them and who love them.

Resilience is, ultimately, a product of will—and a result of values lived as well as preached. Not everyone will have to cope with losing a foot or recovering from an IED blast like my Green Berets. Sooner or later, everyone will have to cope with a failed romance, with losing a job, with losing a loved one, with having to get up at the crack of dawn to be at work earlier than your boss. No one can do these things for you. Resilience is a choice, and a deeply individual one. But what we can do is create a culture that honors and affirms the choice to be resilient. We had that culture once. We can and must have it again.

Every one of us in a position of responsibility—I write here as a husband, a father, an officer, and a congressman—has an obligation to live by example and show resilience. Everyone has their own story of obstacles and disappointments that they've overcome. We have valuable lived experience we can pass on. Our country and our children need us to do it. And America will be far stronger for it.

8

DETERMINATION

I stood on the edge of a dark trail in a pitch-black night, taking a quick drink from my canteen. I had found two points already in the Ranger School land navigation course, and despite my exhaustion, I was ahead of schedule. Things were going well. And then I saw a shadowy figure approaching, emerging from the night, drawing very near. It was a fellow soldier.

"Hey, man," he whispered.

We weren't supposed to say a single word to each other. I thought for a second to keep walking into the woods, but after a few seconds, I whispered back, "What's up?"

"I'm lost," he said quietly, waving his map. "I'm screwed. Real quick, can you point out to me on the map where I am?" I sidled up to him as he turned on a faint red pin light. With a piece of pine straw, I silently pointed to the nearest road intersection.

Out of nowhere, a white flashlight clicked on and shone in our faces. A voice rang out: "What the hell is going on here, Rangers?" A hand emerged from behind the beam of light and snatched both our maps out from us like the hand of God. I don't know how long the Ranger cadre had been standing there in the dark, but it was clearly long enough to hear us speaking when we shouldn't have been.

For the land-navigation portion of Ranger School, aspiring Rangers had to get through some of the densest and remotest terrain in the American South. Between points A and B are dense forests, steep hills, and the dreaded "draw"—ravines so thick with walls of vines that there were times when I would take off my rucksack and heave it forward to crush the vines just enough to take a few steps. Before you even set foot on the course, Ranger School instructors ensured that you were already at a mental rock bottom, thanks to sleep deprivation. You are also at a physical rock bottom, thanks to food deprivation combined with hours on end of torturous exercises. The training cadre then loads you up with a rucksack and sets you off in the dead of night with evaluators lurking in the shadows, watching every move.

At the start, we were given one rule: no talking. The intent was simple: every man had to show what he knew and what he could do, without help.

The evaluator's voice boomed. "You're done!" he said. "Walk up this trail until you see the trucks, get in the back, and wait."

I stood there blinking in shock for a few seconds at how quickly this had just happened. I walked back up the long trail and got on the truck to be transported back to barracks. I had a long time to think about what had just occurred. I was feeling sorry for myself—sorry for getting caught, sorry for being sent back. I was feeling angry at the man who was dumb enough to talk to me and equally angry at *myself* for being dumb enough to talk back and, above all, dumb enough to go along with the plea for help we both knew he should never have made. The anger faded into a dull ache of terrible realization: I was going to be kicked out of Ranger School, a towering personal and professional ambition of mine since I was a kid reading about Rogers' Rangers in the American Revolution, Merrill's Marauders in World War II, and of course the Second Ranger Battalion at Pointe du Hoc. Instead of joining their storied ranks, I was going to be sent back to my unit in Big Army in failure and shame.

I was on this course because I was eager to earn the Ranger tab, both for myself and for the statement it would make about me to the greater Army. As a cadet at VMI, every time an officer or sergeant walked into the room and we saw his Ranger tab, we instantly held him in higher regard. We immediately knew he had shown himself to be tough, tactically sound, and full of grit. These men had been tested to the extreme. Ranger School is the most physical and mental punishment meted out by people who are not actually trying to kill you. You are expected to perform nearly impossible tasks while functioning on less than a thousand calories per day and less than an hour of sleep per night.

The level of testing is extreme because the Ranger missions are extreme.

The men, and now women, who go to Ranger School are also extreme, not in an ideological sense but rather an overachiever compared with their peers. They are usually superior athletes, have displayed exceptional mental endurance, are high achievers in academics, and are usually leaders in sports. The people who come to Ranger School are aware that they are already very good. The job of the Army's various gatekeeping mechanisms is to see which of them are the best of the best.

I was none of those things. I wasn't a valedictorian or starting quarterback. I wasn't the guy who was out in the woods hunting with his dad every winter. I had only one quality that set me apart: I had *determination*. I endured, I was resilient, and I sucked it up and pushed through exhaustion, demoralization, and bad fortune. I never, ever quit. One indispensable element of determination is handling the prospect of crushing failure. Pulled abruptly off the land-navigation course, after so much training and preparation to be there, was one of the greatest mental and emotional beatdowns I'd ever known.

Despite my exhaustion, I was too numb and shattered to sleep. The awful realization of what had happened kept me awake.

In the morning, I was ordered to go see the training company commander in his office. The captain was wearing the black sweatshirt typical of all cadre, a gold-lettered RANGER in an arc across the chest. He sat back in his chair and rubbed the side of his high and tight. Dip protruded from his lower lip.

He opened by telling me what I already figured: I was out

of this Ranger School class. I felt like I was punched in the gut. I looked down at my boots. This was a nightmare.

"Look at me, Lieutenant," he said. "In the Ranger Regiment, we follow orders without question. That is how we get a four-hundred-man battalion of super-troopers out the back of a high-speed transport aircraft at low altitude over hostile territory in minutes, take an airfield, destroy the enemy in close combat, and kick ass for the USA. It's by *following orders*!" He smacked the desk, leaned forward, and spit into a Mountain Dew bottle. "It's what we do. It's what you *didn't* do."

Then he opened a tiny window of hope.

"Lieutenant, I'm going to give you a choice." He paused to spit again. "Option one: you can start over with the next class. But know this, you are going to be tested even harder now. One slip, one mistake, and you're *done*. You're an officer, so the cadre is going to take you from very uncomfortable to extremely fucking miserable. More will be expected of you than you ever thought you had in you. Because you're the one that will be giving the orders that those sergeants might have to follow one day!" He smacked the desk again.

"If you fail, you will be barred from ever attending Ranger School again. No return." The captain paused and spat again into his dip bottle. "This is your last shot. And you're lucky I'm in a good mood today to give it to you.

"Or you can leave now, go back to your unit. Rest up. Get some experience. If you want to come back here at a later date, you're still welcome to apply."

I had the tantalizing thought of a warm bed, a cold beer, and a juicy cheeseburger just before I said, "Sir, I'll stay. I'm determined to be a Ranger. Extremely determined."

I got four more words from the captain: "We'll see. Get out."

By the grace of God and this captain, I was pulled back from the precipice of failure. Recycling back to the beginning of the next course was not without consequences. The next Ranger class was six weeks away, and I spent those six weeks literally painting rocks, packing parachutes, and mowing grass. The tedium wore people down mentally and emotionally. One officer, who had also been granted a chance to recycle, quit one day after receiving a letter from his fiancée wanting to break things off. I looked forward to the next cohort, where I would try again—but also dreaded the fact that this time I would be suffering in the dead of winter. I'd had my chance at Ranger School in the mild weather of fall, and I'd blown it.

When I went through it the second time, you bet your ass I didn't say a word to anyone on the land-navigation course.

Here's the important thing about the experience. I could have faced the prospect of a new Ranger School class with dread, and I could have regarded the mistakes that sent me back to the beginning as a punishment. If I had done that, I would have guaranteed my own failure—for a second time, and this time permanently. I needed to see this as a stroke of luck rather than punishment. My success depended on my determination to make the most of the captain's act of grace.

Without that attitude, I would never have worn the Ranger tab.

Years later, when I had to endure the Special Forces Assessment and Selection course twice thanks to an injury, I did not experience it as any sort of demoralizing passage. I'd been there before. I'd gone through the hellish experience of extreme testing, *times two*, before.

None of this is to suggest that I am some type of badass or special in any way. The ability to turn defeat into the seeds of future victory—through introspection, through resolve, through pure grit—is common in Green Berets throughout history and what is expected in the community. Some guys seem to just sail through all types of hardship. Others, like me, have to grind it out. I was inspired by the thought that within every adversity is the seed of a great triumph. It's not that you fail at a task, it's whether you have the mental fortitude to cope with it, learn from it, and move forward.

My second attempt at Ranger School came during an unusually harsh winter. As I forced myself through the sleet and frozen mud up and down the mountains of North Georgia, I refused to feel sorry for myself. I got a little perspective by thinking of Green Berets that I had read about growing up and who had endured far more. I often thought of one man in particular, Master Sergeant Roy P. Benavidez. At seventeen years old, the native of El Campo, Texas, volunteered for the Texas Army National Guard. At thirty-three years old, Benavidez—a Green Beret, of course—volunteered to assist a twelve-man

Special Forces patrol encircled by nearly one thousand North Vietnamese soldiers. Told that the rescue chopper wouldn't wait while he grabbed a gun, Benavidez climbed aboard armed only with a Bowie knife. Once on the ground facing a hail of enemy bullets, he organized a successful defense, carried half the wounded to waiting aircraft, called in air strikes, administered first aid to everyone around him but himself, and directly defended the evacuation helicopters in hand-to-hand combat as North Vietnamese soldiers swarmed the landing zone.

Benavidez's battlefield endurance would seem unreal if it were fiction. He was bayoneted, and he killed the Viet Cong soldier who did it. He was clubbed from behind and killed that man, too. He was shot and kept shooting back. Altogether, he suffered seven bullet wounds, multiple bayonet slashes, twenty-eight fragmentation-grenade wounds, and a contusion from being clubbed on the head. His entire body was riddled with shrapnel and injury. A bullet hole extended clean through from his back to just below his heart. His right lung was destroyed. He was the last man to load himself on the last medical evacuation helicopter while holding his intestines against his stomach. On his return to base, he was declared KIA and placed in a body bag. He could not see because blood had dried his eyes shut. He couldn't speak from a rifle butt blow that had fused his jaw shut.

As he heard the body bag zipper coming up over him, he screamed, "No!" By the grace of God, the attending physician knelt over him just to double-check that he had no pulse.

Benavidez scored the luckiest shot of his life by spitting in the doctor's face.

Roy Benavidez earned the Medal of Honor for his exploits. When Benavidez received that medal from Ronald Reagan, the former actor commented that the master sergeant's feats were too unbelievable to ever make it into the movies. But the seeds of Benavidez's exploits—and his survival—were planted long before that fateful day in 1968. Benavidez knew *extreme determination*, and when faced with the ultimate test, he embodied it.

He knew that to win—to *live*—you must *fight*. And above all else, you cannot quit.

Thinking about the insane amount of abuse Roy Benavidez endured snapped me out of the pity party I was hosting for myself in the mountains. It motivated me. It put my suffering in perspective, and it helped me put one foot in front of the other to deal with the brutal cold. As my Ranger class navigated the mountains of the North Georgia-Tennessee divide, we were in near-perfect weather for the onset of dangerous hypothermia: temperatures of about thirty-five degrees Fahrenheit, the dead of night, and incessant rain and sleet. Full-on misery.

Ordinarily, the Ranger cadre sergeants, our instructors, had access to emergency bags; big, weatherproofed sleeping bag–type cocoons into which students in real danger of hypothermia could crawl and get some warmth. This weather, though, deprived them of that recourse. The ground transformed the near-freezing rain into slick ice, and the trucks could not reach us with supplies. Every one of us out there was soaked to the bone. The Ranger cadre suffered with us, but they were not weak from sleep and food deprivation, as we were. Ranger students, in a frigid stupor, began to wander off. The first sign of hypothermia is mental delusion. It was clear that we were in real danger—and if the exercise continued, there was a chance a student would be lost to injury or exposure. We all had in the backs of our minds the national news from a year earlier, where four aspiring Rangers had died when their platoon got stuck all night in a flooded, frigid swamp in the Florida Panhandle.

So, our cadre made the right call. They called an end to the exercise, gathered us together, told us to fall into a line with our flashlights on, and said, "We are going to march." It didn't matter where we were marching. We had to keep moving to stay alive. It was that simple. There were no trucks coming to take us to a lower altitude or to shelter. There was no help on the way. We were in the mountains, and it was keep moving or die.

We stumbled all night. I remember at one point reaching down to take a drink from my canteen, and nothing came out. It was frozen. I shook it and got a few drops. At one point, one man hit his limit. I watched his shadow as he walked up to a cadre and said that he couldn't take it. He quit. He was done. I suspect that in his fogged brain, tired and half-frozen, he expected his quitting to trigger a return to the rear, to some warmth, some relief.

The cadre sergeant stared at him. Finally, he replied, "Got it, you quit. But guess what there, stud? There is nowhere to go. This isn't BUD/S with the SEALs. There's no bell for you to ring and then walk to the chow hall for a pizza. There is no quitter's limousine that's gonna come pick you up with a toasty cup of hot chocolate. Get back with your squad and keep walking."

I saw his shoulders slump dejectedly as he turned around. He got back in line and stuck with us. He didn't have a choice. We walked all night, and when the sun came up, we were still walking. We reached the bottom of the mountain, where the trucks could reach us with our survival gear, and we did it without losing a single candidate. The sun broke through the clouds, and it was a real deliverance—except for that one man, who was surprised to be told that when the trucks came, he could get on board and ride back to the base with them.

"You quit!" said the cadre sergeant, more than a little exasperated that the candidate had the gall to walk up and ask if he could continue the patrol.

"Yes, Sergeant, but I ended up sticking with it all night," he protested.

It did not matter. In the moment of crisis, he had made his choice and shown his character.

"Look at these men," said the sergeant, gesturing toward the rest of us. "They can never trust you again. If you quit on your platoon last night when it got tough, out here in training, where no one is shooting at you, then I'm damn sure you will quit on them in combat."

The cadre sergeant pointed toward a truck that was filling

up with others who had apparently also tried to quit but had had nowhere to go until now. The candidate walked away looking utterly crushed. I could see in his face that he knew he would never have another chance at earning the Ranger tab. It was over for him.

Determination is a defining characteristic of someone who was going to be successful in the Special Operations community and in life. I had to find reserves of determination I didn't know I had. I did that by drawing inspiration from the stories of heroes like Roy Benavidez, and I did it by drawing on the extraordinary examples from within my own family—especially my mother.

The first time my mother, Brenda Waltz, heard an operator say, "Ma'am, you have a call from Air Force One," she hung up. Of course, it was me calling from the President's plane. When the operator placed the call a second time, and my mother realized it wasn't a prank, she got emotional. It was as though in that moment, all her struggles, all the years of scraping by to create better opportunities for her son, were vindicated. My mother possesses determination in spades. She never had to do Ranger School, but as a single mother committed to lifting us out of poverty, she had clawed her way up the corporate ladder of an insurance company in Jacksonville, Florida. She had faced down rampant misogyny, had been dismissed as a lightweight, and had been relegated to countless no-win positions. And yet she kept climbing. Despite not having a college degree, with her own extreme determination, my mother outperformed her male peers time after time over thirty years to eventually become a senior executive at their national headquarters.

My mother expected determination from me as well. I was bused across town as part of a mandatory desegregation program and assumed I'd eventually go to the local middle school with my friends. However, my teachers recommended I get tested for the gifted program and apply to a new advanced academic school, Stanton College Prep. My mother forced me, over my objections, to attend this demanding charter school with mandatory advanced placement courses and set the expectation that I attend college after high school. To her credit, she ignored the whining and complaining from a teenage boy who was more interested in having fun with friends than studying hard. She parented. Her determination to expose me to one of the best schools in Florida was nonnegotiable and changed the direction of my life. I finished college in four years. It took her fifteen years—of nights and weekends—but my mother and I ended up graduating the same year.

She did her best to insert positive male role models in my life to compensate for the absence of my father. One day, my mother walked up to a group of men talking after church and said, "The sermon today was about being fishers of men, about being male role models in our community. I have a teenage son trying to find his way. I need you guys to put your money where your mouth is and include him in your weekly Bible study." And just like that, I started attending a men's group that provided me with strong and influential mentors in my life. I also spent time with the fathers of my childhood friends, all self-made men who were just as demanding of me as they were of their sons. Many Saturday mornings were filled with digging ditches next to my buddy Felix or moving heavy equipment for my friend Vikram's family veterinary practice.

My father, a Navy chief petty officer, left us when I was an infant. My mother was twenty-five and working multiple jobs. He sent me postcards periodically when I was young and once took me to visit my grandparents in Iowa. Otherwise, he really wasn't involved. As a boy, I looked forward to his episodic outreach or visits. When I was a teenager, however, that turned into anger and resentment as I watched my mother struggle. My father's brother, my uncle Greg, a Vietnam veteran helicopter pilot, stepped in on the big occasions like graduations and my commissioning into the military. Standing in front of the barracks at VMI, I'll never forget Chief Warrant Officer 5 Greg Waltz giving me my first salute as a brand-new second lieutenant. Years later, we visited Arlington National Cemetery together, and he surprised me by saying, "I'm glad your mother was the main influence in your life, and you should be, too."

I looked back at my uncle, puzzled that he seemed happy that his own brother had left a huge hole in my life—a wound I still resented. He continued, "Your mother had a huge impact on you. You wouldn't be the same person you are today if things were different. She did everything she could to set you up for success. Now it's up to you what you do with it. Don't let bitterness hold you back."

I gazed out across the rows of white headstones. My uncle was right. And with that, I let it go. All those years of anger and feelings of abandonment for not having a father were gone. The point was that you can be very talented and very determined in life, but emotional baggage, angst, and drama will slow you down like a boat dragging an anchor. To achieve your goals, to go after big things in life, you have to cut that emotional anchor away. You have to have the focus and determination to find a way to move forward.

I was thinking of my mother and all her struggles—the years of working night shifts, scraping by in a nine-hundred-square-foot home, raising a child alone, *everything*, surged forward in that very moment when the Air Force One operator patched us through.

"Bear, is this really you?" she said, using my childhood nickname.

"Yes, Mom. It's me. Who would have thunk it? Who would have ever thought in a million years I would be calling you like this?" I choked up.

She choked up, too. "You never cease to amaze me," she said. "I'm so proud of how far you've come. And how far I know you are going to go."

I made that phone call from Air Force One on May 30, 2020. I was accompanying President Trump as he traveled from Washington, DC, to Florida. We were traveling to see the SpaceX Dragon crew launch from Cape Canaveral. It was the first new manned American spacecraft in nearly forty years, and I had pushed hard for the President to be there.

The SpaceX Falcon 9 rocket was itself the product of a very determined man. Whatever you may think of his public persona, few entrepreneurs in history, to say nothing of our own time, have had the extraordinary record of endeavor and achievement of Elon Musk. From his initial successes in investing in PayPal after immigrating to this country, to his record of serial disruption of industry upon industry, Musk exemplifies a unique and very *American* brand of determination. Most men of his stature would be content to have transformed one industry and pocket the millions he made as a result. Instead, Musk bet it all to achieve big hairy audacious goals in the auto, space, and now media industries as well.

Achieving great things takes more than smarts. It takes *extreme determination*. And that determination and his willingness to risk it all has been the key to Elon Musk's extraordinary innovations. For years, I have greatly admired Musk's resolve, and in May 2020, I knew I was going to need more than a small share of it to persuade the President to go to the Kennedy Space Center for this launch. We were two months into the COVID-19 pandemic, and much of the country was still in lockdown. People were terrified; businesses were going bankrupt. The pandemic had ground the nation to a halt. In the midst of crisis like this, convincing the President to come to a rocket launch was crazy. But I thought it was critical for him to be there.

"Mr. President," I said to him on a call in April, "in about six weeks, for the first time in over a decade, we will launch American astronauts, both colonels, on an American rocket, from American soil. I think it would be fantastic for the commander in chief to be there for this SpaceX launch."

"Michael," replied the President, "I admire those men. Would you launch on one of those rockets?"

"Hell yes, Mr. President, in a heartbeat! I have a secret ambition to be the first Green Beret in space," I replied with a grin.

"That's amazing, Michael." Then, in a typical Trump coda: "I think you're a little nuts, but okay." I knew him well enough by then to know that he said it with affection. I also knew I had the green light to press him on the topic.

"Here's a couple of reasons it would be tremendous to have you there," I continued, "First, since Obama canceled the replacement to the space shuttle, we have been paying the Russians ridiculous amounts to launch our astronauts to the space station. They originally charged us a few million, and now they are charging us nearly ninety million per launch."

"That's just crazy," said the President. "Obama and his people backing us into a bad deal with the Russians. But they want to say it's *me* cutting deals with the Russians!"

"Second, Mr. President," I pressed onward, "do you know how many jobs in central Florida we lost when the space shuttle ended? Thousands. They were literally lined up along the runway when the last space shuttle landed, in tears because they knew they would be getting pink slips the next day.

"Third, the whole country is locked down right now. People are scared. There is nothing like a launch into space to symbolize a relaunch of America out of COVID, a relaunch of our economy from the lockdown, and relaunch of America's technological greatness—led by the private sector, not government. Led by you.

"This launch, Mr. President, is a rebirth of America dominating in space. And it's going to happen on your watch, Mr. President." I saved the best line for last. "We can't be number one on earth if we are number two in space."

The President didn't miss a beat, and I knew he was on board. "Okay. I like it, Michael," he said.

The next day, I got a call from the President's chief of staff and gave him the same pitch. I was determined to make this happen. This was what my district needed, what our space program needed, and what America needed.

The thing about determination is that it gets tested. First, I got a call from NASA Administrator Jim Bridenstine. "Mike," he said, "I heard you talked to POTUS about coming to the launch."

"Yes, I'm very excited," I said while thinking I probably *should* have given a heads-up to the NASA chief.

"Mike, that's great. But you know these things don't always go well." As Bridenstine said it, I knew we were both thinking of the exact same thing.

"Damn, Jim, I was in sixth grade when the *Challenger* blew up," I replied. "That can't happen this time. If you have to call off the launch, do what you gotta do. We obviously don't ever want the perception out there that you pushed some boundary just because the President was on-site."

I knew it was a gutsy move encouraging him to come. But true to his word, the President made it a priority to be there.

Equally true to his word, the NASA administrator *did* have to call off the launch—with only sixteen seconds left on the countdown. In typical Florida fashion, lightning rolled in at the last possible moment. The President had brought his entire family down on Air Force One. Don Jr.'s kids were running up and down the aisles. I sat in Air Force One's conference room with my wife, Julia. She wasn't accompanying me as much as I was accompanying her: she was serving as the President's Homeland Security Advisor. As everyone piled back onto Air Force One just after the cancellation, Bridenstine and I stood at the door of the President's office at the front of the plane.

"Jim," asked the President, "when will that rocket get another shot?"

"The next window is this Saturday, Mr. President," he answered.

It was a Wednesday afternoon. "Okay," said the President. "We are coming back."

Everyone's eyes widened. The Secret Service supervisor immediately stepped out, and I could hear him telling his men to stop packing. "Everyone stand down. Mogul is coming back."

I was astounded and impressed. Donald Trump was determined to see this through, despite everything else commanding his attention. The pandemic was consuming the country—the Paycheck Protection Program was due for a congressional vote the very next day—and the tragic killing of George Floyd had just begun to send the nation into a dark and convulsive summer of protests, riots, and violence.

Within all this, the President instinctively *knew* that America needed to return manned launches to space. He was decisive and resolute that he would be there for it.

Four days later, I again had the honor of flying down with him. It was on this second trip that I remembered to call my mother—and then Julia made her own call sitting next to me. My wife's mother, Hayat, cried when she answered the phone. She had immigrated to the United States from Jordan as a persecuted Christian. Her family scraped their way upward in life, as so many immigrants do, with five children in a one-bathroom home in rural Umatilla, Florida. My mother-in-law lost her husband in a tragic accident when her kids were still young, and she scraped by as a nurse, often on night shifts. They didn't wallow in their circumstances or become victims or demand that the government take care of them. Through faith, strong will, and determination, those five children are now doctors, lawyers, and diplomats. I could hear Julia's mother's joy through her tears. All those years of resolve paid off. Only in America does such sacrifice have the opportunity to pay such rewards.

Both of our mothers were living examples of determination. Both women embodied a never-quit attitude. They would have made excellent Green Berets. Sitting there on Air Force One, I remembered how the stories of determined men like Roy Benavidez had kept me focused while I went through the hardest parts of the Ranger course. Then it hit me—I wouldn't even have been in the course in the first place if it weren't for my mother's grit. It put a lump in my throat.

Moments later, in the Air Force One conference room, Trump went around the table, asking for thoughts on his speech he was due to give after the launch. I repeated the line I used while pitching him to attend: "You can't be number one on earth if you're number two in space." He loved it and asked his speechwriter to fit it in.

An hour later, we stood on the viewing stands, President Trump and Vice President Pence standing side by side. This time, the countdown clock struck zero. The delayed sound of the Falcon 9 rocket boomed across Cape Canaveral. The crowd standing behind both men held their breath and then started to cheer as the rocket punched its way into the sky. Moments later, a member of the President's advance party approached. "Congressman, would you like to join the President in his visit to the SpaceX launch center with Elon Musk?"

"Hell yes!" I shot back.

The President's speech that day was one of his best. He addressed the George Floyd crisis with compassion for the dead and steadfastness against the spreading unrest. Elon did a dance as he stood up to be recognized. Everyone could tell he was overcome with emotion. Years of brutally hard work, a famously difficult childhood, a divorce, and huge risks had paid off in a historic way. And for a moment, the entire nation then in the midst of riots and a terrible racial divide paused to come together to cheer those colonel-astronauts on. America loves it when bold people achieve big things.

We can't all be Roy Benavidez, Elon Musk, or Donald Trump. But as a father, as a Green Beret, and as an American, I know the kind of resolve these men exemplify can be *taught*. We can't all be Special Forces operators. We *can* all learn to face challenges and crises with fortitude to never give up. In Ranger school, my most crushing failures became the seeds of my future success—not because I was special but because I refused to quit. Ever.

Determination moved my mother to build a better life for her son. It moved my mother-in-law to escape persecution and seize the American Dream for her children. It moved Elon Musk to take on nations like China, India, and France to join the ranks that conquer space. It is a Green Beret virtue, to be sure—but it is also, I think, something intrinsic to our way of life in this country—from the settlers scraping out a living in the Wild West to immigrants traversing the ocean in a wooden ship. For the sake of the American future, it is a quality we must instill in our children. First, we must find it in ourselves.

9

BOLDNESS

"Haji Azam's back in Khaki Kalay," said my intelligence sergeant.

It was big news. The little village of Khaki Kalay, populated by the Mandozai tribe, had been terrorized by Azam for years. In a war replete with bad men doing unthinkably bad things, he was among the worst. Fueled by fanatical ideology and unyielding hatred, there was little he and his band of Taliban wouldn't do. No resort to violence, brutality, or cruelty was beyond him—and that, alongside a canny operational instinct that kept him one step ahead of us, was why he was so hard to catch. Azam was infamous for having had his men machine-gun a local girls' school after the principal bravely refused to shut it down. Partly it was because he felt the locals hadn't provided him with sufficient recruits. Mostly it was because he simply hated the idea of girls learning anything.

Despite Azam's sadism, the villagers of Khaki Kalay felt there was a lot more risk in alienating him than us. They were rational, and they were right. We weren't going to kill them if they refused to cooperate with us. Azam, on the other hand, would not hesitate to kill them if they refused to work with him.

So when my sergeant said he was back, I knew it was a breakthrough. A village elder had decided to trust us, using a cell phone we had provided to call in the tip. Now it was time to vindicate that trust. I was determined to do it.

We knew how Azam operated. The problem was he knew how we operated, too. An overland approach, on vehicles and on foot, was out of the question. Azam would have sentries watching all approaches, and we were certain that we'd be ambushed before getting near him. I knew our only option was an air assault. That meant Chinooks. The big twin-rotor aircraft would carry my team plus the platoon's worth of Afghan commandos we'd need to take down Azam.

From getting the word to designing the operational plan took less than an hour. It had to move that fast; Azam was perhaps spending the night in Khaki Kalay, or perhaps he was leaving any second. There was a village elder out there, risking his life and the lives of his family—because Azam would kill them all if he knew—and he expected us to move *fast*. Like five-minutes-ago fast.

We moved quickly. The Army bureaucracy did not.

Getting the Chinooks meant contacting the commander responsible for the Chinooks. He expected a full briefing on the tactical concept.

Getting the Chinooks also meant contacting the commander

responsible for the Apaches—because the Chinooks, by regulation, did not go anywhere in this region unless accompanied by their rotary-wing attack cousins. This second commander also expected a full briefing and, of course, wanted time to coordinate.

Getting the Apaches triggered a further requirement from the overall aviation commander: he wanted a Predator drone to check out the village before *any* helicopters went there. So now we had to put in yet *another* request to the commander responsible for allocating the Predators—a completely separate bureaucratic silo.

Right about the time we were requesting the Predator, the village elder in Khaki Kalay called my intelligence sergeant. Long hours had passed since he risked his life calling the Americans, and he was desperate. "*Where are you?*" We didn't have a good answer for him. Azam was drinking tea one compound over from him, and here we were, the Americans, wrapped up in red tape. A group of heavily armed men loitered outside his gate. He was petrified. I had come to Afghanistan to fight a counterinsurgency; instead, I was spending my time fighting a counter-bureaucracy.

Long hours passed awaiting the requisite approvals. I was ready to go. My team was ready to go. The Afghan commandos were ready to go. Unfortunately, the Army bureaucracy was not. We never got all the approvals. Dawn came, and we stood down. The mission never happened. Azam escaped. The village elder who trusted us, literally with his life, never trusted us again. We lost the village of Khaki Kalay and its Mandozai tribe— permanently.

It wasn't the turning point of the war. But this wasn't an isolated incident. This sort of episode happened over and over and over again. There was simply one signal difference between us and our enemy, and it determined the outcome of the conflict:

The enemy knew how to be bold, how to be aggressive up and down their chain of command, and we did not.

The Taliban was focused relentlessly on an outcome: driving the coalition forces out so they could take over Afghanistan to reinstate their twisted form of Islamic extremism. Our desired outcome was to stop them from achieving theirs. We knew their outcome meant allowing international terrorists like al-Qaeda and ISIS to flourish and attack the West. The problem was that while the enemy didn't much care how they accomplished their goal, we were as concerned with the process as with the outcome. It wasn't enough for us to do the right thing—we had to check the right boxes first. We could rain down hell on our enemy, but too often, we had to wait too long to get the authorization to do so.

To be bold—to be aggressive—requires not just courage but a sense of urgency. Purpose and its associated virtues— determination and the refusal to quit—are advantages in life and in battle. They carry with them the possibility of paying a high price—and sometimes the ultimate price. This is precisely why many shy away from them. It is what made men like my friend and Green Beret Matt Pucino so rare.

Pucino was one of our most talented Green Berets, an elite operator in a field of already-extraordinary men. He was smart, funny, built like a linebacker, and an exceptional intelligence analyst. There wasn't anything he couldn't do. After tours in Iraq, Africa, and now Afghanistan, Matt Pucino was working hard on the problem of IEDs.

We had been through a few phases of IEDs in the war at that point. The Taliban, very much like their counterparts in the Iraqi insurgency, favored remote-detonated IEDs that used nearly any form of electronic broadcast to detonate their explosives: cell phones, garage-door openers, simple radios, and so on. Our technical people worked hard on the problem, and we got to a point where we had portable electronic jammers that worked surprisingly well. We'd get into range of an IED, but thanks to our jammer, the waiting Taliban could not detonate them. It saved unnumbered lives.

The Taliban were nothing if not determined. They simply innovated backward and went back to basics: they moved from electronic detonation to old-fashioned mechanical detonation. Instead of radio frequency triggers, the new generation of Taliban IEDs were straight from the Viet Cong arsenal of four decades prior, with pressure plates and trip wires triggering hidden explosives. Technology could not solve this evolution in enemy tactics. There was only keeping a lookout the old-fashioned way, and risk. All the risk was squarely on the shoulders of the lookout up front. Remote-detonated IEDs would often hit the men or vehicles in the center of a line, for maximum disruption, or at the end, for maximum terrorization. The mechanically detonated IEDs mostly hit the men or vehicles up front—a first-mover disadvantage.

In response to this evolution in the IED/counter-IED contest, our conventional counterparts dealt with the risk by staying inside the wire until the risk could be reduced to nearly zero. The infantry battalion sharing our base were allowed to venture out only in mine-resistant vehicles. If the mine-resistant vehicles were down for maintenance (which was often the case) and only the lightly armored Humvees were available, the infantry were not authorized to go beyond the wire. Further, every convoy, even with the mine-resistant vehicles, had to be preceded by a mine-clearing convoy of specialized vehicles staffed by explosive ordnance specialists. These mine-clearing convoys were particularly slow and gave the Taliban plenty of time to position themselves to ambush them—or to escape the areas to fight another day. Only a few of the dirt roads and rudimentary bridges could handle the heavy mine-resistant vehicles, so once the convoys started, it was obvious to every insurgent in the area where the conventional units were going and therefore when to ambush them. The end result was whole units that rarely left their base or telegraphed their routes because of the highly armored and heavy vehicles they were forced to use.

Another way to reduce the risk and better accomplish the mission was to use unconventional methods. My Green Berets usually traveled at night only under night vision. They didn't use any headlights, so the local insurgents couldn't see them coming, and therefore couldn't arm the IEDs. When my teams did travel during the day they often sent a decoy convoy out the main gate that we knew the insurgents were watching and then slipped out a side gate. Matt Pucino always volunteered to be up front, riding ahead of the armored convoy on a motorcycle or four-wheeler. He wanted to be close enough to the ground to see signs of digging or trip wires.

Just before heading out on yet another mission, I stopped Matt and told him, "I love your team's aggression, brother, and that you guys are embracing the risk smartly and getting after the enemy. I'm proud of you guys for being bold, for being aggressive, for continuing to push hard while virtually every other unit has shut down patrols unless they're virtually guaranteed there is zero chance of an IED. I know I've been pushing you guys to get after it."

Matt smirked. He knew the "But . . ." was coming.

"I can't believe I'm saying this, but you're pushing too hard." I asked him to spread out the risk. It was too much for him to always be on point—"You're pushing your luck. Your teammates are just as willing as you are to be up front."

Matt shook his head. "Hey, sir, I hear you. But if a pressure plate gets missed or if we don't see the trip wire, the IED will only get me, not my four teammates in the vehicle behind me.

Besides, I don't trust those knuckleheads not to miss something," he said, smiling.

He wanted to be the one to take the hit, not one of his brothers. That's the kind of man he was.

On November 23, 2009, Matt Pucino was once again out in front. It was dark, and his team was coming back from an unsuccessful raid. We later determined that the enemy most likely guessed the team's route back to our base and armed a pressure plate IED. Matt took the hit while scouting ahead of the convoy on a four-wheel all-terrain vehicle as they came out of a wadi. He was killed instantly. No one else on his team was hurt. Matt's audacity and self-sacrifice saved his brothers' lives.

The economist Nassim Taleb writes about this instinct toward self-fortification. We think of the opposite of fragility as flexibility. As Taleb points out, the opposite of fragility is actually anti-fragility, in which the stressors that might break something that's fragile go on to strengthen something that's anti-fragile. As is often pointed out, being bold and courageous is not the absence of fear but rather the commitment to overcome it. Some might assume that someone like Matt or other elite special operators somehow weren't afraid. That's ridiculous. Of course they were. But they consciously chose to battle their fears. They trained for every scenario to build the confidence to face it head-on and step right through it to move forward. In politics or business (or even those stepping onstage in front of a large group for the first time), you obviously aren't facing the same sort of life-or-death decisions. I never underestimate what it takes to push past fear. I don't expect everyone to have been to war. What I want to do is encourage a culture of smart risk-taking in those around me. I need to lead by example, and when I'm in doubt, I think of those who've been an example to me. In so doing, I hope to convey the skill of anti-fragility: not just bending to or withstanding the obstacles before us but using them to become better, stronger versions of our true selves.

When leaders boldly, and very publicly, miss and fall short, they cannot let that miss lead the team into hyper-caution and risk aversion. Analysis paralysis is dangerous. Even after setbacks and failures, leaders must continue to set (and embody) bold expectations. They must continue to set bold expectations above and beyond what their subordinates believe they can attain.

In combat, serious injury or death is sometimes the price of determined aggression. Matt's death hit all of us hard. It still does. I was Matt's commander. He was my responsibility. I approved that mission and knew Matt's team was heading into a Taliban-infested area. I will live with that guilt the rest of my life.

One can live a long time dodging risk. One can choose to live comfortably, opting out of the cold, avoiding discomfort, and letting others make the tough sacrifices. But that's not how Green Berets roll. We didn't want to lose a single man. We also knew that it was wishful thinking that we could just keep every soldier home and hope the terrorists would just leave us alone.

As Americans, we have boldness in our DNA. Our nation was born in battles and feats—from the stand at Bunker Hill to the Lewis and Clark Expedition to Chuck Yeager breaking the sound barrier. Americans have demonstrated time and again that risk-taking was a prerequisite for liberty and progress.

Every American knows the famous Emanuel Leutze painting of George Washington crossing the Delaware. You may recall from history class that the crossing was part of a surprise—and highly successful—attack on a superior British position manned by Hessian German mercenaries. What's more important to remember is that Washington was taking an extraordinarily bold risk while at the brink of total defeat.

The first full year of our rebellion—1776—had been disastrous for the Americans. George Washington had lost a series of battles, and by Christmas, his Continental Army was down to some five thousand troops. That small force was America personified—without it, there was no country—and so long as it existed, America existed, too. As 1776 came to an end and the desperate army reached the south shore of the Delaware River, there was every reason, strategic and tactical, to accept the refuge and play it safe for the sake of what was left of the American cause.

Not far to Washington's rear, the American government had already given its verdict on their army's prospects: Congress abandoned Philadelphia. Winter and the icy Delaware would protect the small and beaten Continental Army for some months, but when the weather warmed with spring, the British would surely resume their advance and complete the victory. That was the universal assumption, and it was held by both the fleeing Continental Congress and the British commander Lord Cornwallis, who confidently settled into winter quarters at New Brunswick, New Jersey.

General George Washington had spent months in a series of operations mostly meant to avoid the total destruction of his army. He understood that sooner or later he would run out of space to retreat. Furthermore, he knew it was possible he would run out of men before that. As the Continental Army fled, men drifted away from it—or worse, switched sides to be among the winners. The American crisis at the end of 1776, Washington perceived, was not simply operational: it was moral. If left unaddressed, the moral aspect would doom the Revolution more certainly than any battlefield setback.

Because he understood what was at stake, Washington chose to do the opposite of what was expected, what was obvious, and what was safe. Beaten, driven hundreds of miles southward, his forces diminished, plunged into the depths of a hard and freezing winter, and faced with overpowering British arms, Washington did the last thing expected of him. He *attacked*.

At Trenton on Christmas 1776, Washington had to motivate his men to become the aggressors for once and mount a high-risk nighttime raid on the garrison of Hessian mercenaries on the north shore of the Delaware. Then, knowing a British counterattack was certain, Washington had to *persuade* his army to stay in the field—for most of the enlistments were expiring at year's end—and then meet and defeat the enemy at Assunpink Creek. Electrified by their unexpected victory at Trenton, the Continentals held at Assunpink on January 2. Washington then conducted a masterly disengagement, tricked the British facing him, and deftly positioned the bulk of his forces to attack and destroy the unsuspecting British garrison at Princeton *the next day.*

In nine days of daring, the Continental Army erased months of defeat. They also revived desperately flagging morale. For the first time since the opening months of the conflict, the Americans began to believe they could win the war. The British, stunned at the string of American victories and surprised by the American willingness to fight in high-risk scenarios, responded with what turned out to be fatal caution. They retreated to their base at New York, ceding momentum to the Americans.

Our first commander in chief saved the nation through boldness and *aggression*. Those qualities can save America again, if we can properly understand how to channel and use them.

As I write this, we are nearing fifty years since the end of the draft and the creation of the all-volunteer force for America's defense. A quarter century after my own commissioning and multiple battlefield tours, I know from experience that the men and women who volunteer really are some of America's best. I also know from experience that an all-volunteer force incentivizes risk aversion in combat. I don't mean that volunteers are less brave or aggressive than their draftee forefathers. This fear of risk is more institutional than individual but does all the greater harm as a result.

An all-volunteer force, in which every enlistment or commissioning into military service holds the promise of a *career* rather than an effort for the duration, actively discourages risk-taking. Quite the opposite. A commanding officer was rarely, if ever, relieved in Afghanistan or Iraq because of enemy advances in his area of operations, or for a decline in popular sentiment toward us—all things that are very hard for superior officers to measure. But should that same commander have a base overrun, a patrol wiped out in an ambush, a helicopter shot down, or a high-profile civilian-casualty incident because of a risky or aggressive operation that he approved, it would likely be devastating to his or her career. It certainly does not reflect well on their next evaluation report when they are being compared with other officers who had zero incidents. For even the best-intentioned career officer, the easiest and least risky action becomes *inaction*.

Our own lack of aggression, our risk aversion, in my wartime experience, lost us many villages and tribal support.

Sometime after that fiasco of planning and bureaucracy about Haji Azam, my same intel NCO brought me the news: "We've got him again. It looks like he's going to stay the night in the K-G pass." The Khost-to-Gardez pass was remote, inaccessible, and overrun with Taliban: exactly the sort of place Azam and his like would spend the night. He'd been terrorizing villages there, raising money and recruiting fighters—or more accurately, extorting money and forcibly conscripting teenage boys into his group of fighters. The pattern was well established across Afghanistan and always included commandeering a local compound for a good night's rest.

The villagers largely hated it, but they also endured it. They didn't see a choice. They were also well accustomed, in this region especially, to the ravages of war. The Soviets never controlled the K-G pass in their war in Afghanistan—and neither did we. It was a uniquely tough area, even in an Afghan context: resistant people, jagged cliffs, high-altitude terrain, and a single road winding through it.

I knew that the bureaucracy that denied me permission to air assault into Khaki Kalay was never going to agree to an air assault in the vastly more forbidding K-G pass. I also knew that a single brave informant was, *right then*, calling in information to us that required us to act *now*. This lone and heroic man not only told us where Azam was, he actually placed an infrared beacon adjacent to the commandeered compound. It's a trope, but it's true: courage is often being afraid but doing the right thing anyway. This man was courageous. He did the right thing. He was also deeply frightened. "He's going to find it," he rasped over the phone, his panic unmistakable. "He's going to find me."

We owed this man our action in return for his courage. We owed it to him to be bold and do whatever it took to take Azam out.

My staff discussed options. An air assault was out of the question; it would be the same outcome, both in terms of resources denied and target lost. We also knew that driving up the only road into the pass wasn't going to work. We'd be identified by Azam's lookouts before we got within a mile of him. Azam would escape, and we would be ambushed. We needed a third option.

One of my sergeants raised his hand. "Hey, sir, what about a jinga truck? It's the only thing that regularly gets through the pass. Maybe we pile into some of those. I know it will never get approved by higher, but I'm just sayin' . . ."

Long-distance trucking is a huge subculture across South Asia and Afghanistan. In places with no railroads or ports, it's the only way goods move. Truckers there, like truckers in America, will personalize the trucks in which they work and live for months on end. In the States, that might mean a custom paint job or some accessories in the cab. In South Asia, it goes to a whole new level: gaudy decorations and bright paint transform ordinary beat-up trucks into traveling works of art. Beads, calligraphy, papier-mâché flowers, Islamic iconography, and more: all this goes into the creation of what is called the jinga truck. You can't miss them—and they don't aim to be missed. They're the exact opposite of the sort of transportation you'd take when you don't want to be spotted.

In the spirit of bottom-up leadership, we took the sergeant's bold idea and ran with it.

The jinga truck was our only surefire way into the K-G pass that wasn't going to be immediately noticed by all present. On paper, it seemed like it might work: load up a platoon's worth of Afghan commandos and a Special Forces team into a few jingas, drive up to Azam's compound, dismount, and fight. In reality, it was fraught with risk. The trucks were completely unarmored, for one thing—and they weren't fighting platforms of any sort. In an ambush, the men within would be essentially unprotected sitting in a metal box and unable to effectively fight back. One wrong passage, and a daring raid would become an infamous fiasco. An additional challenge was that we couldn't even be sure that our jinga-truck drivers wouldn't betray us at the first opportunity. These men drove through the K-G pass with some regularity; who knew whether they had Taliban friends or family there? The chances were high.

The easy thing for me to do as a commander would be to reject the mission as too risky. Another easy way out would be to float the idea up the chain of command, knowing they would deny it, and save face with my men. The best way to avoid the risk was just not do the mission. If Azam caught the informant and killed him—or worse, punished the whole village brutally—it would cost me nothing in the eyes of my superiors. On the other hand, if I pushed my men to be bold, unconventional, and daring—and it turned out badly—there would be hell to pay. I knew I would likely be relieved of command, if not worse.

I informed headquarters that we'd be going out on a low-level patrol, escorting some jinga trucks with supplies. This was partially true, but not the whole story.

We also managed downward. To mitigate the risks of driver betrayal or defection, each of our drivers was joined by two men in the truck's cab: a trusted Afghan commando, and a Special Forces soldier, his face appropriately wrapped. They loaded up, and they drove into the pass.

I monitored the entire mission all night from my operations center, my heart pounding. We got lucky, and the jinga trucks encountered no Taliban checkpoints—a fatal oversight for the normally paranoid Azam, who no doubt felt securer in the K-G pass. Everything was going right until the moment one of the jinga-truck drivers nearly sent himself, his truck, and half a team of Green Berets and commandos off a cliff.

There is no driver-qualification course for navigating large vehicles across the high mountain passes of Afghanistan and Pakistan, and it showed in moments like this. One of the jinga-truck drivers needed to get down and check a turn for clearance on the high mountain road. He stopped his vehicle and got out to look—without setting the brake. The truck, of course, began to roll toward the cliff's edge with a dozen men inside. Fortunately, the Special Forces operator in the cab lunged for the emergency brake and locked it down. Thankfully, he had been quietly paying attention to how the driver operated the truck.

It was a miraculous deliverance and, even more miraculously, the only real surprise on the inbound mission. They rolled into the village, posted the Afghan commandos in an outer perimeter, neutralized the surprised and complacent lookouts outside the compound, and entered it. It was a silent entry: no explosives at the doors, no entryways battered in, no noise. The men put ladders up against the compound walls on either side of the gate. One man scaled it, dropping into the locked compound by himself. Another man stayed atop the wall to provide cover. The man inside unlocked the main gate, and the whole force entered. They literally walked into Azam's bedroom without waking a soul.

There they found Azam sleeping peacefully in his stolen bed. He woke with a tap to the forehead from the cold metal of an M4 muzzle.

"Wake up, motherfucker."

Azam's face shifted from confusion to raw and guttural fear as he saw the shadows of Green Berets and Afghan commandos standing above his bed in the darkness, only the faint green glow of their night vision splashing on their faces.

The target was bundled into the back of a jinga truck, and the team set out on their return. This portion was considerably more fraught. The operation had taken longer to unfold than we had planned, and we ran out of darkness. With the sun coming up, my teams and commandos would be sitting ducks in a fight. One of our interpreters sat on Azam's back in the bed of the truck, holding the captive's cell phone and responding to texts in Pashto, pretending to be him. We had no way of knowing if that would be enough, or if news had traveled from the village about us snatching Azam. I called in a favor and asked the operations officer of the aviation unit stationed at our base and asked him to divert his scout helicopters from their normal morning patrol route to the road leading from the K-G pass. We had deliberately made friends with this captain at our regular barbecues with smuggled booze. He didn't ask any questions. A half hour later, my phone rang.

"Sir," the aviation officer said as I picked up. I held my breath. "My birds reported seeing nothing but a small convoy of jinga trucks coming out of the mountains toward our base. No sign of enemy activity or anything else unusual."

I sat down, leaned my head back, and exhaled. They did it.

We avoided a Taliban ambush, but now my career was squarely in the sites of the Army bureaucracy. The phone rang again. It was my higher headquarters operations officer. "So lemme get this straight: You guys bagged Azam—the Taliban most wanted that you've been chasing our entire tour—by just stumbling upon him while escorting some jingas?" His tone dripped with skepticism.

"That's right," I replied, deadpan. "We got a tip that he was nearby. So, we just pulled over and grabbed him."

"That's quite a coincidence. You jackasses should buy some lottery tickets since you're so lucky. Well, here's the deal. Headquarters is calling bullshit about your made-up logistics run.

They think this was incredibly reckless. The colonel wants you relieved. But the boss is fighting for you."

I shot back, "If the colonel wants to send me back home to my civilian job for taking a murderous Taliban thug off the street by using some unconventional methods, *like a damn Green Beret should*, he can go right ahead." I hung up without waiting for a reply.

For this—for being too bold in battle and not following the prescribed process—I nearly lost my Army career. I was told that the colonel in charge of the entire Special Operations group in Afghanistan was determined to relieve me. I was saved only because the officer between him and me went to bat for me, for which I remain grateful. His defense of my actions succeeded only because we succeeded. Had we failed to capture or kill Azam, or had I lost a single man, or had the raid gone catastrophically wrong (say, the emergency brake didn't hold and that one truck rolled off the cliff), my time in command would have been over.

But I was willing to risk it. I understood that it is risky to be bold, *but it is often riskier not to be.* I also knew that while I was willing to put my career on the line, that was nothing compared with my men—and our brave informant—who were willing to put their lives on the line. We had lost out on this mission before, thanks to our own bureaucracy. I was determined that we weren't going to lose it again. Aggression was, in the end, the risky choice, but also the right one. Failure to risk would cost us more. Eventually, risk aversion would cost us the entire war.

To prioritize avoiding risk above all other goals is a recipe for disaster. If Matt Pucino had prioritized avoiding risk, he might not have saved his team. If George Washington had prioritized avoiding risk, we'd have the face of King George III on our money. If I had prioritized avoiding risk, Haji Azam would have killed more innocent Afghans—and Americans.

When we have prioritized avoiding risk, we have emboldened our enemies. Our frantic and bungled withdrawal from Afghanistan sent a clear message that America was not willing to stay and fight. Vladimir Putin got the message: the United States will not risk much to defend its friends, allies, or interests. Six months after our disastrous Afghan pullout, the Russians invaded Ukraine, calculating that we might complain but would not confront. A still more formidable enemy—China—has noted the message as well. An increasingly confrontational Chinese military is testing our limits and threatening our friends, probing the limits of our aversion to risk.

A foe who knows we will take risks to defend our interests is a foe who respects those interests. The reverse is also true: The more fearful we are of our own aggression, the more we encourage the aggression of those who mean us harm.

Risk aversion isn't just found on foreign battlefields. It's found in a culture that is hostile to traditional masculinity, labeling boldness, aggression, and the desire to protect as "toxic."

It's found in the cultural obsession with "safe spaces" and the desire to insulate our children from anything that could upset or challenge them. At its most extreme, risk aversion paralyzes individuals and societies. We all witnessed what that looked like during the COVID-19 pandemic.

In April 2020, I called Governor DeSantis. The pandemic had been spreading for weeks. Much of the country had locked down, and states like New York, California, and Michigan were demanding still more aggressive measures. They wanted to shut down schools, businesses, and churches. My office was flooded with calls from the families of my constituents trapped in countries around the world. I wanted to better understand how the governor intended to approach all these issues and more in Florida.

"Mike, we are going to follow the data," he said matter-of-factly. "We don't have as much information as we would like yet, but from what we can tell, this thing disproportionately affects the elderly and those with some type of comorbidity. We are going to focus all the resources we can—the National Guard, our testing facilities, our PPE purchases, and any type of therapeutics that get developed—on our nursing homes and older communities. But for younger workers, and especially in schools, this thing is proving to be more like a bad flu. Kids might get sick, but thankfully, only a fraction of a percent are ending up in the hospital. I've shut schools down for the rest of this school year, but I'm leaving day cares open so working people can still work. And I'm absolutely reopening schools at the end of this summer . . . five days a week, with in-person teaching."

I paused. We were only a month into this pandemic—so much was still unknown. It was incredibly bold to pledge to open schools for the fall.

"For kids with grandparents at home or parents with immunity problems, can we create some type of remote option?" I asked.

The governor jumped in, "Exactly, Mike, we're going to do that. This is about choice and leaving it up to parents. If they agree with my analysis of the data, their kids can go to school. If they need to do remote, they can do remote. There is no reason we can't set up some type of camera in the classrooms and stream it. But families should make that decision—not bureaucrats or teachers' unions. Our job is to give families options and resources and let them decide."

DeSantis turned to what I could do. "Your messaging on cable news is helpful. We must stop the Left in Congress who are talking about creating national mandates and locking everyone down like California and Michigan. If the data changes, then we will change our policies. But we are the ones following the science, not them."

The governor was taking an aggressive stance. It was a calculated risk, but it was based on a sober analysis of the impact of the lockdowns. A year into the pandemic, Michael Barone of the American Enterprise Institute pointed out something we'd already grasped in Florida:

> *One oddity of COVID-19 responses in the United States has been the one-dimensional perspective of liberal decision-makers. They claim to be following "the science," but with a narrow focus.*
>
> *To prevent the spread of a virus that is often asymptomatic and less lethal than influenza to people under age 65, they have imposed restrictions that have reduced lifesaving medical screenings and produced mental illness and stunted development among children and adolescents.[2]*

In other words, the remedy did more harm than the disease itself. In Washington, President Trump and those of us in Congress came to the same conclusion. The desire to avoid all risk pertaining to COVID ended up creating a ripple effect of greater risks. As the years pass, we see more and more evidence of the harm that the blue state lockdowns caused, harm rooted in a frantic impulse to avoid danger. As the title of the Barone piece put it, "Too Much Risk Aversion Is Too Risky."

---

2 Michael Barone, "Too Much Risk Aversion Is Too Risky," American Enterprise Institute, April 2, 2021, https://www.aei.org/op-eds/too-much-risk -aversion-is-too-risky/.

There are untold costs and consequences of our national allergy to aggressive action, and those costs are felt the most by the most vulnerable people. One can only imagine the consequences if President Trump had not boldly ordered a halt to all incoming flights from China in the early days of the pandemic and invoked the Defense Production Act for everything from ventilators to personal protective equipment for first responders.

In his famous Rice University speech, John F. Kennedy pledged to get a man on the moon by the end of the decade. Not because it is easy, he said, but because it is hard. Within living memory, we were committed to aggressively pursuing our ideals and our priorities. We understood the costs, accepted the risks, and we dared. We need that same boldness now in fields like artificial intelligence and quantum computing, and in launching mankind to deep space. George Washington took an aggressive risk; Matt Pucino did as well. The former saved the cause of our country; the latter saved his friends and gave his life for freedom. Each man knew that the risk of *not* being brave and bold outweighed the risk posed by their daring and aggressive actions. We need more George Washingtons and John F. Kennedys—even more, we need more Matt Pucinos.

We need leaders who think and lead like a Green Beret. We need leaders to deliver hard truths.

10

SERVANT LEADERSHIP

Our combined platoon of Afghans and Americans patrolled down the dry wadi of the Tagab Valley. Dusk descended upon us. We were in the heart of Taliban country.

You'd think the Tagab would have been secure. It was just to the east of Bagram Airfield, the repurposed Soviet-era base that was the gigantic epicenter of the American war in Afghanistan. But in a pattern familiar to any student of insurgency (and Afghan history), our authority did not extend far outside our own gates. Although within easy distance of Bagram, the Tagab was an epicenter of a different sort. It was a Taliban hub. Through the Tagab Valley ran IEDs, men, and resupply for the forces seeking to kill as many Americans as possible, take over the Afghan government, and slaughter those locals brave enough to cooperate with us.

The force in the wadi was an Afghan National Army platoon, with two fellow embedded Green Berets and me. Arab coalition soldiers from the UAE provided overwatch from their armored vehicles at a local police station. We had been on foot patrol with the Afghan soldiers all day, and as nightfall approached, their discipline deteriorated. They were tired—and they did not want to be out in this dangerous valley, away from our base at the local police station, after sunset. They were not wrong to be worried.

The lead soldier on point was Sergeant Major Sumar Ghul. Sumar had already impressed us over the last several weeks of patrolling. Now he was walking slow and steady, scanning the labyrinth of mud-walled compounds, drainage ditches, and small farm plots lining the dry riverbed. He was a strong, disciplined example to his men. Every time they bunched up behind him like horses smelling the barn, he angrily motioned for them to slow down and spread back out.

"My Ranger School instructors would be proud of him," I whispered to myself.

Our Afghan platoon leader ought to have been providing that leadership himself, but after watching that lieutenant for weeks, I had concluded that he was incompetent. He was typical of far too many officers from developing countries. Men like him took their positions for prestige, authority, and—all too often—access to corruption. Officers like this certainly weren't about to sacrifice themselves for their country, and still less for their men. If there is a definition of servant leadership, men like this are the exact opposite.

This particular lieutenant's sole virtue was that unlike many Afghan officers, he let his sergeant major step in to lead. By contrast with his lieutenant, Sumar Ghul was the living archetype of servant leadership. He always volunteered to walk point. He always took care of his men first. He always ensured they all had adequate food and water before he did. We observed him checking every one of his soldiers' gear, weapons, and supplies—before *every* mission.

I wish that Sumar had heard my whispered praise. Only a moment after his methodical scan of the wadi, the sound of a bolt slamming forward rang through the stillness of the evening and echoed off the village's mud walls. I saw Sumar swing to his left and raise his weapon. But he was too late. The ambush was incredibly close. A machine gun directly in front of Sumar let off a burst—I could see the flames spurting from the muzzle—and raked him, the lieutenant, and our interpreter as the weapon's trajectory swung down the length of the wadi. I saw all three crumple to the ground. The machine gun sprayed fire up and down the straggling Afghan line, hitting some and missing others and generally sowing deadly anarchy in an already loose formation. The machine gun nest was barely thirty feet away from me.

I raised my M4, put my sights on the belching muzzle flash, and began pulling the trigger as fast as I could. And then everything went into slow motion. I saw the brass casings ejecting, fluttering to my right as I fired—and then I saw them stop. I pulled the trigger, and nothing happened. As if in slow motion, although in reality in seconds, I went through the failure drill my first team sergeant, Marc, had me practice a hundred times to ensure the magazine and rounds were seating properly.

I pulled the trigger again. Nothing.

Another machine-gun burst raked the wall to my right. A second, smaller muzzle flash opened up. Then a third. These were single shots—likely from AK-47s. Another burst from the machine gun flew about a foot over my head. The snap-crack of the bullets breaking the sound barrier was unmistakable. They were shooting at me—and I still couldn't shoot back.

In the dusk, I realized I had a double feed. It was fixable, but there was no time. I slung the useless M4 to my left and went for my 9 mm pistol.

Though I was not reflecting upon it in that moment, there was a little bit of irony in unholstering the 9 mm. In our role as Special Forces in uniquely dangerous spots across Afghanistan, we never lacked for firepower. Heavy machine guns, light machine guns, grenade launchers, you name it, we had it.

During our pre-deployment training, Marc insisted upon what seemed like nonstop pistol-range practice. Given all the other weapons we had at our disposal, I thought it was a little ridiculous and unnecessary. One day, when I was still a brand-new team leader, I watched him talking the team through yet another pistol drill at the range, and I decided to say something. I pulled Marc aside and asked whether it might not be better for us to train on some other skills.

"Hey, man, I'm just saying that if we're at the point at which we are drawing 9 mm pistols on the enemy—it means crew-served weapons, rifles, artillery, and air support have all *failed*.

Won't that mean it's probably time to get the hell out of there?"
I asked.

In most units in the Army, if the commanding officer thinks something is a poor use of valuable training time, the unit will probably change the training. That isn't how Green Berets work. We practice bottom-up leadership, which is why my team sergeant replied with a nice dose of sarcasm, "Great insight, sir. We're going to keep working with pistols today. You will see, when we get overseas, that fire support can be slow, and we might find ourselves out of range of our heavy weapons. More often than not, you'll be in some mud hut in tight spaces, or where you can barely raise your rifle, while facing an enemy that's very up close and personal. Trust me on this one," he said as he patted my shoulder, turned around, and walked back to the range so he could continue leading the session on magazine changes. I wasn't sure I bought what he was selling, but I trusted him and did as he asked. It turned out to be a damn good decision.

So, there I was, pistol in hand, standing in the middle of the riverbed, steps away from a Taliban machine-gun nest, putting as many rounds as I could on the enemy with my ridiculously small handgun. I saw two heads pop up above the wall; I fired, and the heads dropped. I have no idea if I hit them or if they dove for cover. But their disappearance gave just enough pause in the firing to allow one of my sergeants time to run down the wadi—and chuck a grenade onto them.

I dove over a short wall, rolled over, and inserted a fresh magazine into my pistol just as my sergeants had trained us. Then I heard a sound that sent a shiver down my spine. Behind me, the boom of a Mk 19 grenade launcher opened up from the UAE overwatch position. We dove into the dirt as a string of grenades exploded on the compounds and trees all around us in a fury. One of my sergeants embedded in the patrol had launched a red flare to mark our position—a prearranged signal—and the UAE personnel took it as the point to shoot *at* rather than avoid. Next we saw the tracers from their .50-cal heavy machine guns flying over us with the rounds thumping into the mud compound nearby. I looked over and saw my sergeant screaming into his radio, "Cease fire, damn it!"

It took me a moment to realize that while I had been only thirty feet from the ambush, Sumar was only *ten* feet away when the machine gun opened up. His dedication to leading from the front, and his sacrifice as a servant leader, meant he was cut down in that first burst of deadly fire.

Now we had two tasks. One was to fight and survive against the converging Taliban. They tried to maneuver on us as dusk turned to dark. I grabbed the interpreter, who was in a fetal position, and consolidated the patrol. I later learned that our UAE overwatch could see the dozens of Taliban fighters but didn't feel able to fire upon them without hitting us.

Our other task was to recover the body of Sergeant Major Ghul.

The Afghan soldiers began to drift away from our hastily

established perimeter and away from where Sumar's body lay. Again, the 9 mm pistol proved useful. I blocked their exit, raised the gun, and fired it in the air.

"You never leave a fallen comrade," I said, falling back on the Ranger Creed. "If you won't go with me, I will go alone." I kicked my interpreter and told him to translate. I could not compel them to *feel* honor, but I was damned well going to force them to *act* honorably. The Afghan soldiers didn't come with me, but at least they stayed put and didn't flee. My sergeants covered me, and I reentered the wadi and engaged the enemy fighters. Inbound rounds from small arms pinged about as I crawled up to the dark mound that I thought was Sumar. At first, I tried to drag him by his gear, but the strap snapped off in my hands. I then sat him up and bear-hugged him from behind. As I heaved him backward, I heard a sound that haunted me in nightmares for years later—a slow, deep exhale that was his dying breath. Eventually, I dragged the lifeless Sumar out of the wadi and onto a ladder, which I used as a makeshift stretcher. I was covered in his blood. We spent the rest of the night dodging Taliban ambush teams, and we maneuvered our way back to friendly lines at the police station. They gave me a Bronze Star for valor, but I would much rather have Sumar back.

In another life, Sumar Ghul would have spent his days as a well-loved local teacher in an out-of-the-way village somewhere in the vast Afghan hinterland. He believed in education and understood its power. Education did more than teach—it elevated and ennobled. He understood this clearly, which was why Sumar dreamed of laying down his weapon and returning to his love of teaching. He had a personal motivation as the father of six children; his dream for them was to transcend ignorance and poverty. He had a larger dream as well: to bring education to the Afghan people, men and women alike.

Sumar had the heart of a servant leader.

The life that Sumar was actually given was not what he had planned for himself. The man whose father taught him the value of service and education was raised in the midst of a long and bitter war against the Soviet Union. He grew into adulthood in the civil war that followed. He saw his community—and his own children—relentlessly attacked by Taliban fanatics who despised education and reviled teaching unless it was of a puritanical form of Islam.

Instead of fleeing to a refugee camp, Sumar chose to stay, and he chose to *fight* in the new Afghan Army after the Americans came. His belief in protecting education now led him to soldiering. He was not simply a former teacher who chose to become a soldier; Sumar was a soldier who was exceptionally aggressive (and exceptionally proficient) at his new profession. This set him apart in the ranks of the Afghan National Army.

Sumar worked constantly to master the soldiering skills. Where the typical leader in most third world armies would send others into danger to save themselves, Sumar went himself and led from the front—setting the example in embracing the risk of nearly every patrol. He was everything we, as Green

Berets, wanted to promote as we trained and advised our counterparts. Sumar wasn't doing any of this to please American
soldiers. He was serving with us because we were serving the
cause of freedom for his country.

That boldness, and that embrace of risk in the pursuit of
servant leadership, is how Sumar came to be with me in the
Taliban ambush that took his life.

In his famous 1970 essay "The Servant as Leader," Robert
K. Greenleaf pointed out the importance of those who were
driven to *lead* as a result of their greater desire to *serve*. Greenleaf was writing about corporate America, and he worried that
too many big companies were stuck in the model of authoritar-
ian leadership. In that model, the drive to lead derives from a
desire for power, position, or resources. What America needed,
Greenleaf argued, was executives who saw their most important job as serving their workers, enabling their employees to
flourish and become the best that they could be. Greenleaf
made his case that "servant leadership" is not a new concept
but rather an old one embedded in our history. It was, he
argued, a tradition America needed to rediscover.

Servant leadership can be found everywhere. The life of
Sumar Ghul is a shining example. But though Sumar was
Afghan, he found the fullest expression of his innate call to
servant leadership fighting alongside the Americans. He was
not a Green Beret, but I considered him a brother. Alongside
us, with our imperfect-but-authentic value of sacrifice, Sumar
found an opportunity to serve he might not have had otherwise.

Servant leadership may not be limited to any one race, but history shows it is uniquely expressed among Americans. The great model is George Washington, a man who could have been king but who stepped aside for love of America. Later, we see servant leadership in Abraham Lincoln, Ulysses S. Grant, and George C. Marshall—all men who laid themselves on the nation's altar in different ways, not for glory but for country.

Most other people recognize and elevate their own subduers. America recognizes its liberators. Or to put it in modern terms, we are a nation of servant leadership.

Obviously, servant leadership has a great deal to do with bottom-up leadership. Think of it as the flip side of the coin. If bottom-up leadership is the empowerment of the lowest levels to accomplish the mission, then servant leadership is the ethos and approach of the highest levels to facilitate that empowerment. Servant leadership, however, is not just an obligation for the top tier. It is an ethic for *anyone and everyone* with subordinates for whom they are responsible—and to whom, in the servant-leadership framework, they answer. A general officer has an obligation to servant leadership, and so does a newly promoted sergeant.

When I became the CEO of a rapidly expanding small, veteran-run business, I did my best to implement the concept of servant leadership. In his influential work *Good to Great*, the scholar of American entrepreneurship Jim Collins identified five levels of leadership, ranging from "capable individual" at the bottom rung to "level 5 executive" at the top. The variable that moves an individual up the promotion ladder is his effect upon others, and the distinguishing quality of the top tier is what Collins calls a *paradoxical* combination. That paradox, in his telling, is the right blend of "personal humility" and "professional will." Collins gives us Abraham Lincoln as the classic historical example of humility plus will. As Collins points out, Lincoln—simultaneously modest and iron-willed—is the exact opposite of how our culture normally depicts business-executive leadership. Television shows enshrine the brash, larger-than-life figure: the swashbuckling tycoon who moves fast, breaks things, and imposes his vision on everyone around him. What Collins showed, and what I have observed time and again, is that though these figures do exist, they are not typically among the most successful. The level 5 leader is a leader but not a ruler, and his success is less about himself than it is about those he leads. The level 5 leader is the most elite because they focus, often quietly and always relentlessly, on the effective maximization of the talents of others.

To put it more simply, the level 5 leader has a mission focus and a desire to do things *by*, *with*, and *through* others. This is, of course, also the Green Beret ethic. This approach to leadership—found at the very top tier of the business world—is expected of *every single* Green Beret from day one of his training.

There is a postscript to the story of Sumar Ghul. One might expect that a widow of a hero like him would be an honored figure and cared for by her community. Unfortunately, the opposite was usually true: a widow with six children was immediately vulnerable in Afghan society.

There was no explanation of how he died, no survivors' benefits. The widow of the man who so admired a classical education was forced to send her sons off to madrassas—Islamic boarding schools that taught only the Koran, and usually became factories producing young jihadis. When I heard about it from one of my interpreters, it broke my heart. Sumar deserved better. *Afghanistan* deserved better. I was determined to prevent those children from being pulled into extremism. I set up a charity to send the widow the annual equivalent of Sumar's salary in the Army. That money enabled her to withdraw her children from the brainwashing of the madrassas and bring them home. Seventeen years later, each of her children has graduated from a secular high school, and several of the boys have attended trade schools.

It was only one family that I was able to help, but the war on extremism had to be fought one family, one village, at a time. With Sumar's death, we had lost one battle—but with his family, we won another. His story is a reminder that given the chance, servant leaders can arise in unexpected places—and do extraordinary service.

The need for servant leadership is acute in places like Afghanistan, but it is no less important in America.

I have spent a lot of time reflecting on how best to re-inculcate the ethic of servant leadership into American society at large, especially now that we are generations away from the draft and the Greatest Generation. There's good news. We remain a people who volunteer, who join associations, and who cooperate with our neighbors toward a common good. Anyone who has seen parents rise up to challenge a misguided curriculum put forward by school boards, or seen the Cajun Navy come to the rescue after a storm, or watched a volunteer firefighter company do its work, knows this personally.

Veterans understand this ethic firsthand, and in America today, we understand it better than most—because we have seen the terrible alternatives to it. My time in Congress has only validated the belief I held when I launched my first campaign: that one of the reasons our political system has become so dysfunctional is the record-low number of veterans in our politics. It's not that as veterans we agree on all issues. Of course we don't. However, our service tends to mean we bring a certain ethos to the public trust. If at an early age we were willing to die for our country, then we are likely willing to roll up our sleeves and do the hard work, and take the tough votes, necessary to move the country forward *now*. We have to be mission focused, driving toward objectives and coming together to move the ball forward for America, rather than allowing problems to fester and linger.

Though the discord and arguments tend to make headlines, we come together more often than people realize and find common ground.

In the summer of 2019, during a hot and difficult summer of

impeachment investigations, contentious hearings, and seemingly everyone in Washington calling each other names, I sent
a note around to each of my fellow veterans serving in the
House of Representatives. I asked them to meet me at sunrise
the next day at the Vietnam Veterans Memorial. Over two
dozen showed up, both Republicans and Democrats. We met
with the Park Rangers and, together, helped them wash the
black granite wall. Bret Baier from Fox News brought a camera
crew. I thought the public needed to see us coming together to
honor those who died for our country. I thought we needed the
reminder that no matter how intense our debates might be, we
could not let our disagreements define us.

It was a powerful moment, washing those fifty-eight thousand names and seeing our own reflections in the black granite
as we did so—as if we ourselves reflected the country for which
they fell. This has become something of a bipartisan tradition,
and we wash the wall together now on the morning of Memorial Day.

On another occasion, Representative Jason Crow, a fellow
Army veteran, and I were in France observing the seventy-fifth
anniversary of D-Day. Jason is a Democratic member of the
House, representing Colorado, and he is also a former Ranger
who served in Iraq and Afghanistan. Jason and I met up with
the "Horse Soldier" Green Berets who had liberated Afghanistan on horseback and jumped over Sainte-Mère-Église, the
small French town upon which many of the Eighty-Second
Airborne descended on June 5, 1944. We parachuted from the

original C-47 that led the invasion fleet on that fateful night. The name of the aircraft was *That's All Brother*, and we jumped in vintage Second World War uniforms. Fortunately, the parachutes were new!

One memorable part of that day was the ninety-two-year-old paratrooper who jumped tandem, hooting and hollering all the way to the ground.

"How was it?" I asked when we landed.

He replied, "Hell of a lot better than being shot at by the Germans! A lot more fun this time!"

Also amazing was the reaction of the French people in Normandy. I jumped in a vintage OSS uniform of the kind that was worn in Operation Jedburgh, the clandestine (and very successful) plan to parachute special forces into occupied France. It's very possible that an older Frenchman might have recognized my uniform. Every town had wall-size banners with slogans such as "We love you, America," and "Thank you for our freedoms," and "Welcome to our liberators." I landed about a mile off course and had to walk in my vintage uniform through a French village that looked like it hadn't changed since D-Day. The locals walked alongside me by the dozens and handed me bottles of wine and bread. I got plenty of kisses on the cheek. Young kids ran around with pictures of Eisenhower and Patton on them. I initially thought they were the children of American reenactors, but it quickly emerged that they were French kids. One would have thought D-Day had happened the previous week, not seventy-five years earlier.

It was a powerful reminder of the countless Americans who died for other nations' freedom. And it was a powerful reminder that those nations *remember*—and are grateful. Jumping with Jason Crow, whose politics and party I do not share, was a reminder that the ethos of servant leadership can still unite us. Our divisions are real, but we are still Americans.

Not everyone can go to Normandy and experience the gratitude of the locals and visit the graves of our fallen heroes. We must inculcate servant leadership in those who will not have those opportunities. This is why for several years, I have promoted the idea of returning America to a nation of service through a National Service GI Bill. The idea behind it is to take the tremendous benefits of the old military-draft system and revive them without reviving the draft. Instead of mandatory military service, the federal government can incentivize a voluntary corps of citizens who come together to serve their country in certain defined ways. You don't have to wear a uniform to serve your country. You can teach, help maintain national parks, work on Corps of Engineers infrastructure projects or with FEMA on disaster relief, or assist with rural or tribal medicine. There are tons of possibilities. The incentives range from loan forgiveness, to in-state college tuition, or tuition to learn a trade. We can and must be bold and creative in how we imagine the scope and scale of a national service program.

The bottom line is that society deserves something in exchange for the benefits paid for by fellow taxpayers. In return, our next generation deserves to learn leadership, discipline, and teamwork in service of a higher cause. Perhaps most important is that they will do it with other Americans who don't look like them. One of the benefits of the draft was that it forced elements of society to come together. This came home to me in speaking with a Korean War–era veteran after an event in Jacksonville, Florida. He shared with me that, growing up in the segregated South, he never had any type of meaningful relationship with a person of color. Next thing he knows, at nineteen years old, he is rounding the corner in his first ship in the Navy and discovers that his bunkmate will be a Black man from Detroit. They became lifelong friends. He told me that had he not served, he likely would have remained biased and bigoted out of ignorance. Today, as our siloed news sources and social media promote the perspective of like-minded "friends," we need this forcing function more than ever.

The other thing service provides is perspective, especially if it can be done overseas in the military or Peace Corps. I regularly encounter people who can only focus on the ills and mistakes of America. They believe our nation is inherently racist and that our income disparity is the worst in the world. I wish they could serve in places like West Africa, Central America, or an Afghan village. I wish they could meet people like Sumar Ghul and understand the deep devotion so many have to America. If they saw the world as it is, they would quickly appreciate how good we have it in the United States. There is sacrificing comfort to be an activist for a cause in the United States—and then there is literally putting the lives of one's entire family at risk. When you see the difference, you know what we have—and you know we have to defend it. We defend it best when we defend as servants.

But you don't need to be a Green Beret or have fought alongside heroes like Sumar to embrace servant leadership. You just need to love this country, to want it to prosper, and for America to continue to be a beacon of freedom to the world.

11

TRUTH TO POWER

"Sir, we have a problem back home with Brian's funeral arrangements," one of my sergeants said as he walked into my operations center.

I was in no mood to hear it. The death of Sergeant First Class Brian Woods, early in our deployment to eastern Afghanistan, hit me hard. Brian was a sterling example of America's best: a dedicated soldier *and* a Marine, having served in the Marine Corps before enlisting in the Army and qualifying for the Special Forces. When he was mortally wounded during a Taliban ambush in volatile Ghazni Province, he was doing what he truly loved—being a Green Beret medic and leading a squad of his local Afghan police. Brian paid the price that any one of us was willing to pay for our country. We knew it was always a possibility. That awareness never softened the blow.

I grieved for Brian. My loss, of course, was nothing compared with what his family experienced. They didn't lose a great teammate or an exemplary medic; they lost a man they loved, and a man with whom their hopes rested for care, for protection, and for a future that would remain unwritten.

My sergeant had infuriating news. "Sir, apparently the Department of Defense is going to send a fucking bill to Brian's family for an additional flight to a burial site," he said.

I was *livid*.

"Brian's parents want to memorialize him in Missouri—and his wife wants him buried in North Carolina," my sergeant said.

"So why the hell can't we make that happen?" I asked.

"It means his body has to be flown to multiple locations. Apparently, the Defense Department only pays for one flight to one location. The casualty assistance officer that is assigned to the family is saying the spouse will have to pay for Brian's remains to be flown to a second location. Sir, it's thousands of dollars," he replied, throwing up his hands in disgust.

"Hundreds of billions of dollars every year in a defense budget, and yet they want to nickel-and-dime a Gold Star family. Such colossal bullshit," I replied.

Apparently, there was no flexibility in the regulations. There we were, running missions every day on the other side of the world, knowing that the grieving widow of one of our brothers was about to get *billed by the Army*.

Keeping my emotions under control, I said, "You do whatever you have to do to stop the Army casualty officer from delivering the bill. I'll pass the hat to see what the guys or some charities can pitch in, and I'll cover the rest." It was the only option.

If the Army and its ridiculous policy couldn't do what's right, then we would.

Although I had a lot of reasons for running for Congress, wanting to correct the treatment of Brian Woods's family and injustices done to Gold Star families in general were among the most important. I wanted to lead the charge in correcting many of the wrongs I experienced in uniform. I wanted to speak truth to power and then be in a position to put changes into law. I wanted those with the power to make policies to understand the real-world impact of their decisions.

The billing of families for the transportation of their loved ones' remains was the tip of the iceberg. There are a whole slew of problems with how we fail to care for the Gold Star community after that coffin with their loved one goes into the ground. One of the most upsetting things I found after my election was that we were taxing the Gold Star family survivors' benefits at the *highest* IRS tax rate. As Republicans were in the minority in the House of Representatives at the time, we were able to work with a veteran Democrat in the majority to get the policy repealed.

Yet another ridiculous policy was the rule *penalizing* remarriage by a surviving spouse. If a soldier is killed in war, there are survivor benefits that go to the widow or widower. In my view, these benefits are not sympathy gifts from the government;

they are *earned*. It is a core obligation of the American government to see that they are given. Abraham Lincoln's own second inaugural address charges the nation with this sacred duty: "to care for him who shall have borne the battle and for his widow and his orphan." The nation's obligation to that spouse doesn't end when she takes a vow to love and cherish another.

Soon after I was elected to Congress, my office learned that because of this cruel policy, there is a whole universe of Gold Star widows who live in shadow marriages. They cannot lose their survivor benefits, so they form informal partnerships with new people. This denial of civil recognition also carries with it tremendous consequences: for health benefits, wills, hospital visitation, and children.

The fact that Department of Defense policy creates a disincentive to marriage struck me as deeply immoral.

On another occasion, Master Sergeant Richard Stayskal, a father of two and a Green Beret, came to see me. My congressional staff know my rule: if a Green Beret wants to see me, we make the time.

Master Sergeant Stayskal walked into my office, shook my hand, and looked me in the eye. "Sir, it's an honor to meet you. I came to you today because I'm dying. The military medical system got it wrong, and because of the law, there is nothing I can do about it for my family." The doctors had missed a diagnosis of lung cancer until it was too late. He was just thirty-six.

We had the master sergeant come to Congress, testify before our committee, and tell his story. Stayskal explained that his symptoms were overlooked and ignored at the military hospital for six months, until he was finally permitted to go off base to see a specialist, who immediately diagnosed him with terminal lung cancer. When Stayskal learned he could not bring a medical malpractice claim for the care he received at the military hospital—thanks to a Supreme Court case in the 1950s called the *Feres* doctrine—he knew he had to do something to change it.

The purpose of the *Feres* doctrine was to protect medics, doctors, and emergency care in combat overseas from liability. That made sense. But Stayskal, and those of us who supported him, made the case it shouldn't apply to regular doctors here in military clinics in the United States. Anyone else with a terminal prognosis would have traveled the world, checked items off their bucket list, and enjoyed the few years they had left. Not this Green Beret. He lobbied tirelessly, making hundreds of calls and trips to Washington. He was bold. He was determined. He was the epitome of resiliency. When Senators and lawyers made objections, Stayskal adapted and kept moving forward. Most of all, he stood tall as a servant leader, sacrificing his last days to make sure his family was cared for—and making sure that future soldiers had some sort of remedy. One of my proudest days in Congress was to stand tall next to him as my fellow members of Congress and I announced the SFC Richard Stayskal Military Medical Accountability Act.

* * *

Green Berets know that power can come in many forms—in tribal tradition, in a single strongman, in a cabinet official, in intractable bureaucracy, or in a national media platform that allows one to reach millions of Americans. In the case of taking care of Gold Star families, speaking truth to power meant confronting the last two of these. A lot of good people come to Washington, DC, and after a while, they are dismayed and worn down by seemingly insurmountable barriers to change. Even obvious cases of right and wrong are adjudicated slowly, if at all. It can be maddening. Yet Green Berets are trained to alter the trajectory of ancient ethnic feuds in the name of America's national interests—often at the ends of the earth, and with little support. It puts moving the federal government into perspective.

In baseball, it's often better to think about base hits rather than home runs. As a Green Beret, I'd learned to be patient. When you're the guest of a tribe who might turn on you at any moment, hours from any help, and utterly dependent upon circumstances well beyond your control, you learn that achieving small victories is a matter of simple survival. When you have a tactical-size force and you're ordered to generate a strategic-size effect, you think in terms of base hits. You might not have the firepower to hit it out of the park, but stringing together a series of singles achieves the same result. You just have to be patient, cunning, and persistent.

Sometimes, you'll strike out. Yet in politics—as in baseball and Special Ops—a strikeout can still be an opportunity.

That's what happened the first time I spoke truth to the highest levels of power.

Not long after I'd returned from Afghanistan, and just before I returned to my policy job at the Defense Department, I pushed back on then Secretary Donald Rumsfeld and later Defense Secretary Robert Gates. Both were dedicated public servants, worthy of the trust that was placed in them. That doesn't mean they got everything right, though. One thing that was well intended but had negative secondary effects was Secretary Gates's directive to mandate the use of heavily armored mine-resistant ambush protected (MRAP) vehicles for all patrols in Afghanistan. It was a textbook case of a policy intended to solve one problem causing a myriad of other problems because of a lack of feedback, or truth to power, to the policymaker.

His directive was understandable. The insurgents in both Iraq and Afghanistan were getting very good at IEDs and mines, and they were costing the lives of American soldiers and our coalition partners alike. The MRAP mitigated that threat; its heavy armor and V-shaped hull meant a direct IED blast might break some bones and cause concussions for the crew but would not kill them. On the other hand, a strike on the flat, unarmored underbelly of our Humvees typically resulted in death or dismemberment for those inside. So, the order went out: when Americans left their base in Afghanistan, they had to do it in an MRAP.

Those of us who lived and worked out in the field knew immediately why this was going to be a problem. The MRAP's armor made it exceptionally heavy—and the roads in Afghanistan simply couldn't handle it except for a select few. The policy looked like a success on its own terms because American lives lost to IEDs and mines went down, but that metric entirely missed the real measure, which was *whether we were winning the war*. Were we able to reach Afghan villages, meet our potential allies, and take down the insurgents who were terrorizing them? With this directive, we weren't able to do those things, because the MRAP-only policy had the effect of cutting us off from huge swaths of Afghan territory—territory in which the Taliban, al-Qaeda, and eventually ISIS moved around unchallenged.

One of my Green Berets once said to me as we were discussing the new policy, "This is playing not to lose, rather than to win. It's like pointing out the quarterback hasn't thrown an interception lately while ignoring the fact that he's losing the game."

A young platoon leader told me, "Sir, this MRAP policy effectively keeps me out of nearly seventy percent of my own area of responsibility, because I'm not allowed to leave my base unless I have my men in a convoy of four MRAP vehicles. I only have five total, and two of the damn things are typically down for maintenance issues. That means my platoon can't patrol and go be out in the villages. And even when we can leave the wire with four operational vehicles, we can only use the few roads wide and thick enough to handle these big things. It also makes our routes very predictable and easily ambushed.

These things are actually getting us ambushed more often! It's nuts, sir."

Meanwhile, my Green Berets, who did not fall under the mandatory MRAP rule, were allowed to use ingenuity, deception, and adaptability to deal with the IED problem. They operated from the same bases as our conventional units, but they used the cover of darkness, different entry and exit points, and feints to keep the Taliban off-balance and guessing to where and how they traveled. We did our best. But there was no question that the MRAP policy, well-intentioned as it was, ultimately benefited the enemy.

Telling all this to the Secretary of Defense and his staff was not a popular move. But I did it—and though I wish I could say it resulted in dramatic change, it did not. Secretary Gates genuinely appreciated my candor but felt strongly that American casualties were a strategic issue that was eroding popular domestic support for our presence in Afghanistan. I pushed back, telling him, "That's playing not to lose." I suggested we might as well bring our troops home if they had their hands tied while riding around in armored boxes. Some of his staff didn't appreciate my frankness, but I felt obligated to give him the hard truth. Gates's right-hand man at the time was a former classmate of mine, Ryan McCarthy. Over drinks one night, Ryan told me, "The Secretary takes every casualty very hard. They are like his own children. He feels completely responsible." I nodded when I heard that. Gates was a consummate servant leader.

Ultimately, Gates didn't revoke his mandate, but he did

tell his generals to consider allowing exceptions to the MRAP rule when common sense and the commander on the ground required it. It was a small win. I took it.

Years earlier, I spoke up from the back row of a meeting with Secretary Rumsfeld. He was telling his team of assistant secretaries that dealing with the drug problem in Afghanistan and the Middle East wasn't the Defense Department's problem. It was State's and DEA's problem. As I heard this, my heart beat through my chest. No one spoke unless called upon in Rumsfeld's meetings, but what he was saying was correct in theory but ran squarely against my experience on the ground. I took the risk and spoke.

"Mr. Secretary, these Islamist extremists, whether it's the Taliban or Hezbollah, make hundreds of millions off selling drugs to fund their terror. They justify it in their warped view of their religion because, number one, it's killing Western infidels, and number two, it allows them to buy the weapons and explosives to kill even more Westerners—including American soldiers. Eventually, it becomes our problem, sir," I said.

Rumsfeld furrowed his brow, stared at me long and hard, then looked at my boss, and said, "He needs to leave, and you need to make the State Department do their job."

I got up and walked out, thinking I was going to be fired. I wasn't, thank God, but it was a long time before I was invited to any more briefings with Secretary Rumsfeld.

Speaking truth to power doesn't mean you will get your way. Often, you won't. Often, speaking that truth will be a bad career move. I didn't care. As a servant leader, you have a moral obligation to think beyond your own career. I knew what it was like to be one of the only Americans in some of the most remote and dangerous places on earth. I owed it to my men to be candid with those responsible for crafting policies that could cost us the mission—and our lives.

Secretary Gates was firm but cordial to me. That's not always the case when you speak truth to power. While I was deployed with my reserve unit in eastern Afghanistan, Mike Vickers, the assistant secretary of defense for all Special Operations, came to see me at my base, after asking for me by name. The assistant secretary knew the war was not headed in the right direction, and he asked me—in front of two colonels who accompanied him—what was going wrong.

At the time I was a lowly major but I told him the truth. "Sir, we are often our own worst enemies, hamstrung by convoluted and bureaucratic approval processes. I have to fight the bureaucracy almost as hard as I fight the Taliban and al-Qaeda. My men call the fight out here counter-bureaucracy instead of counter-insurgency" I gave the assistant secretary a specific example. "Sir, when I wanted to go kill or capture a mid-tier Taliban commander, I have to seek *twelve* approvals from twelve different headquarters. It's insane."

The colonels present, who each helped design and implement exactly this system, were livid. I could see their faces distort. "Major Waltz, that's horseshit," said one. He turned to the assistant secretary. "We do *not* regularly disapprove missions."

The assistant secretary, himself a former Green Beret and CIA officer in his own right, didn't reply and looked back at me. I took that as a sign to continue. "Mr. Vickers, that's true. They don't regularly disapprove missions. They just question them to death until the target has moved on. What all those twelve layers of staff do is micromanage the mission, add on extraneous requirements needed for final approval, and dull the tip of the spear."

I explained to the assistant secretary that the approval process was so cumbersome that we had to plan attacks on the enemy a minimum of *one week* in advance—not because that's what was needed to take out the bad guy but because that's how long it took to obtain all the necessary approvals. It was war by committee, against an opponent that was nimble and had no bureaucracy to bog it down. The Taliban were outfoxing us not because they were better or smarter but because we had walked away from our principles as Green Berets and mired ourselves in risk aversion.

That exchange was a big deal in the Army world. When a colonel tells you that what you're saying is "horseshit" in front of an assistant secretary, it's career-on-the-line time. But I cared about my career a lot less than I cared about soldiers. That wasn't just courage. The great thing about being a Special Forces officer in the National Guard, mobilized for only a year, was that I had a whole other civilian career and life back home to go to. I had far less on the line than my active-duty

Brenda Waltz and six-year-old "Bear" (author) on the family farm outside Jacksonville, Florida, 1979.

Junior Class year at the Virginia Military Institute.

Dealing with a tough and crafty G-Chief during the Robin Sage exercise; the final step toward earning the green beret.
(Courtesy of Special Warfare)

Mother's Day in the mountains of eastern Afghanistan. We believed there was a realistic chance of being overrun by Taliban fighters in this isolated position so I wanted to be sure my mother had this photo.

A new class of special forces soldiers donning the green beret for the first time. The years of rigorous training instilled a new way of thinking and leading focused on strategic missions "by, with, and through" local forces.

(K. Kassen/Army)

Author advising and operating "by, with, and through" the Afghan National Police while on patrol alongside United Arab Emirates Special Operations Forces.

Author in local garb designed to blend in. Green Berets are specially trained on local cultures and languages.

Training Nigerian Navy SEALs on mission planning regarding operations to rescue school girls kidnapped by the terrorist group Boko Haram.

Winning the hearts and minds of the next generation in Niger through soccer.

Afghan "Jingle Truck," of the type used to hide a team of Green Berets, to conduct a raid on a Taliban commander. It was a risky, unconventional tactic that almost got me relieved of command.

Afghan Sergeant Major Sumar Ghul kneeling to the right while on patrol. My family has cared for his family since he died in my arms and kept his children out of Islamic extremist madrassa schools.

Leading the charge during the search for the deserter Private Bowe Bergdahl. His was the ultimate betrayal of his fellow soldiers and his country.

Discussing with President Trump and his National Security Advisor Robert O'Brien the need to keep Bagram Airfield in Afghanistan—the only base in the world neighboring China, Iran, and Russia. *(Courtesy of Doug Coulter)*

Afghan interpreter "Spartacus," who fought alongside my Green Berets and ultimately was beheaded by the Taliban. He was waiting on his Special Immigrant Visa approval to come to America.

Congressional hearing after the withdrawal from Afghanistan, pointing out that we now had zero bases to conduct counterterrorism operations against al-Qaeda and ISIS. *(Courtesy of C-SPAN)*

Washing the Vietnam Memorial Wall before Memorial Day with the National Park Service and veteran members of Congress from both sides of the aisle.

Bipartisan jump over Normandy out of the original C-47 that led the invasion fleet to honor the seventy-fifth anniversary of D-Day with ninety-two-year-old paratrooper Vincent Speranza.

On Air Force One with President Trump and minority leader Kevin McCarthy. RNC Co-Chair Tommy Hicks is discussing next steps in the US-Israel relationship.

President Trump and Vice President Pence at the historic SpaceX launch of two colonels into space from American soil for the first time in a decade.

(White House Archives)

Selfie with Elon Musk, an innovator and risk taker who embodies the Green Beret traits of adaptability and boldness while speaking truth to power.

An "American Dream" moment: My wife and Army veteran Julia Nesheiwat calling her mother, Hayat, a Jordanian Catholic who immigrated through Ellis Island, from Air Force One.

Discussing how national service leads to entrepreneurship with Israeli Prime Minister Benjamin Netanyahu.

Meeting with Prime Minister Narendra Modi. As Co-Chair of the India Caucus in the House, I believe the US-India relationship is one of the most critical of the twenty-first century.

(Courtesy House of Representatives photographer)

King Abdullah of Jordan: A true ally with the mindset of a Green Beret and one of the most impressive leaders I've met.

The ad that the NBA and the Chinese Communist Party didn't want you to see, featuring NBA player and human rights activist Enes Kanter Freedom, calling out the hypocrisy of corporations that preach social justice in America but turn a blind eye to genocide in China.

counterparts whose military careers would get cut short with one bad fitness report.

"Sir," I continued, speaking to the assistant secretary, "Taliban commanders regularly escape before we get the green light to kill or capture them. One of my Special Forces teams," I continued, "is required to submit our PowerPoint slides outlining our mission through twelve headquarters before we go after just one Taliban chief."

The assistant secretary's brow furrowed. "Name them," he said. It was a fair challenge. I needed to be ready. I was.

"The team must submit the mission request through me, the Special Forces battalion and group headquarters above me, and then to the commanding general for all Special Operations—that's four there. At the same time, the mission request has to go through the conventional battalion, the brigade, and their regional commanding general—that's seven. If they are using helicopters, then the aviation battalion and brigade will want to have eyes on it. That's nine." I ticked them off on my fingers.

"And finally, we always have a partnered force of Afghans, and their battalion, brigade, and Special Operations headquarters also want to know." I held up ten fingers, closed my fists, then held up two fingers on my left hand. Twelve.

The assistant secretary looked at me, shook his head, and turned to the colonels. "What the hell are we doing here?"

Before the colonels could respond, I decided to go for broke. I had something else I needed to say.

"Sir, the other key strategic issue is improving the fighting ability of our Afghan partners. It's our first priority. But let's not kid ourselves—it's going to be many years of advising and assisting them until they're ready to defend this country by themselves."

"That's not what I'm hearing at my level," the assistant secretary replied. "I've been briefed repeatedly that the Afghan Army is just around the corner to being able to operate on their own."

The thing about speaking truth to power is that once you start, it inspires others. Before I could answer the assistant secretary, one of my older Green Beret sergeants, a grizzled warrior who didn't give a damn about being diplomatic, spoke up. "They suck, sir. They're terrible. Most are illiterate or just need a job, and a meal, even though they don't get paid half the time. We will get them to a better place. We have no choice. It's the only way we will be able to leave here one day so that the Afghans can take care of the Taliban and al-Qaeda themselves. But it's going to take a very, very long time, just like it has taken decades with the Colombian, the Philippine, and South Korean armies. If anyone is briefing you otherwise, they're bullshitting you."

I nodded my agreement with my sergeant. I thought one of the colonels was going to have an aneurysm.

The "truth to power" moment didn't come without consequences. The colonels complained about me up through my chain of command, as I knew they would. The commanding general demanded my boss, a lieutenant colonel, fire me. To his credit, and my relief, he refused for the second time that tour. It was rare, but always welcome, to find a superior who positively valued hearing uncomfortable truths.

Over a decade later, as a member of Congress, I found myself in President Donald J. Trump's office in the front of Air Force One. Unlike how the media portrays him, President Trump loved gathering opinions. He truly listened and, in my experience, always welcomed hard truths. I took the opportunity to give my opinion about the situation in Afghanistan, and the Doha Agreement with the Taliban. "Mr. President, you're absolutely right that eventually all sides have to come to some sort of political agreement. But the Taliban will never honor the terms of this deal. They are evil, sick bastards and are telling us whatever they have to say to get us out so they can take over the country. I know you want our troops home, Mr. President. We all do. But we have to keep Bagram Airfield. It's the only base in the world sandwiched between Iran, Russia, and China. We can change the focus of what our guys are doing there, to only provide training, intelligence, and support while the Afghan Army does all the fighting."

"Michael, you are a warrior," President Trump replied. "We've been there so long. It's time. I told the leader of the Taliban that we will bomb the hell out of him if he gets out of line."

"Right on, Mr. President. We just have to leave some kind of Special Operations and intel there to keep a lid on al-Qaeda and ISIS, or they will come roaring back. Obama didn't have a plan when he pulled out of Iraq, and that led to the rise of ISIS and their attacks all over the world. Then he had to send *more* troops back to clean it up."

"Yes," acknowledged the President, "I had to clean up Obama's mess, and we destroyed ISIS. Okay, Michael. I hear you. I saw you on TV talking about this. If they don't honor the deal, we'll see. Keep talking to O'Brien and Pompeo about it. Thank you for being such a fighter."

Ultimately, he reduced the number of U.S. troops, but listened to his national security team when they told him the Taliban hadn't lived up to the conditions in the deal. He kept a small force and that critical base just a few hundred miles from China's western border.

In President Trump, we had a commander in chief willing to be challenged. He made himself available, listened, and welcomed opposing views. He was constantly probing, "What do you think of this position? How is Secretary So-and-So doing?"

I didn't have that relationship with his successor. Like many who had served, I was stunned and horrified when a newly inaugurated President Biden announced a full withdrawal of Afghanistan to be complete by September 11, 2021. Unable to reach the President, I found myself speaking truth to the ultimate power in our democracy—the American people. Along with several Democrats who were also veterans, we held multiple press conferences about the need to get American citizens, our interpreters, and the Afghans who fought alongside us out before we withdrew our troops and shut down our bases.

What appalled and worried us was that the State Department had made no plans to include Americans, our interpreters, and other key figures of Afghan civil society in our withdrawal plans. When I questioned the general in charge of the Middle East on the matter, he gave me a very concerning reply.

"Congressman," said the general, "my mission as it stands is to get our troops out. As you know, a withdrawal in the face of enemy pressure is the most dangerous type of mission. If I'm ordered to slow down to help with certain groups of Afghans or our NATO allies, then we will be prepared to do so, but that will increase risk to our forces."

I was astounded. In effect, this general was telling me that there was no serious plan to get our people out in time.

I went on television and social media sounding the alarm bells and questioning the administration's overall policy. I noted that never in our history have we pulled our troops out in the face of the enemy before we have our civilians and allies safe. I demanded that we establish Guam or our bases in the Middle East as refugee centers, and I asked that the President keep our presence in Afghanistan until we honored our promises to those that stood with us.

None of it happened. President Biden stubbornly pressed on. Disaster followed. And the entire world tragically learned how important it is for those in power to have a receptive ear to the hard truth when it is spoken to them.

I am only one of 435 members of the House. Nonetheless, I have constitutional authority as a member of Congress. Since the day I was sworn in, I have done everything I can to be the sort of leader to whom truth can be spoken—even if it's not what I want to hear. To be a representative doesn't just mean listening to hard truths. It means that once I've heard them, I have an obligation to use my power to take meaningful action. My office has become a place where active-duty military and veterans can bring their issues with the Defense Department. A number of cadets, soldiers, and their families have brought me material on a quasi-whistleblower basis, asking me to look into serious matters.

Much of the material that has been passed on to my office concerns some highly politicized curriculum taught at our military academies. In 2020, one West Point cadet approached my office with information about a lecture given at the academy by a Dr. Carol Anderson. Entitled "Understanding Your Whiteness and White Rage," the lecture made the case that white people are outraged by Black advancement and that the Republican Party platform is rooted in white supremacy. Before acting, I spoke multiple times to the cadet, who was very nervous about some form of retribution from their superiors at West Point. I wanted to ensure they were comfortable with how I intended to call the Army leadership to the carpet.

With the cadet's consent, I sent a letter to the Superintendent of West Point. An excerpt:

These critical race theory teachings . . . pit cadets against one another through divisive indoctrination under the pressure of "wokeism." There is no doubt our country has had to overcome atrocious racial bigotry. We have made enormous progress and there is still much to be done in our country. But, the United States military, uniquely in American society, must strive to unify. Unfortunately, these seminars imbue in our future military leaders that they should treat their fellow officers and soldiers differently based on race and on socio-economic background. In a combat environment, where every soldier must equally share the burden of danger, I cannot think of a notion more destructive to unit cohesion and morale.

Consequently, as a member of the U.S. House Armed Services Committee I am requesting that you provide the full presentation of these seminars, presentations, assemblies, and other related curricula to my office so that the Congress can execute its oversight responsibilities of the U.S. Army and the U.S. Military Academy. I look forward to your prompt response.

I did several follow-up segments on national television, raising awareness of the issue.

On June 23, 2021, Secretary of Defense Lloyd Austin and Joint Chiefs Chairman Mark Milley testified before the House

Armed Services Committee. Responding to a query from Representative Matt Gaetz, the Defense Secretary claimed that critical race theory is not taught in the military. I was next in line for questions and said, "Mr. Secretary, I find your statement remarkable. I have here my letter to the West Point Superintendent and his reply, indicating that this 'White Rage' lecture was indeed provided at West Point and that *Critical Race Theory 101* is a textbook offered in the curriculum."

After some back-and-forth, Secretary Austin conceded that neither the lecture in particular nor an overt focus on race in general are appropriate at the academy. General Milley then jumped in and offered an astonishing diatribe on the importance of cadets understanding the history of race relations. He added, "I want to understand my white rage."

In his four-star dress uniform, at a public hearing that went viral, General Milley became a symbol for a politicized military.

The issue wasn't a concern about about history courses. We were pushing back against indoctrination that sows suspicion and mistrust. Critical race theory tells our soldiers that the United States and the U.S. military are systemically racist *today*, not generations ago. How can we expect our best and brightest to put their lives on the line for institutions that they are taught are inherently misogynist, colonialist, and racist? As I told General Milley, "Our enemies' bullets could not care less about race, religion, or gender. They only care that they are killing Americans."

I was pilloried by the media for the exchange but stood my ground. Keeping our military, a meritocracy, focused on winning wars isn't just my pet issue, it's critical to our survival as a free people. And it was an important reminder. Sometimes speaking truth to power isn't summoning up the nerve to have some straight talk with your boss, or even the President. Sometimes, it's challenging conventional wisdom at the risk of tremendous blowback. Cancel culture is all too real—and it takes real courage to challenge the political agendas that have captured so many of our institutions and done such harm to our common life as Americans.

In order to speak truth to power, you need more than courage. You need to first discern what that truth is. As Green Berets, we prize our ability to listen, to connect, to navigate past emotion and danger to find out what really matters most. We strive not just to be smarter but to be wiser. We want to be sure that when we do find the courage to say what needs saying, we are saying the right thing.

Some of the greatest regrets of my life are moments when I could have spoken truth to power but did not. Some of the proudest moments of my military, business, and congressional career have come when I have found the guts to take the risk to speak up and drive change. In these uncertain—and frankly, dishonest—times, we all need to find the courage to confront power with truth. And those of us who have power? To borrow a line from a famous movie, we have the moral obligation to be strong enough "to handle the truth."

Truth spoken to power can change the course of history. In May 1940, even as Hitler had much of Europe on the ropes, President Franklin Roosevelt was under tremendous pressure to cut rather than increase defense spending. As hard as it may be to believe in retrospect, most Americans at the time thought we spent too much on the military. FDR, anxious to preserve his popularity in an election year, was inclined to agree. Treasury Secretary Henry Morgenthau and Army Chief of Staff George C. Marshall went to the White House to try to talk the President out of his planned cuts. The meeting was brief. FDR was firm, telling Marshall and Morgenthau that his decision was final.

As the President dismissed them, Marshall stood and asked for three additional minutes to make his case. Everyone else in the room was stunned—FDR had fired generals for less. Something in the urgency in Marshall's tone got through to the President, and he chose to listen. In a brief, impassioned tirade, the general risked his career to make a single point: Hitler was a much graver threat than anyone realized. America's survival—the survival of democracy—hinged on not only on reversing the decision to cut the defense budget but increasing it substantially. Marshall could barely field fifteen thousand soldiers while Germany was equipping nearly two million. America had to get ready.

His three desperate minutes up, Marshall waited. FDR looked at him. Finally, the President spoke: "Come back tomorrow, and we'll discuss this." When Marshall returned the next day, the President agreed to take a proposal for a massive increase in defense spending to Congress. Had Marshall not risked his career by challenging a very determined (and often short-tempered) commander in chief, the entire course of history would have been different. He could have easily convinced himself that he tried alongside the Secretary of the Treasury, and that was good enough. Put simply, the Western world survived because Marshall had the guts to go the extra mile, risked telling the most powerful man on the planet that he was dead wrong, and convinced him to change course.

As a Green Beret now in a position of some authority, I have an obligation to foster an environment that allows truth to be spoken to me. Encouraging my team to speak truth to power is essential for bottom-up leadership and servant leadership. I also have to make myself available to my constituents who are living with the consequences—good and bad—of the policies we create in Washington. We owe it to the men and women we represent to leave everything on the table, even— and *especially*—if we know it is unwelcome and may even put our careers and reputations at risk. One simply cannot exercise the traits outlined in this book—trust, determination, resilience, restraint—if they are not allowed the freedom to challenge power. It's absolutely essential to thinking, leading, and tackling life like a Green Beret.

12

PERSISTENCE

August 15, 2021. I was half-awake when my phone buzzed. A text news alert: Kabul had fallen.

I lay back, stared at the screen, and felt the emotions course through me.

I had seen this moment coming. It was still hard to take in. So much sacrifice given, so much blood spilled, so much time and treasure spent—and all so the enemy could take over Afghanistan and create a sanctuary for terrorists to threaten America once more. I was angry, of course, and worried for those we had left behind. I was also deeply concerned about the message that a reckless, rushed, and irresponsible withdrawal would send to the rest of the world—especially our enemies.

In the years since we left Afghanistan, I've come to see the withdrawal as something else: the direct opposite of the virtues I've put forward in this book. Each of the previous chapters has highlighted a particular quality that the Green Berets exemplify. Each of those qualities is something the leaders of the Biden administration either willfully ignored or failed to understand. The administration failed to adapt, it failed to allow for bottom-up leadership, it failed to be bold, it failed to show discipline or resilience. Above all else, the Biden administration lacked persistence and betrayed the trust of our Afghan allies, of our brave American servicemen and servicewomen, and of our Gold Star families. What happened with the fall of Kabul and the subsequent fiasco was the culmination of a series of failures, bad policy decisions, and foolish choices. In sum, our withdrawal was a textbook example of how rejecting the most important virtues leads, invariably, to failure.

The defenders of Biden's Afghanistan policy point out that he inherited a mess that had snowballed over twenty years. That's true. There are many things we should have done better in the conduct of the war. We made many mistakes long before President Biden was sworn in: allowing the Taliban sanctuary in Pakistan, outsourcing the lead for the effort to our European NATO allies during the depths of the Iraq War, and doing a poor job of holding the Afghan government to account. Only later in the war did we focus on the vital job of mentoring the Afghan military. These were just some of our failures, and none of them started with Joe Biden. Other presidents had grown frustrated with the slow pace of progress and the tremendous cost of the war.

As Green Berets, we rarely got the opportunity to pick the cards we were dealt. We played the hand we were given as best we could, according to our training, our experience, and by our moral compass. President Biden didn't pick the cards he was dealt. But he chose to play those cards horribly and then refused to take responsibility for it.

Americans do not live in a bubble. I have argued for years that terrorism will follow us home if we allow it. Avoiding all "foreign entanglements" in the hopes that isolationism will buy us peace and security is an idea that has tempted people across the political spectrum for generations. It is, with respect, a naive fantasy to imagine that our enemies around the world are only our enemies because of our foreign policy. Dictators and terrorists hate us, not because of our actions, but because our basic principles are a threat to their rule. They don't hate Americans because the United States has military bases abroad. They hate us because they despise our ideals and our identity. If we don't fight the war on terrorism in places like Kandahar, that war will come to places like Kansas City. That's not hyperbole—it is historical fact.

The voices pressing for withdrawal from Afghanistan were loud on the far left and right. They missed the fact that we have had troops in Colombia for decades dealing with cartels, in South Korea and Japan for seventy years providing stability to Asia, and still have troops in Iraq targeting ISIS. "Bring the troops home" is an easy slogan to say. We all wanted them home. I didn't want to attend one more funeral at Arlington National Cemetery any more than anyone else. But perhaps the only thing worse would be to attend another civilian funeral from another attack on the homeland.

Biden's defenders like to claim that his hands were tied

by the Doha Agreement, which was negotiated during the Trump administration. I want to be clear; nothing in the Doha Agreement called for such a shambolic and chaotic withdrawal. Nothing in the Doha Agreement required America to abandon our allies and more than eight hundred American citizens.

I pointed out on a national television interview, "President Biden has had no issue backing away from many of his predecessor's policies. From canceling the Keystone XL pipeline, to reentering the Paris Climate Accords, to trying to reenter the Iran deal, to reversing polices on America's southern border like Remain in Mexico. On a dozen different fronts, Biden reversed the decisions of the Trump administration. Yet Biden expects us to believe that when it came to Afghanistan, his hands were tied. It's a bunch of crap."

When President Trump left office, we still had a small force of twenty-five hundred U.S. troops in Afghanistan, accompanied by a much larger NATO force and contractors to advise the Afghans on technical issues such as keeping their planes flying. The Trump administration very deliberately kept Bagram Airfield operational, the only American base in the world sandwiched among China, Russia, and Iran. At the end of the day, even though he wanted out as well, President Trump listened to his advisors like Ambassador Robert O'Brien, Director of National Intelligence John Ratcliffe, and Secretary of State Mike Pompeo when they told him the Taliban had not lived up to their end of the deal. Trump adapted. He said the deal was off. He left a contingent force of Special Operations

Forces and intelligence officers to keep a lid on terrorism and an eye on China.

In April 2021, when Biden announced the final timeline for withdrawal, I held a joint press conference with fellow Republican and Democrat veterans in Congress along with the American Legion. We demanded the State and Defense Departments start getting our people out immediately. We called on President Biden to begin evacuating any Americans still there and to make sure that our interpreters and others who had fought with us were granted the Special Immigrant Visas (SIV) we had promised.

The SIV program allowed an interpreter to qualify for a visa to the United States after fighting alongside U.S. forces for two years. This was about loyalty. Our interpreters didn't just put their lives on the line to fight alongside us; they put their entire families' lives at risk, too. The Taliban didn't just come after the person that they believe betrayed their narrow version of Islam—they went after every last relative they could find, mafia style. We badly needed them, too, because going without an interpreter was like going without a radio. As Green Berets, we needed to win hearts and minds. We have language training, but we would never master the local vernacular as a native could. That's not just true in Afghanistan—it's true all over the world. If the world saw that we didn't honor our promises, who else would trust us? Without that trust, we couldn't operate abroad.

I was as clear as I could be in the press conference. "How

many future Afghan families, how many great American contributions will we not have if President Biden does not act, and act now?" I said. "If he does not act and does not get these people out, blood with be on his hands and his administration's hands.

"The time for talk and debate is over. We have a moral and national security obligation to get these people out. Evacuate them now. We've done it before; we can do it again. If the President doesn't start pulling our allies out, if you pull our military assets out before our allies, you are consigning them to death. These people shared our values and were willing to fight and die for us. We must honor our promises."

We also called on the White House to surge State Department employees to accelerate the processing of the tens of thousands of backlogged visa applications and consolidate the already approved Afghans in various hubs around the country while we still had some military capability there. We pleaded with the administration to keep the major air base in Bagram open, so they could start evacuating people to Guam or one of our bases in the Gulf. Those of us who had witnessed the Taliban's ruthlessness up close knew exactly what they were going to do when they took power. I got some pushback from people who were worried about the immigration issue. I told them that if there was ever an immigrant who deserved to legally come to America, it was those who were willing to fight and die with U.S. soldiers, and most, if not all, agreed.

We reminded people that in Vietnam, President Gerald

Ford did the right thing. Ford showed leadership and loyalty, and he directed Henry Kissinger to come up with a plan. He directed the military and State Department to form a task force dedicated to airlifting those who stood with us and faced certain execution from the North Vietnamese. Through Operations New Life and Frequent Wind, the United States successfully evacuated or rescued over 138,000 people over a period of several months in 1975. With the unhappy exception of the Montagnards tribespeople, the Ford administration didn't abandon our allies, and two generations later, we have a thriving Vietnamese American community, including my former executive officer France Hoang, who graduated West Point and became a successful entrepreneur. For Afghanistan, Joe Biden had the means and the moral obligation to do what Ford had done in Vietnam. Biden chose not to do it.

In congressional hearings, I pushed to ensure we were capable of getting our people out. The Defense Department representative was cagey on the subject. In response to my question, he carefully replied, "Yes, if ordered by the President, DOD could begin airlifting our allies to Guam, bases in the Middle East, or anywhere else so directed."

I asked the Chairman of the Joint Chiefs, General Milley himself, and he confirmed the military was focused on getting our troops out as fast as possible and that they *could* shift operations to evacuate. All these "coulds" bothered me. Resilience, determination, and loyalty—those require more than "coulds." They require commitment. Instead of commitment, the people who had given us their devotion were abandoned and left to the mercy of the Taliban. They weren't abandoned because we lacked the *ability* to protect them. They were abandoned because we lacked the will.

All that was needed to save countless lives was an order from the President—and that order never came.

I've made the case that it's essential to speak truth to power. It's also a basic requirement of leadership that you listen to the truth when it's spoken. That didn't happen. As documents later confirmed during the investigation into the withdrawal, the White House was warned repeatedly that without U.S. air support and without the contractors that maintained the Afghan Air Force, the Afghan military wouldn't last long. Three four-star generals—the field commander, General Austin Miller; the commander for all forces in the Middle East, General Frank McKenzie; and the Chairman of the Joint Chiefs, General Milley—all recommended the U.S. leave a residual force in a supporting role for the Afghan Army. More than two dozen diplomats in Kabul issued a formal (and rare) cable directly to the Secretary of State dissenting with how the withdrawal was being conducted. The diplomats predicted that the government would fall within weeks of our final withdrawal. The diplomats and generals spoke truth—bottom-up leadership at its most vital. Power wasn't listening.

In July 2021, Afghan President Ashraf Ghani made a last-ditch visit to Washington, DC, to see Congress and President

Biden. At a dinner the night before his Oval Office meeting, he had a singular request—airpower. "The Taliban forces are out in the open. If you hit them now, you can destroy large numbers of their forces and blunt their momentum."

Standing at a long table of forty people from across the country who had invested decades of their lives in the Afghanistan war, Ghani pleaded, "Please do all you can to press President Biden for American air support in the short term. Secondly, please—we must find a way to allow your contractors to return to provide maintenance for the Afghan Air Force. Without your contractors, we are literally grounded. Without them, all is lost. We are not asking for any more U.S. troops in Afghanistan. We understand that decision is past us. But we need to provide our army some air support to buy us time until the winter. Then we will regroup and go on the counteroffensive."

President Ghani didn't just ask for air support and contractors. He explained that the Taliban were winning the messaging war, telling Afghan forces that they might as well surrender—the Americans were sure to abandon them. Ghani pleaded for a "different narrative," from Washington, one that said that while the American military might be leaving, America would not abandon the Afghan people.

I was the first to speak after Ghani's plea. I stood up across the table from Generals David Petraeus and Jack Keane. "Mr. President, I want you to hear me loud and clear. The Congress stands with the Afghan people against the brutality they will face if the Taliban are successful. We could fill this room with stacks of think tank reports on the mistakes we've made—both your government and mine—in this war. But that does not mean we can now turn our backs on terrorism and evil and pretend like it will magically go away. We know this cancer will spread. What happens in Afghanistan will not stay in Afghanistan."

The next day, when President Ghani walked into the meeting with Speaker Nancy Pelosi and Minority Leader Kevin McCarthy, I'll never forget thinking I was seeing a dead man walking. The mood was heavy. The message he had received from President Biden was grim: "You are on your own."

Just weeks later, Kabul fell to the Taliban. The way it fell was not inevitable. It was a consequence of inaction, dithering, and misplaced trust in some of the worst people on earth. It was inexcusable, unconscionable, and a scandal that shocked the soul of this nation.

As I watched the news, I kept thinking of my interpreter Spartacus. He had saved our lives, been our friend, and loved America. The Taliban had beheaded him in front of his family. The thought of that happening over and over again as they hunted down every Afghan who believed in America, who believed in our ideals of liberty and freedom, was too much to bear. I watched in anger and deep sadness as desperate Afghans fell from our cargo planes as the enemy took Kabul. So many people had believed until the end that America would be resilient, determined, and relentless in fighting extremism. They clung to those planes as they took off from the airport in

Kabul because somehow, they still believed in us. It was soul crushing.

As the situation deteriorated, I received a flood of texts, emails, and direct messages on social media from Afghans I had worked with over the years. Many were harrowing:

> *Pres. Biden, We are your allies. America promised us.*
> *Now we are left behind and live in prisons. No routes*
> *open to escape this prison. Waited 4yrs & was in last*
> *stage of SIV. No call & email. Sir, you breached your*
> *Promise. Last tweet.*[3]

My office was flooded with calls. I was in a position of influence—but not in charge. It was the most frustrating experience of my life. The stories I heard were harrowing. I received desperate call after call from my interpreter Rahim. He is on the cover of my first book, *Warrior Diplomat*, and is now an American citizen in Texas. "They caught my cousin," Rahim sobbed. "You remember him; he served you food in the mess hall. The Talibs tied him behind one of their trucks and dragged him to death through the village and said this is what happens to anyone who worked for the Americans."

3 Ahmad (@Ahm88672531Amir), Twitter, August 29, 2021, 5:02 p.m., https: //twitter.com/Ahm88672531Amir/status/1432086220046278662.

I spoke to another just-evacuated Afghan during a visit to a relocation camp in Quantico, Virginia. He told me of his harrowing ordeal of being beaten night after night as he tried to pass through the Taliban checkpoints, only to be repeatedly rejected by the State Department officers at Kabul airport for having incomplete paperwork. He started over again, day after day, until he was finally able to hand a phone to the Marine standing post on the barbed wire. On the other end of the line was a veteran back in the United States that the interpreter had served with years before. The Marine took pity on him, and he finally made it out. Once safely in the States, he got a call about his favorite nephew, only ten years old, still back in Afghanistan. "We have him," the voice of a Taliban fighter said on the other end. "Either you come back here, coward, to face Taliban justice—or your nephew will." The Taliban's sadistic reach followed refugees around the world.

It was not limited to Afghans. For days, we had an American couple, both in their eighties and diabetic, stuck near a bridge that marked Afghanistan's border with Tajikistan. The Taliban let them through on one side of the bridge, but the Tajik border guards would not allow them to pass on the other side. They were Americans, but they didn't have the right papers. They did have a cell phone and somehow managed to get in touch with one of the veterans' groups and even a celebrity, John Ondrasik of the band Five for Fighting. They desperately contacted my office. For days, my team and I called every Tajik official we could. I fired off a formal letter to the Tajik ambassador and foreign minister. Eventually, word filtered down from the capital, Dushanbe, down to the border guards on that bridge who finally let the couple across to safety. Those poor people shouldn't have been left behind in the first place. Once we knew their location, we should have sent a helicopter in to get them. But all our military assets were gone. The Defense and State Departments didn't get them out, so we did. I'm proud of that—but also frustrated. It shouldn't have fallen to a congressman's office and veterans' groups to do the State Department's job. And every time Secretary of State Antony Blinken came on national media essentially blaming the U.S. citizens left behind saying, "Americans in Afghanistan were repeatedly warned to leave," I wanted to throw my phone at the television.

My former executive officer on my last tour to Afghanistan, France Hoang, himself a refugee immigrant from Vietnam, stood up the organization Allied Airlift 21 from scratch because he couldn't just stand by and do nothing. He soon found himself figuring out how to charter private aircraft that were willing to go into the war zone, all while clandestinely communicating with former Afghan soldiers and interpreters to gather them in safe houses and try to coordinate their escape. After the last U.S. forces closed the gates and left Kabul, France and his team refused give up. He figured out how to remotely charter buses to get dozens of allies across Afghanistan through Taliban checkpoints from Kabul to the only remaining airport in the northern part of the country still accepting international departures. He and his team shuffled them from house to house to stay a step ahead of Taliban search teams. They virtually collected documents, created manifests, raised money, and pitched in huge sums of their own savings to honor America's promise to our fellow Americans and those who fought with us. He had to beg the State Department every day to give assurances to the governments of Qatar, the UAE, Kosovo, and other countries that the U.S. government would take responsibility for these refugees if they were allowed to land.

"Every day, my disgust with the U.S. government is countered with how proud I am of my fellow vets for giving so much of their time or treasure to do what they know is right. What's happening right now is the opposite of everything we learned at West Point. It's un-American," France told me during one late-night conversation. I felt the same way. The only glimmer of light in these dark days was the grassroots groups like Task Force Pineapple, Save Our Allies, and Digital Dunkirk—many of them Green Berets—that stepped up to bring out as many comrades as they could.

For me, all of this was happening as I was getting married. My wife, Julia, is also a veteran of Afghanistan and Iraq, so thankfully, she was understanding that I was constantly checking my phone for the latest desperate plea for help. I walked out in the middle of our rehearsal dinner to do an appearance on Bret Baier's show on Fox News. President Biden had said that the Taliban were letting Americans through their checkpoints with no problems and that al-Qaeda was gone. "This administration is either lying, ignorant, or both," I replied, shaking my head.

When I was done, I looked at Julia and said, "Honey, we have to postpone the honeymoon. I can't in good conscience go sit on a beach and drink fruity drinks while our brothers are begging for help." My bride was in full agreement with me. Vacation could wait.

We flew straight back to Washington, DC. Days later, thirteen Americans and more than 170 Afghans died in the Abbey Gate suicide bombing that took place in the final tumultuous hours of the withdrawal. Every veteran watching the throngs of people pressing against the U.S. perimeter knew it was only a matter of time. The Pentagon and White House had agreed to the completely asinine construct of having the Taliban help us screen the crowds for ISIS suicide bombers. But the instinct to lock everything down in response to the threat of suicide bombers conflicted with the mission to help Afghans get out. Those Marines and soldiers were ordered to do an impossible mission—to both protect the gates to the airport but also keep them open.

When the news broke of the bombing, I was on the phone with the Vice President of Afghanistan, Amrullah Saleh, who had not fled the country but was rather holed up north of Kabul in the historic stronghold of the Panjshir Valley. He was with Ahmad Massoud, the son of the famous Lion of the Panjshir, Ahmad Shah Massoud, who had heroically resisted both the Soviets and the Taliban in the 1980s and '90s. They had begun calling me their new Charlie Wilson, after the Texas congressman who helped the mujahedeen fight the Soviets and was made famous by the movie *Charlie Wilson's War*. I tried my best to manage their expectations and reminded them that President Reagan was on board with Congressman Wilson's efforts while Biden's team would no longer return my calls. I was able to arrange several national media interviews for Saleh and Massoud to raise awareness that some Afghans were still standing strong in the face of terror. We also pointed out that America still had policy choices other than making a deal with the devil in the Taliban.

"Congressman, my sincere condolences on this attack," Vice President Saleh said. "You and I know the terrorists will not stop with this bombing. Their jihad will not stop at the borders of Afghanistan. They will never stop until someone stops them with steel. We will fight them as long as possible. I know you will do your best to send us whatever support you can."

"I will," I replied. It was a desperate plea. I could barely speak.

Weeks later, the once impenetrable Panjshir Valley fell to the onslaught of the Taliban riding in American-made armored vehicles with American weapons. The proud people of the Panjshir, who had resisted invaders from Alexander the Great to the Soviets to the Taliban in the 1990s were slaughtered.

The last plane went wheels up on August 30, and I was

physically sick, exhausted, and angry. Most of all, I was disappointed in myself. I felt I was in a position to effect change and failed.

My old friend Lieutenant Colonel (Ret.) Scott Mann, the man who built Task Force Pineapple (one of the most effective and remarkable ad hoc groups that rescued our interpreters), tried to reassure me. "No, Mike. You did make a difference. You channeled the moral injury every one of us are feeling every time you went on television. We all knew your outrage was coming from the heart. We needed a messenger that was authentic and knew what the hell he was talking about. You might not have been able to get Biden to listen to you, but we all knew you were listening to us. And that mattered."

I hope he was right.

In my congressional offices in DC and Florida, my staff who normally dealt with expired passports and social security checks were working 24/7 fielding desperate calls from soldiers seeking help for their Afghan contacts—or directly from desperate Afghans themselves who heard my office was helping people.

Officials at the State Department stopped returning our calls. It probably didn't help that I was raking them over the coals on national television on a daily basis. We were enraged every time Secretary of State Blinken stood before the cameras and said that fewer than one hundred Americans who wanted to leave were still left behind. We knew that number was way off, and he was downplaying it. A year later, that number was quietly revised to "over eight hundred." Adding insult to injury, President Biden stood before the world and declared the evacuation was an "outstanding success."

The sacred principle to never, ever leave a fallen comrade on the battlefield was drilled into me and every veteran out there on day one of taking the oath. Now we were abandoning twenty years' worth of relationships that were born in blood.

Special operators are used to solving the most complex problems imaginable. The sense of powerlessness in the face of this betrayal hit many of them hard. In the days and weeks that followed the fall of Kabul, I spoke to Green Berets who quit their jobs to be able to devote themselves full-time to helping their former Afghan brothers escape. Many of them were blowing through their personal savings. One even exhausted his kids' college savings accounts.

"I just can't stop answering the phone," he told me with tears welling up in his eyes. "I can't abandon them and leave them to die. I hope my kids will understand one day." His marriage had survived multiple combat tours—but it did not survive the aftermath of the botched evacuation. Scott Mann told me he had to bring in mental health professionals to counsel these veterans. "Mike, these guys will not let it go. They won't just walk away. So many of them had found a way to heal and move forward after their tours downrange and now this. It's eating them alive." Once again, they were being asked to be mentally and emotionally resilient, to callus their hearts, to suck it up. Sadly, this time, it wasn't from the actions of our enemies in combat; it was from the incompetence of our own government.

I reminded my fellow Afghanistan veterans that their sacrifice was not in vain every chance I could.

"For all of you veterans out there wondering, 'What was all of it for? What was the point?' You kept an entire generation of Americans safe from terrorism. No one had to wonder if another plane was going to fly into a building or if a suicide bomber was going to blow up a school bus, because you kept the fighting over there and not here. You should be proud of that."

The courage, determination, resilience, adaptability, and discipline our soldiers showed for twenty years in Afghanistan had kept the homeland secure. Green Berets in particular understand that not everyone can do what we do. However, we hope that our leaders share our values and understand our sacrifice. For countless veterans, the Biden withdrawal was shattering because it was so painfully clear that too many of our leaders did not share those values, much less understand the sacrifice. I was not surprised to learn that calls from veterans to the suicide-prevention hotline skyrocketed after the fall of Kabul.

As worried as I was about getting those who had helped us to freedom, and as concerned as I was about the mental health of my fellow veterans who were moving heaven on earth to help, something else upset me more. I knew that sooner or later, future Green Berets and American soldiers were going to have to clean up the mess. I made the case relentlessly in hearings, on television, and at yet another hearing with the Secretary of Defense, the Chairman of the Joint Chiefs, and General McKenzie:

"Let's compare Barack Obama's 2011 withdrawal from Iraq. He yanked all of our troops out with no follow-on plan to help the government keep terrorism there under control. Three years later, al-Qaeda morphs into ISIS; an even more extreme and brutal version of itself, and explodes on the scene to quickly take over an area the size of Texas. They launched a bloody reign of terror across the Middle East, Europe, and even the United States. We all remember that ISIS fighters gruesomely beheaded Americans and posted it on jihadi websites—and inspired the attacks in San Bernardino, the Pulse Nightclub, and all over Europe."

Holding up a map of the Middle East in the first hearing with the Joint Chiefs Chairman, General Milley, and Secretary of Defense Austin, I stated, "Here's the big difference: when we had to send troops back into Iraq, we had bases in Turkey, Israel, Jordan, and the Gulf States. We had local allies on the ground in the Kurds to help us, and we had the cooperation of the Iraqi government and army in our ultimately successful fight against ISIS. But here's my question: Should we face attacks on the homeland from Afghanistan yet again, General McKenzie? Do we have any bases in Afghanistan?"

"No, Congressman, we do not," he replied.

"Any bases in a neighboring country?" I asked.

"No, Congressman."

"Any local allies?"

"Congressman, we have some options—" he started to reply.

"No, we don't," I snapped back. "If you are referring to the former Northern Alliance, you know that they are being hunted down as we speak with our own damn equipment. Every day, I'm receiving videos of beheadings and torture from people in hiding and desperate for help.

"And what has me so damn mad is that future soldiers, the next generation after you have retired, will have to go back to deal with the mess this administration is leaving them. That you, gentlemen, are leaving them."

We later learned that the suicide bomber at Abbey Gate was with ISIS and had been released from the prison at Bagram Airfield weeks earlier. We also learned that our Marine snipers identified the suicide bomber early on the morning of the attack. Marine Sergeant Tyler Vargas-Andrews, who would lose both legs and an arm in the attack, sought permission to take out a man who matched the description of the bomber. His commanding officer denied him permission. As he would later testify, "We made everyone on the ground aware. Plain and simple, we were ignored. Our expertise was disregarded. No one was held accountable for our safety."[4]

---

4 "McCaul Requests Interview with Sniper's Commanding Officer at Abbey Gate on Anniversary of Fall of Afghanistan," Foreign Affairs Committee, August 15, 2023, https://foreignaffairs.house.gov/press-release/mccaul

The uproar from the hearing drove a follow-up investigation that concluded the commanding officer made the right call. The actual bomber was a different man. For years the Marine believed he could have stopped the attack and, sadly, it took Congressional pressure to bring him the truth.

What infuriated me most was that this was a betrayal of the families of the thirteen servicemembers lost at Abbey Gate. For two years, these families suffered in silence searching for answers and accountability for what happened to their loved ones. I periodically met with some of them, but as a member of the House minority, I was powerless to demand hearings and subpoena witnesses. I had engaged the Gold Star community and their grief throughout my career, but I had never come across families so frustrated and angry with their own government. Once in the majority, I worked with the Chairman of the Foreign Affairs Committee, Mike McCaul, along with fellow veteran members like Representatives Darrell Issa, Brian Mast, and Cory Mills to have hearings and give a voice to these families. Mark Schmitz, father of fallen Marine Corps Lance Corporal Jared Schmitz, perhaps summed up the frustrations of the Abbey Gate families. "We're knee-deep in bullshit," he said after two maddening years of trying to get answers to their questions while coming to grips with the total lack of accountability in the Biden administration for the debacle.

-requests-interview-with-snipers-commanding-officer-at-abbey-gate-on
-anniversary-of-fall-of-afghanistan/.

Several mothers recounted how they had received differing stories on how their sons and daughters died and had difficulty in receiving all their personal effects.

The next day, I called President Trump and asked if he would mind visiting with the families up in his club in Bedminster, New Jersey. It was a quick conversation. "Michael, let's get them up here. I would be happy to spend time with them. They have sacrificed so much. Let's do it. See you soon," he said.

President Trump was originally scheduled to spend an hour and a half with the Abbey Gate Gold Star families. He ended up spending the entire evening. He spoke to each of the families individually, held a round table to listen to their issues collectively, took photos with them, and signed their loved ones' photos. To top it off, he invited them to dinner at the club restaurant. By the end of the evening, we had closed it down. These mothers who had suffered so much were laughing, crying, and telling stories of happy times with their fallen heroes. The President pulled out his iPad and played Frank Sinatra songs and selections from his favorite musicals. When Paula Knauss Selph, mother of Staff Sergeant Ryan Knauss, and her husband, Mark, got up to dance, several other couples joined them. Two of the mothers told me that it was the best thing that had happened to them since losing their children.

In this disastrous withdrawal, we painfully witnessed what happens when our national leaders display the *exact opposite* of the essential qualities of a Green Beret. The way we walked away from Afghanistan in 2021 is not just a footnote in history or an unhappy story rapidly fading into memory. It is an indictment of a rudderless and morally bankrupt Washington, DC. Personally I will continue to fight, as long as it takes, for a much fuller reckoning with what happened before, during, and after that debacle.

We don't need that reckoning for the sake of settling political scores. We need it to remind ourselves of the immense cost of abandoning our allies, of backing down in the face of evil—and of betraying our own American character. We must be persistent in the search of the truth and accountability for those Gold Star families, for our veterans, for our allies left behind, and for our fellow Americans who could once again be in harm's way if we don't reckon with hard truths.

13

Those of us who stand for a strong military that keeps the peace are sometimes called hawks or even warmongers by those who would rather we retreat into wishful isolation than do what it takes to lead the free world. There are very few in Congress who have seen the horrors of war. I have seen the consequences of both boldness and appeasement, and I know full well that the latter is far deadlier. I have felt a man's dying breath, seen friends killed and families destroyed. There is nothing I want more than to prevent that from happening ever again. I know, too, as Ronald Reagan knew, that lasting peace comes only from the projection of strength. At the 1980 Republican convention, he said, "We know only too well that war comes not when the forces of freedom are strong, but when they are weak. It is then that tyrants are tempted."

Unfortunately, I know too well that nothing emboldens those same thugs and tyrants as much as the attempt to placate them. That's the lesson I saw in Afghanistan; it's a lesson we see over and over again in history; and it's the lesson we must remember as we consider how to confront the likes of the aya-tollahs in Iran, the Mexican cartels, Putin—and the Chinese Communist Party.

A month before the war began in Ukraine, with Russian forces massed on the border, I flew to Kyiv with a small group of congressmen. It had been less than four months since Biden's calamitous withdrawal from Afghanistan, and the signs were clear that our enemies were emboldened by that disaster. Now, sensing that the United States had grown timid, the Russian president amped up the rhetoric. It was increasingly obvious Putin was going to invade the whole of Ukraine and, if successful, likely keep going to take other countries in the former Soviet Union.

I'd heard as much weeks earlier, when a small group of Defense Department officials briefed the House Armed Services Committee.

The message from Defense was sobering: They'd been monitoring a massive Russian military buildup on their border with Ukraine. It didn't seem to be a bluff this time. The coming invasion would likely involve massive missile and artillery barrages, ground invasion operations, a decapitation of the Ukrainian government by Russian Spetsnaz special forces, and an amphibious assault from the Black Sea.

Politicians are rarely quiet in these briefings, but one could have heard a pin drop in the room. The consensus from the briefers was that the Ukrainian military would become completely overwhelmed very quickly. This was going to be a land war in Europe the likes of which the world had not seen since World War II—and no one knew how far Putin was going to go.

I distinctly remember thinking that if we did nothing to stop Putin from Ukraine, he'd feel emboldened to move on to attack a NATO country like Poland or Lithuania. And if he did that, the U.S. would be treaty obligated to go to war. In Putin's mind, he had already gotten away with it in 2014 during the Obama administration when he took Crimea without a shot or even a strongly worded outcry from the Europeans. When it was my turn, I peppered the briefers with questions. "So, what is the administration going to do about it? What is your plan to support a Ukrainian resistance or insurgency in a Russian-occupied Ukraine? And finally, what the hell are the big economies of Europe, the Germans and French in particular, doing to step up to defend their own backyard?"

I reminded everyone in the room that the Germans and French had opposed providing lethal aide to Ukraine under both Obama and Trump. They had appeased the Russians through the building of the Nord Stream 2 pipeline and allowed themselves to become hooked on cheap Russian gas that Putin could use as leverage to sideline several European nations.

Just after the briefing, the Chairman of the Special Operations subcommittee (on which I also served) walked up to me. "If I can pull a trip to Kyiv together in the next few weeks, you want to go?"

"I'm in," I replied. "It's Green Berets that are training Ukrainian Special Operations over there—and the Florida National Guard is training their conventional troops. I want to talk to them and see what the hell is really going on besides a canned Pentagon brief. We need some ground truth."

When the congressional delegation landed at Kyiv's airport, I was immediately struck by how normal life looked in the capital. The sidewalks were bustling with people bundled up against the harsh Ukrainian winter, going about their daily business among Kyiv's beautiful and elegant buildings. In talking to ordinary Ukrainians, I could sense that there was a definite sense of disbelief that their "cousins" the Russians would actually attack them in a large-scale invasion.

"The Russians do this every year. Putin wants something and will try to scare the government into giving in to it," one Ukrainian agribusiness executive said, shrugging, as he talked to me at the hotel bar. I was a little surprised at his optimism given the taking of Crimea in 2014 but understood that they had become accustomed to living at the end of a barrel.

We spent the next day receiving briefings from the U.S. embassy on the situation. I was struck by the frustration and candor from both State Department and military officials at what could only be described as an appeasement strategy from the White House and Pentagon. We asked about anti-tank Javelin missiles, Stingers, and anti-ship Harpoon missiles—all vital defensive weapons in the event of an invasion. Exasperated, the embassy officer threw his hands up and told us that "the Ukrainians had been begging for all of those weapons systems and more." The Ukrainians knew that Putin might think twice about an invasion if he saw Ukraine armed with modern Western weaponry. Right now, Putin had too many reasons to believe that an invasion would not be very costly.

"Those systems you are asking about are viewed by Washington as too 'escalatory' and provocative,'" another official vented. "The administration thinks rushing arms to the Ukrainians would 'poke the bear' and not give the President's threat of sanctions and diplomatic isolation a chance to work."

I remarked that our strategy was risk aversion at its most dangerous. We needed to make Putin think twice about invading, and perhaps he would pause if he *believed* his military would pay too high a price. It was the only way to hopefully prevent this war. I remember half the embassy staff nodding. No one disagreed.

The next morning, we visited Ukrainian Special Operations headquarters. The commanding general was right out of central casting; short and stocky with a shaved head and deep wrinkles across his forehead. The Ukrainian parliament had recently passed a national mobilization law to authorize gun ownership and partisan resistance, and I was very interested in how his command would implement it. I channeled my Green Beret training: "Respectfully, General, we need Putin to believe that not only will every single Ukrainian citizen fight but that they will have the organization, basic training, and weapons necessary for guerilla warfare." I didn't want to lecture a fellow special operator, but I wanted to be sure he got the point.

He leaned forward as he replied in broken English, "Our people will fight. Every citizen will resist. The entire world will see their determination to fight for freedom." The general added with a smile, "And thanks to the training the last six years from your Green Berets, we know how to put a sniper on every rooftop—and a Javelin missile on every street corner. Most important, we have changed our old Soviet tactics. We will have small hunter-killer teams in every village."

As we walked out, I was so proud of the many rotations of Green Berets that had trained them. The Ukrainian special forces had adapted decades' worth of highly centralized Soviet tactics and thinking to bottom-up leadership. They were clearly determined and loyal to their cause. They were showing that they had absorbed how to think and lead like Green Berets.

I had dinner with some of the Florida National Guard officers that night to get their assessment and to hear about the training they'd done with the Ukrainians. Knowing that the Ukrainians were likely to have their senior ranks destroyed or communications cut off during the invasion, we needed to ensure junior officers could understand basic strategic intent and execute using their own judgment. The reverse was true: since the Russians still used the strict Soviet top-down system, we taught the Ukrainians to target their officers with snipers, their command vehicles with anti-tank systems, and their headquarters with artillery.

"The Ukrainians get it," the Florida Guard officer replied, "but the problem is that the Pentagon and White House won't allow the long-range missiles the Ukrainians keep asking for. It just seems like Washington is petrified of Putin. The irony is that their half-assing of this effort is exactly what is going to make Putin think he can get away with invading."

Back in Washington, as 2021 became 2022, I watched in horror as a series of strategic missteps basically invited Putin to invade. President Biden's abandonment of our allies in Afghanistan, his lack of response to the Colonial Pipeline hack that shut down gas supplies to the East Coast of the United States, the lifting of sanctions on the Nord Stream 2 pipeline from Russia to Germany, and pulling our ships out of the Black Sea—all these moves were intended to de-escalate, to make war less likely. But as had happened before, what was meant to de-escalate was seen by Russia as appeasement. President Biden's remark that the U.S. response might be different if there was only a "minor incursion" gave Putin the green light.

On February 25, 2022, Vladimir Putin launched a complex invasion that quickly bogged down. A few months after the war began, I returned to Ukraine. This time, there was no commercial flight into Kyiv because missiles were literally flying. Instead, our delegation flew into Poland and then took a very slow, ten-hour train to Kyiv.

"Why do we have to move so slow?" I asked one of the train conductors.

"So I can see if Russian saboteurs or missiles have broken the track," he replied, deadpan.

"You go as slow as you want, my friend!" I replied.

The walk into the Presidential Palace to meet with President Volodymyr Zelensky reminded me of stories I read about Churchill's headquarters during World War II. All of the floor-to-ceiling windows were blacked out. Sandbagged bunkers stood at the intersection of every hallway and the base of every stairway. Because of the KGB's proclivity to poisoning its opponents, Zelensky's inner security informed me I was not allowed to present him one of my challenge coins. The meeting with Zelensky and his national security team took place in a baroque, chandeliered conference room for over two hours.

Along with many Americans, I had concerns about how the Ukrainians were using our money and our matériel. I pressed Zelensky to allow more American military advisors to help with oversight of logistics, maintenance, planning—and accountability of our equipment.

To my surprise, the Ukrainian president replied, "I welcome them. I have asked your administration for a joint planning team in strategic communications, logistics, and intelligence. The hesitation is with the White House, not us.

"Please give us the long-range weapons we need to win," he pleaded. "We can end this war quickly. We are grateful, but the

MIKE WALTZ

slow pace is dragging out the war. We must go to any negotiation from a position of strength."

As I discovered in my previous trip, we were handicapping ourselves with risk aversion. Biden was playing not to lose, rather than taking bold action to ensure a win and put an end to the war. I feared this incremental approach would settle into a stalemate, a war of attrition that would be incredibly costly in lives lost and in American dollars.

While waiting for our return train to Poland, a casualty train unloaded soldiers wounded fighting in the east. Waiting on the terminal was a line of ambulances as far as the eye could see. No one made a sound as they unloaded hundreds of heavily wounded men into the ambulances. The train quickly pulled out to make room for the next train—this one with wounded civilians. The next line of ambulances pulled up and swallowed up the next trainload of people grievously wounded from cities under bombardment in the south and east. I saw the grim resolve on the faces of the paramedics—and on the faces of the wounded themselves. The Ukrainians had the same spirit of resilience I'd seen with my men and our Afghan allies. It is always humbling to witness.

As I watched the women and small children loaded into ambulances, it hit me that deterrence had utterly failed. All of President Biden's grand threats of economic sanctions and international isolation failed. Bottom line, dictators only understand hard power. When given a chance, they will push and push until met with cold, hard steel. It's the only thing that stops the strong man from moving in as he pleases. The hard truth is that only hard power keeps the peace. In Washington, people were patting themselves on the back that Russia had failed to easily overtake Ukraine. But the cost in blood and treasure was enormous and should have been avoided.

Further, I repeatedly voiced my frustrations with our European NATO allies. In television appearances and in congressional hearings, I pointed out, "For decades, the United States has carried the vast burden and share of the cost of defending Europe while two-thirds of the alliance failed to live up to their commitments of two percent of their GDP toward defense, especially the large economies of Germany, France, and Italy. This is an awesome deal for European politicians to have the American taxpayer subsidizing Europe's vast social programs while the U.S. goes further and further into debt. NATO was an extraordinarily successful alliance at preventing war with the Soviet Union. To now see the largest land war since World War II on their doorstep and only a few of the Eastern European countries plus Britain doing their best has been infuriating."

Biden continued to send request after request for billions in aid from Congress. Finally, I had enough and released an op-ed titled "The Era for Blank Checks from Congress for Ukraine is Over." In it, I made the argument that rubber-stamping each request when there was no strategy, no stated goals for what victory looked like, insufficient burden-sharing with our European allies, and an energy policy that ultimately fueled Putin's war machine was not acceptable.

"Why is the burden always on the American taxpayer to dig deeper and deeper in their pockets and there are no demands from the White House for European taxpayers to dig deeper into *their* pockets?" I asked in an interview just after its release. The op-ed also argued that until the U.S. southern border was under control and America released its vast energy reserves, we could not continue spending such vast sums on assistance. Our allies weren't doing their part: unbelievably, Europe was still buying Russian gas. They were just doing it through brokers in India and Hong Kong and having it shipped via tanker rather than through overland pipelines. President Biden's ban on exporting American LNG only drove global prices higher and gave allies in Europe little alternative than buying from Russia. The Speaker of the Parliament in Lithuania told me that her country bought 80 percent of its gas supply from the terminals in Texas and Louisiana. Further, U.S. aid wasn't limited to military equipment. There were also vast sums of cash going into the Ukrainian economy to pay for things like first responders and teachers' salaries. It was important to keep the economy going, but none of those things were going to end the war. I could not in good conscience go back to my district and explain to underpaid teachers and first responders why we were continuing to approve billions to pay foreign first responders and teachers. Given the scope and scale of our contribution, other nations should have picked up the tab for those types of humanitarian assistance, not the United States.

My additional frustration was the constant dithering about

giving the Ukrainians the types of weapons they needed to win and end the war. The vacillation on what to provide, from Patriot air defense systems, to tanks, to anti-ship missiles, cost many more lives, lengthened the war, and dramatically increased the cost to the taxpayer once the conflict settled into a stalemate with World War I–style trench warfare. With the lack of a desired end state or goal and a strategy to achieve it, I couldn't just keep rubber-stamping more money.

Regardless of the mistakes made in supporting Ukraine, the biggest mistake was not preventing the war in the first place. Deterrence failed, period. Because of our weakness, Putin was not afraid of continuing his war in Europe, and a year and a half later, Iran was not afraid of planning and supporting a war through Hamas in Israel. We cannot undo the past. What absolutely matters now is focusing on how we can apply those lessons to the future. And right now, the future involves our existential struggle with the Chinese Communist Party.

Both the Trump and Biden administrations have listed the Chinese Communist Party as the most dangerous challenge to the United States and the main threat to our global leadership role. Too often, our response to China's rise can be boiled down to purchasing more tanks, planes, ships, and satellites and ensuring ours are more modern and capable than theirs. This is what the Defense Department calls the "pacing challenge" to keep pace with China's rapid military buildup. The problem is that we are also facing threats from Russia, Iran, North Korea, and global terrorism while saddled with more than $35 trillion in debt. We can no longer assume the traditional way of American warfare—build better military equipment than the other guy—will work in the future. This is why I've consistently tried to instill the mindset of the Green Beret—asymmetric, unconventional operations—into our national security institutions. The inability of the establishment to grasp that need became painfully evident in hundreds of briefings, hearings, and policy forums.

For example, the Secretary of the Air Force came to our committee asking for funding for additional stealth bombers. "Mr. Secretary, I'm all for additional bombers to be able to keep China at bay. But I have a question for you. What do you think gets inside Beijing's thinking more—a few more stealth bombers, or the possibility of unrest with the Tibetans and Uighurs, or in Hong Kong, that are seeking basic human rights and freedoms? The thing the CCP fears the most is its own people, not the U.S. Air Force."

The Secretary said he didn't disagree but he was there to discuss more funding for stealth bombers. I was hitting my head against a wall.

We are decades behind the Chinese in adopting unconventional thinking in our defense establishment. In 1999, after witnessing the overwhelming military might the United States brought to bear in the Persian Gulf War, two Chinese colonels authored the book *Unrestricted Warfare*. They argued that the United States was overly focused on hard power and only modernized its doctrine when technological advances forced it to do so. They also argued that if a nation like China were willing to engage in economic warfare, lawfare, and dominating international rule-making institutions, they would have sufficient leverage over their opponents to negate the need for military confrontation. They were using Sun Tzu's teachings to employ all elements of power to win without ever needing to fight.

I'm not saying we shouldn't be bold with our own military might. But we need to think like Green Berets in how we do it.

There is a critical lesson we must learn from Ukraine as it applies to our allies in the Pacific facing Chinese aggression: you must arm your allies *before* the enemy invades, not in the months and years afterward as the Biden administration has done. Not only are well-armed allies better positioned to resist an attack once it starts, but sufficient arms can also deter the invasion in the first place. Dictators want to pick on the weak little guy, not one that's armed to the teeth. And they certainly won't want to pick on a neighbor that's been trained by the best—the Green Berets.

I traveled to Taipei, Taiwan, weeks after visiting Kyiv to see the situation firsthand. On the way, I stopped in Pearl Harbor to visit the Indo-Pacific four-star command responsible for the conduct of all military operations in the region. In one of our meetings, I raised the issue of strategic clarity versus the current policy of ambiguity. The deputy commander challenged me. "What problem are you trying to solve, Congressman? The

Chinese assume we will intervene militarily anyway," he said. I stated that clarity about our commitment to defend Taiwan would send a vital message to our allies and the American people.

Clarity means deterrence—and deterrence means peace. The reason Putin attacked Ukraine instead of a NATO country is that it was clear to him that twenty-nine NATO countries would quickly come to the defense of the nation he attacked. Clarity allows us to lead allies with an understood purpose— and clarity allows us to reach common understandings with the American people before a conflict. If we wait to make the case to the American people and our allies that Taiwan is worth defending as Chinese amphibious ships are loading with troops and tanks to cross the straits for an invasion, it could be too late. The clearer we make that case to our own citizens, the clearer the message we can send to Beijing that the cost isn't worth the gain, and hopefully prevent what would likely be the deadliest conflict since World War II.

It has become one of my primary missions in Congress to do everything I can to prevent a conflict with China. That means reminding Americans of the existential threat that China poses to our way of life. Xi Jinping, the chairman of the Chinese Communist Party, is explicitly telling his country to prepare for war. He talks disdainfully about the decline of Western values, the ills of capitalism, and the dysfunction of democracy. Xi promises the triumph of "socialism with Chinese characteristics" with

China as the new global superpower. To that end, the Chinese Navy is now much larger than ours: they are trending toward five hundred ships, while the United States Navy is regressing to fewer than three hundred. They can concentrate their combat vessels in one ocean while ours are spread across the globe. The Chinese space force is launching more into space than the rest of the world combined. They have a new space station in low earth orbit and realistic plans to put a manned station on the moon by the end of the decade. China is tripling the size of its nuclear arsenal and deploying first-strike technologies like hypersonic missiles that the United States is struggling to match and defend against.

As I've explained throughout this book, Green Berets know better than anyone that persuasion and diplomacy are integral parts of the art of war. When I fought in Afghanistan, I made the case to tribal chiefs that working with Americans was in their best interest. Now that I'm in Congress, I'm still making a case—this time, to fellow members of Congress and the American people. Why is stopping the Chinese Communist Party worth some economic hardship or, worse, putting our soldiers in danger? Why is it worth our time, our attention, and our treasure?

The reality is that if the CCP controls Taiwan and the South China Sea, they will then control the shipping lanes into South Korea, Japan, and all of Southeast Asia. They will have leverage over half the world's GDP in the economies of Asia. If they take Taiwan, China would also instantly gain control of

90 percent of the world's most advanced computer chips and will be able to put America at a huge economic disadvantage from which it would be almost impossible to recover.

What distinguishes us as Americans from so many of the enemies we have fought in history is a sense of decency that we not stand idly by as a thriving democracy gets swallowed up by a stronger neighbor. Since the end of World War II, the world has enjoyed the most prosperous period in human history with hundreds of millions lifted out of poverty. If we let Taiwan fall, not only will our prosperity be threatened, so, too, will our moral leadership. Our allies much closer to China—Japan, South Korea, Australia, and Thailand—will realize that they are on their own and cannot rely on America to support fellow democracies. As one member of the Philippine Congress said to me, "We all know that first it was Tibet, then Hong Kong, next is Taiwan, and then us." Our allies in Asia will either make concessions to China to avoid Taiwan's fate—or they will try to arm themselves with nuclear weapons. Either way, the world would become a less safe place, and America would no longer find itself the leader of the free world.

There is much we can do to avoid that fate. The strategy for preventing war with the Chinese Communist Party will require American society to adopt every hard truth put forth in this book. It will be the greatest test of our great nation. That strategy has five prongs.

First, we must arm Taiwan faster and give their military the capability and confidence to fight hard and resist. On my visit to Taiwan, the first issue raised by their security officials and President Tsai Ing-wen essentially was, "Where are our weapons? We have paid for them. Time is not on our side." The Taiwanese have billions' worth of weapon systems that they have paid for and had been approved by the American government—but are tied up in red tape and production delays.

Second, we need to provide clarity to our allies in the Pacific that America will stand strong with them. That means beefing up organizations like the Quad, with India, Japan, Australia, and the United States. Our relationship with India in particular, given the growing economic, technological, and military might of the world's largest democracy, will be the most consequential partnership of the twenty-first century. That's why I currently serve as the Co-Chair of the India Caucus in the House of Representatives.

Third, we have to make major investments in the U.S. military to modernize aging ships and planes that are increasingly in disrepair. But it's not just better hardware. We have to reintroduce a warrior spirit into our military and make sure it remains a meritocracy that promotes only the most disciplined, bold, and determined soldiers that we have among us. As I've said in multiple hearings, "All I care about is that our military is recruiting and promoting the best of the best and that they are focused on defeating our enemies. I can guarantee you that our enemies' bullets couldn't care less about the race, gender, or sexual orientation of our soldiers, so neither should we."

Fourth, we must be disciplined about bringing our supply

chains back to the United States and stem the hundreds of billions of U.S. dollars flowing into Beijing's economy. If it doesn't make business sense to bring the supply chains here, then let's at least get them to the western hemisphere or at least to fellow democracies that won't threaten to cut them off as leverage. China has deliberately created dependencies in everything from critical minerals to pharmaceuticals that it can then cut off in a time of crisis and cripple our economy. We are starting to see some bottom-up leadership in industries looking to protect themselves—and our nation's future—by bringing manufacturing back to America.

Fifth, we absolutely must protect our intellectual property. Our open society will always out-innovate the rigid surveillance state imposed by the CCP, but if we keep allowing the CCP to steal our ideas and technological breakthroughs, it won't mean a damn thing in terms of staying ahead in the long run.

Finally, and perhaps most important, the West must win the war of ideas and cut off the massive flows of money into Beijing's coffers. Green Berets know a basic truth. There's only one thing tyrannical governments fear as much as the U.S. military: global opinion being exposed to the hard truth of their brutality and a backlash resulting in the dictatorship being cut off from access to American capital. We must do more to expose what is happening to ethnic minorities, religious freedom, and pro-democracy movements within mainland China in a way that no corporate board in the West can turn a blind eye. We need to win the messaging war.

No one defends the cruelty of the Taliban or ISIS and their extremist vision of Islam. Yet all kinds of people apologize for the Chinese Communist Party and ignore their brutality for the sake of their next quarterly earnings. The poster child for this hypocrisy is the NBA, which is eager to expand its brand in China and keep making billions on that market. NBA executives and players preach about "social justice" while wearing sports gear made in Uighur forced-labor camps. The same athletes who denounce police brutality in America are deliberately silent when it comes to infinitely worse atrocities in China, where modern-day slavery is happening.

Fed up with the duplicity of many American corporations when it came to China and human rights, I struck up a relationship with NBA player Enes Kanter Freedom. Enes was a lone voice in his league, willing to stand up against the CCP—and to call out corporate America and his fellow players for their silence. He is a true servant leader. I sponsored legislation to boycott the 2022 Winter Olympics in Beijing. Enes and I then made a television ad, highlighting the corporations sponsoring the Olympics. Part of the script read, "The Olympics is the world's greatest athletic showcase, but just outside the show: rape, genocide, slave labor . . . American companies are drunk on Chinese dollars, entangled with Communist dictators committing atrocities and propping up these genocide games staged by the Chinese Communist Party."

At the end of the ad, Enes said, "Stand for freedom, defund

the dictators." I offered a simple call to action: "When you see 'Made in China,' put it down."

My team reserved very expensive prime-time slots during the Olympics for the ad—a large sum just to have it air a few times. We submitted the ad and waited. Sure enough, the night before the opening ceremony, the network's legal team called us and said they would run the ad if we took down the logos for all of the corporate sponsors. Of course, we refused—and then pushed the headline, "Here's the ad that the mainstream media and the Chinese Communists don't want you to see." The ad went viral—for free.

While we didn't succeed in our full boycott, we did pressure the Biden administration to enact a "diplomatic boycott" to hold back on sending any official representatives of the U.S. government. I'm convinced the pressure campaign from us and others in large part caused the Beijing games to have the worst ratings on record for a Winter Olympics, which in turn put a serious dent in the numbers of people absorbing Chinese propaganda about its socialist utopia. When American athletes howled to my office about their right to compete, I asked in reply, "Dear Athlete, would you have fought so hard to be able to compete in apartheid-era South Africa, which was banned from hosting or competing in an Olympics for decades? Why do you take a moral stand about South Africa but turn a blind eye to genocide and oppression in China?"

It's not just sports, or Hollywood, or our universities that are drunk on Chinese money. It's not just the theft of our technology. When I contemplate the half-trillion-dollar trade deficit, the massive investments from U.S. companies and pension funds into the People's Republic, and the trillions in capital that Chinese firms raise on U.S. markets, I sense that future historians will look back on this era and shake their heads. Our whole relationship with China embodies Lenin's observation that "the capitalists will sell us the rope that we will use to hang them."

President Trump's policies were routinely undervalued, but one in particular was undeniable; he understood the nature of the Chinese threat and was willing to do something about it. From the time he launched his first campaign for the White House, Trump grasped that the best way to prevent conflict with China was by taking them on where it counted: their economy.

In my first term in office, I was appalled to learn that the federal government's 401(k) plan—the Thrift Savings Plan, or TSP—was investing our military members' retirement savings into the Chinese market. After trying to reason with the TSP oversight board and getting nowhere, I asked Matt Pottinger, the Deputy National Security Advisor and China expert, if it would be helpful if I raised the issue with President Trump. "We have discussed it with him, but another push from you would certainly help," Matt replied.

"Hello, Michael. What's up?" the President asked after his aide patched me through. I got straight to the point. I explained that the board overseeing the TSP (all Obama appointees, with

$800 billion in assets under management) were investing the international portion of the funds into the Chinese market. I knew the President wanted straight talk, and I gave it to him:

"Let me put it to you this way, Mr. President. As commander in chief, you have sailors on aircraft carriers out in the Pacific Ocean, sending portions of their salary home for retirement, and this board on Wall Street overseeing the military's 401(k) plan is investing those funds into Beijing's market that hosts the very same Chinese defense industry that is manufacturing the missiles and ships that could kill those sailors one day. For example, a shipyard that's listed on the Beijing stock exchange just built new ballistic missile submarines that can launch nukes and destroy America. Mr. President, this is nuts!"

The President's reaction was instant. "That's bullshit, Michael. Work with O'Brien on the best way to stop it. The Chinese are desperate for our money. We can put a stop to it. Thank you for being such a fighter, Michael."

I don't know how he did it, but the President made himself very accessible and received dozens of calls a day. I did indeed hear back immediately from the President's chief of staff. A week later, Larry Kudlow (head of the President's National Economic Council) and National Security Advisor Robert O'Brien sent guidance to the TSP board, instructing it to halt all investments into the Chinese market. Another letter by the Labor Secretary followed shortly, and not long thereafter, three new nominees for the board were sent to the Senate.

"Boom! That's what I'm talking about!" I said to my team when we got word from the National Security Advisor about the President's directive.

"Bold move calling the President directly on that one," my Legislative Director said, smiling.

Here's the thing about President Donald Trump—he got things done. People obsessed on his rhetoric. I focused on his results. *No President in recent history has better understood the nature of the enemy we face.* We need leaders who are absolutely clear about that danger and committed to sending a clear signal to the world, and to the Chinese themselves, that we will stand firm and strong against their aggression.

On the way back from that visit to Taiwan, we stopped to call on the Pacific Fleet in Pearl Harbor. I was able to arrange a deeply moving side trip to snorkel over the sunken wrecks of the USS *Arizona* and USS *Utah* with Navy SEAL Team 8. As we swam over these sacred sites, I thought of all the lives taken far too young in a sneak attack that infamous day launched by an imperialistic, expansionist government. I learned on my visit that Pearl Harbor survivors could elect to have their ashes interred in urns inside the USS *Arizona* so that they may be with their shipmates forever. It was a powerful reminder of what's at stake in preventing war. In the 1930s, far too many Americans couldn't see the looming threat until it was too late. We must learn from the sacrifices of our forebears, employ the virtues that are foundational to the Green Berets, and be crystal clear about the potential for future conflict with China.

I firmly believe the number one job of the federal government, of the Congress in which I serve, is to keep the country safe. That's not just halting the aggression of tyrants like Putin, Xi, ISIS, or the ayatollahs in Iran. It also includes defending our borders, particularly against the Mexican drug cartels that control nearly a third of Mexico and huge portions of the U.S. border. That's why I, along with Representative Dan Crenshaw from Texas, introduced legislation to authorize military force against the cartels and why we will continue to press this issue until we take bold action to end this scourge.[5]

These cartels are far more like ISIS than they are the Mafia. They are equipped with heavy weapons and armored vehicles, have billions at their disposal, and have repeatedly fought the Mexican Army to a standstill. We have to launch a new strategy against them along the lines of Plan Colombia in the 1990s and 2000s, where the U.S. provided military resources to support law enforcement and the Colombian government so they could dismantle the Medellín and Cali Cartels and defeat the narco-terrorist insurgency led by the FARC. Green Berets were the tip of the spear in Plan Colombia, providing intelligence, training, planning, and all types of support to the Colombian military—but rarely engaging in direct combat with the insurgents. We can and should do the same against the cartels in

---

5 Houston Keene, "Crenshaw, Waltz Introduce Joint Resolution to give Biden Military Authority to Combat Cartels," Fox News, January 12, 2023, https://www.foxnews.com/politics/crenshaw-waltz-introduce-joint-resolution-give-biden-military-authority-combat-cartels.

Mexico. As we did with the Colombian government, we must make it clear that we will act unilaterally to defend our national security, but it is in our mutual interests to tackle this menace together.

And no—despite the claims of some media outlets who have pushed clickbait narratives, we are not advocating an invasion or occupation of portions of Mexico. Rather, assets like offensive cyberwarfare, space, and drones that are not available to law enforcement should be used to support them. Put it this way: If it were ISIS and al-Qaeda instead of the Sinaloa and Jalisco Cartels pumping deadly chemicals into our youth, making millions on human trafficking, and infiltrating our cities, it wouldn't even be a debate. We cannot continue business as usual. We must adapt to a changing threat that is on our doorstep—otherwise, the threat will continue to cross our doorstep with impunity.

Whatever the threat, in order to keep the country safe, we have to have a citizenry that is prepared to do so. The virtues in this book are a compass and guide to that end. Not everyone can endure Ranger School or the Special Forces Qualification Course. But crafting a strong, resilient society full of Americans who think and lead like a Green Beret starts with transforming our educational system.

The bottom-up principle that is foundational to Green Berets needs to be foundational in our schools. It was certainly foundational in my own life as a product of the remarkable school that my mother pushed so hard for me to attend. And that means putting parents, not teachers' unions, in the driver's seat. Parents deserve a menu of choices for their children. We must foster competition in education and not leave children behind in failing systems. I am where I am in part because my mother fought so hard to get me into a better school. But parents shouldn't have to fight educational bureaucracies and unions every step of the way. This isn't just about choice—it's about the hard truth that we are not preparing the workforce of the future. The United States is on track to be a million jobs short in the STEM fields in the coming decade. We must reemphasize and incentivize learning a trade and "hard" skills. The pendulum has swung too far toward prioritizing liberal arts degrees at four-year institutions. Far too many young people graduate with huge debt—and without the job skills to repay it. It pays pretty darn well these days to turn a wrench, repair circuit boards, or spot weld; we need to embrace vocations and trades as pathways to prosperity.

Our youth are unprepared to drive the changes many claim to want within our system of government. A majority of people under twenty-five consider themselves activists for some type of cause—yet that same majority cannot name the three branches of government. I've supported legislation mandating civics education. I believe that to graduate high school, you should have to pass the same exam required for new immigrants. We can foster a nation of servant leaders by prioritizing national service in exchange for educational benefits. You want your fellow taxpayers to pay for your college or erase your debt? Get out there and contribute to the common good! Whether it's disaster relief, eldercare, or working in a homeless shelter, we must encourage Americans to serve one another again. Service is about leadership—and smart, loyal "followership." That doesn't mean blind obedience—it means the willingness to work together toward a common goal. Our nation will have better citizens—and a brighter future—if we inculcate in our young people the experience of discipline, teamwork, and sacrificing for a cause bigger than themselves.

Just as we raise young people *to* serve, we must be a nation that honors those who *have* served. We have promises to keep and, as a society, show the trait of loyalty to those willing to die for the rest of us. The number of veterans tragically ending their own lives has remained the same in the past two decades despite exponentially more money thrown at the problem. Medical providers should have a full menu of options at their disposal, not just opioid prescriptions as their primary tool. Great organizations like K9s for Warriors had to fight for years alongside me and other legislators for legislation to force the VA to start providing service dogs to our veterans despite multiple studies showing the dogs have tremendous benefits. We should expand the veterans' choice program that allows veterans to go to private physicians of their choice rather than pouring money into a government-run hospital system. Allow veterans to go to local doctors and bill it to the government, just as we do with Medicare. There's a vital difference between government-run health care—and health care that is private-sector managed but government-funded. Finally, we should take a bottom-up approach and send a large portion of those hundreds of billions from the VA budget devoted to running 1,200 hospitals and clinics directly out to the many fantastic veteran-service organizations that are face-to-face with those who have served and best know their needs.

This is not an easy time in our nation's history. Our political divisions seem enormous, as do our challenges. Sometimes it seems like we're living in alternate universes. We need leaders with the tenacity, the courage, and the vision to stand strong for their convictions—but at the same time push back against the bitterness and the cynicism that have infused our society. We need leadership that inspires others to serve, to learn, and to give back. The ideals of service and patriotism transcend partisan politics, or at least they should. We cannot give up on making the case to the American people that our best days still lie ahead—and we will get there by relying on the values and attributes that made us great in the first place.

I wrote this book because I wanted to honor some of those important attributes of the Green Berets. I wanted to tell the stories of those traits in action, both in combat and in civilian life. There's a bit of a paradox here. Green Berets go through very uncommon training and testing, all to identify the best of the best, to do very uncommon things. The preparation is extreme, and so, too, is the work we are called to do in some of the most dangerous places in the world. Yet the virtues that guide us—the ones I've talked about in this book—are not just for a small elite of special operators. Discipline, boldness, a willingness to speak truth to power, loyalty, restraint, resilience—these are building blocks of what it means to be an honorable human being. Put in practice, they can transform your family, your community, and our country. They are qualities we need to instill in our children regardless of what profession they choose. They are qualities we should try to embody in our everyday lives, because our children will learn less from what we say and more from who we are.

We have a right, too, to expect these attributes in our national leadership. I believe much of the anger and discontent that is so palpable in this country boils down to the fact that too few in our leadership are willing to live these hard truths. If we can collectively learn to think and lead like Green Berets, our communities and our country will maintain their role as a "shining city upon a hill, whose beacon light guides freedom loving people everywhere" for the twenty-first century and beyond.

De Oppresso Liber.

= ACKNOWLEDGMENTS =

One hard truth is that anything worth doing in life is best done as a team. I've been blessed with fantastic, high performing teammates in the Army, business, policymaking, and now Congress. There are few things more satisfying than casting a vision and watching a well-oiled machine come together to implement it.

I would be remiss if I didn't first acknowledge my mother, Brenda Waltz. Her character, drive, and grit not only set us on a course to break out of poverty and rise into the middle class, but she imbued in me the work ethic that allowed me to persevere through countless challenges. Thanks, Mom.

I've had too many wonderful mentors in life who helped me realize the hard truths that matter. I can't thank them all by name, but I promise to always try to pay it forward by mentoring the next generation.

Many thanks to my agents at Javelin for helping me find the right publisher to realize my vision for this book. I am especially grateful to St. Martin's Press, and my editor, Marc

Resnick. Marc continues to bring the sights, sounds, and experiences of combat veterans to life for the next generation of Americans to appreciate and learn from. Special thanks go to Joshua Treviño and Hugo Schwyzer for their tireless research, writing assistance, and editing.

Most of all, I want to thank the Green Berets who served alongside me all over the world in our mission to keep America safe. Non-commissioned officers are what make the U.S. military great, and they have set me straight time and again over the years. Thank you to my VMI mentor, SGM Bill Goodson, and to my platoon sergeants, Freddie Pleasant and 1SG Ray Egan. The key leaders of my special forces teams and company—Marc, Kevin, Trip, Brian, Tom, Graham, and York—were instrumental in teaching me how to think and lead like a Green Beret.

To the families of Brian Woods, Matt Pucino, Alejandro Grenado, Sev Summers, Ron Luce, and Chris Robinson, every day that I walk up the steps of the United States Capitol I tell myself to be worthy of what you sacrificed for all of us.

For the veterans of our longest war, know that your sacrifice was not in vain. You kept America free from major terrorist attacks for a generation. You brought justice to the victims of 9/11 and let the world know that there would be consequences for the perpetrators.

To the grassroots veterans' groups who rose up during the Afghanistan withdrawal: You stepped in where your government failed you and our allies. You are honoring our promises still to this day.

I've had the honor of coming to know the thirteen Gold Star families from the Abbey Gate bombing. We will not quit in our quest for the answers you deserve, and accountability for your great loss.

I've been blessed with a strong and tireless team in my congressional offices in Florida and DC. Thank you for being servant leaders day in and day out in service to our constitutional republic.

Finally, to my supporters in my campaigns, thank you for your trust, your time, and your belief that we should have more veterans leading this country.

All of you embody the hard truths discussed in this book, and the motto of the Green Beret. *De Oppresso Liber.*

INDEX

ABOUT THE AUTHOR

CONGRESSMAN MIKE WALTZ represents Florida's sixth congressional district. He is the first Green Beret to be elected to Congress and a former White House and Pentagon policy advisor. He has served worldwide with multiple tours in Africa, the Middle East, and Afghanistan. For his actions in combat, Mike was decorated with four Bronze Stars, two of them with valor. He is a nationally known leader in national security and with regard to the threats posed by China, Russia, Iran, and global terrorism. Mike is married to Dr. Julia Nesheiwat, also a combat veteran, who served as the President's Homeland Security Advisor. They live in St. Augustine, Florida.